The Making of *Walden*

JAMES LYNDON SHANLEY is professor
of English and associate dean of the
College of Liberal Arts at Northwestern University. He took his A.B. and
Ph.D. degrees at Princeton. In com-
menting on *The Making of "Walden,"*
Professor Shanley points out that he
first examined the Huntington Library
manuscript with the simple intention
of using it to annotate an edition of
Walden; when he discovered he could
determine the order of the manuscript,
he gave up his original project and
turned to the study of how Thoreau
created his masterpiece.

The Making of *Walden*

with the Text of the First Version

By

J. Lyndon Shanley

THE UNIVERSITY OF CHICAGO PRESS

Library of Congress Catalog Number: 57-6990

THE UNIVERSITY OF CHICAGO PRESS, CHICAGO 37
Cambridge University Press, London, N.W. 1, England
The University of Toronto Press, Toronto 5, Canada

© *1957 by The University of Chicago. Published 1957. Composed
and printed by* THE UNIVERSITY OF CHICAGO PRESS, *Chicago,
Illinois, U.S.A.*

Acknowledgments

I AM happy to express my thanks for help in preparing this book. The Graduate School Research Fund and Dean Simeon E. Leland of the College of Liberal Arts, Northwestern University, gave financial aid that was essential to carrying on my work. I owe much to my colleagues, Wallace W. Douglas, Harrison H. Hayford, and Moody E. Prior, who read my manuscript and made valuable suggestions; and to Miss Katheryn Sheehan, who gave indispensable assistance at every stage in the preparation of the manuscript and the reading of proof.

I am deeply indebted to the Henry E. Huntington Library for permission to work with and to publish extensively from the *Walden* manuscript on which this study depends, and to the members of the staff upon whose never-failing help my work depended, especially Mr. Herbert C. Schulz, Curator of Manuscripts, Mr. Tyrus G. Harmsen, Miss Phyllis Rigney, and Miss Haidée Noya. I am also grateful for permission to publish manuscript material in the Henry W. and Albert A. Berg Collection, New York Public Library, and in the Pierpont Morgan Library. The Houghton Library of Harvard University and the Yale University Library provided me with photostats of manuscript material for study.

I have received generous assistance from Messrs. C. Waller Barrett, John L. Cooley, and T. Y. Davis, who sent me manuscripts and photostats or transcriptions of Thoreau material; and from Mr. Herbert Cahoon, of the Pierpont Morgan Library, Mr. John D. Gordan, Curator of the Berg Collection, Mr. Leslie M. Oliver, of the Houghton Library, and Miss Viola C. White, of the Abernethy Library, Middlebury College, who answered many questions about Thoreau manuscripts and books in their collections.

Acknowledgments

I gratefully acknowledge the permission of the publishers to quote from copyrighted works: The Bibliographical Society of America for *The Cost Books of Ticknor and Fields*, edited by W. S. Tryon and W. Charvat; Houghton Mifflin Company for *The Writings of Henry David Thoreau* and H. S. Canby's *Thoreau;* Macmillan and Company, Ltd., for S. Alexander's *Beauty and Other Forms of Value;* The Macmillan Company for *The Autobiography of William Butler Yeats;* and William Sloane Associates for J. W. Krutch's *Henry David Thoreau.*

J. LYNDON SHANLEY

Contents

I

The Walden *Manuscript*

THAT Thoreau did not write *Walden* all at one time has been evident ever since his journals were published in 1906.[1] The journals of 1850–54 contain a very considerable body of material that Thoreau used in *Walden*, published in 1854. But by early 1849 he must already have written a good deal of *Walden*, for in January or February of that year he inquired of Ticknor and Company about publishing it; in February his Aunt Maria wrote of his preparing it for the press;[2] and some copies of the first edition (1849) of *A Week on the Concord and Merrimack Rivers* carried a notice in their advertising pages that *Walden* would be published soon. It is clear, therefore, that he worked on *Walden* at various times, but the real nature and the great extent of his work could not be known until the proper order of the 628 leaves of Huntington Manuscript 924 had been established.[3] Some time ago I was able to establish the proper order and am therefore able to tell how

1. *The Writings of Henry David Thoreau* (20 vols.; Boston: Houghton Mifflin Co., 1906). Unless otherwise indicated, all references to Thoreau's published writings are to this edition.

2. *The Cost Books of Ticknor and Fields*, ed. W. S. Tryon and William Charvat (New York: Bibliographical Society of America, 1949), p. 289; Henry Seidel Canby, *Thoreau* (Boston: Houghton Mifflin Co., 1939), p. 248.

3. Henry David Thoreau, *Walden, or Life in the Woods* (HM 924 in the Henry E. Huntington Library, San Marino, California).

The Making of Walden

Thoreau wrote the first version of *Walden* in 1846–47 while he was living at the pond and how he rewrote it, doubled its length, and reshaped it during the years between 1848 and 1854.

The manuscript has long been recognized as the work sheets of *Walden*. It consists of almost twelve hundred pages of writing on leaves of different colors and sizes, in different inks and varying handwritings of Thoreau, with cancellations and ink and pencil interlineations everywhere; there are some torn leaves and scraps and a few leaves with irrelevant material marked "A Week" or "Civil Disobedience." In 1909 F. H. Sanborn, Thoreau's early biographer and editor, prepared a bizarre potpourri for the Bibliophile Society which combined unpublished material from the manuscript with most of the published text of *Walden;* it is seriously inaccurate in every respect.[4] The only other study of the manuscript was a brief, unpublished paper in which Odell Shepard described and commented on some of the revisions he had traced in it.[5]

When I first obtained photostats of the whole manuscript, I was thinking only that unpublished material in it would be useful for an annotated edition of *Walden*. A brief study of the photostats suggested that something valuable might be said about the way in which Thoreau put *Walden* together. Working with the photostats, I was able to assemble the different versions (anywhere from two to five) of a number of passages in *Walden* and thereby to follow Thoreau's methods in rewriting sentences and paragraphs. But I did not perceive any extended consecutive version of *Walden*, nor did I expect to find one in the manuscript itself. No reliable suggestion had ever been made that there might be a distinguishable version of any length in the manuscript. The general impression seemed to be one of a minimum of order in a welter of leaves of all sorts and conditions: "Then, while he was making his books, his Journal was ransacked, until the author was finally entangled in such a mass of papers as one finds in the work sheets for 'Walden,' now in the Huntington Library. No

4. *Walden* (2 vols.; Boston: Bibliophile Society, 1909).

5. Read before the Modern Language Association in 1937. Professor Shepard generously lent me his paper and notes.

literary man with whom I am acquainted ever worked amidst greater self-made difficulties."[6]

It was not Thoreau, however, who produced the tangle but someone else, who had arranged all the pages of the manuscript according to their relation to the published text. Almost every page bears one or more heavy-pencil notations, "p. 56," "p. 75," etc., variously placed on the page. Each notation indicates where the material at that point in the manuscript is to be found in the edition of *Walden* published by Houghton Mifflin Company in 1889, and in a number of later editions based on that of 1889.[7] Sanborn used one of these later ones, the 1893 edition, in preparing the Bibliophile Society *Walden;*[8] it was undoubtedly he who made these notations on the manuscript, and more than likely he was the one primarily responsible for the order of the pages as I found them. This order produced only confusion since, as I was to discover, Thoreau had written and rewritten and added various parts of *Walden* at different times, and he had also frequently reordered long as well as short portions of his work.

When I went to the manuscript itself to check my reading of the photostats, I found the clues that led to the sorting and proper ordering of all its leaves. Many of the first versions of the passages for which I had assembled the variants were on leaves of the same light-blue paper and of the same size, and they had been written in a smaller hand and in a lighter ink than the other versions; in addition, many of these leaves bore the same embossed stationer's mark: a rose on a stem with leaves and a bud. Furthermore, although the contents of some of these leaves are in passages that are widely separated in the published text of *Walden,* they formed consecutive passages in the manuscript when the leaves they are on were brought together. In one group of leaves, for example, material that is in "Economy," 85 and 96 in the published text, made a consecutive passage in the manuscript; and in another group material of the following paragraphs ran con-

---

6. Canby, *Thoreau,* p. 193.

7. *A Centennial Check-List of the Editions of Henry David Thoreau's "Walden,"* ed. Walter Harding (Charlottesville, Va.: University of Virginia Press, 1954).

8. *Thoreau Society Bulletin,* L (Winter, 1955), 2.

secutively: "Higher Laws," 7, "Brute Neighbors," 10, "Spring," 25, "Brute Neighbors," 9, "Winter Animals," 13.[9]

I therefore assembled all the leaves of this particular kind in the manuscript, and when I had discovered their proper order, they made a complete piece, save where leaves were missing. When their contents are compared with the other material in the manuscript, it is clear that they constitute the first version of *Walden* in the manuscript and, without a doubt, the first version that Thoreau wrote.

Since the color and size of paper, ink, and handwriting, and the stationer's mark had led to the identification of one distinguishable group of leaves, I went on to see if differences in these points in the remaining leaves would identify other distinct groups. They did so. No single criterion was conclusive by itself in establishing further groups, but all the criteria taken together were generally decisive. The relations of the contents of the groups confirmed or corrected the reading of the physical signs. In the end there were seven large groups of leaves and two smaller ones.

The contents of the seven large groups and the relations of these contents make it clear that these groups mark seven major stages of Thoreau's work on *Walden:* the first version of 1846–47 and six sets of additions, cancellations, and revisions that he made between 1848 and 1854.[10] The relations of the revisions from one group to another and the relations of the contents of the groups to Thoreau's journals determined the order of the groups. Both internal and external evidence established the periods within which Thoreau wrote the various groups (see chapter ii). Only the first group, which constitutes the first version, represents a complete

9. See transcript of first version, pp. 132 and 191. Chapter titles and arabic numerals referring to the paragraphs of the given chapter in the published text must be used to identify the material under discussion at any point, but, as will be made clear in the following chapters, Thoreau did not make chapter divisions until 1853; the paragraph numbers are reliable references to the order of the paragraphs only in the final text; and the contents and the order of the contents of the paragraphs varied considerably from the beginning to the end of his work.

10. One of the smaller groups consists of short passages that Thoreau wrote between the major groups; the other consists of preliminary notes for the first version, leaves torn from journals and notebooks, and a few miscellaneous pieces.

piece by itself. But each time Thoreau added the material of a new group of leaves, he also went back and canceled, emended, and rearranged previously written material, and thus he created a new version of *Walden* with each set of additions.

After writing the seventh and last version in the manuscript, Thoreau wrote one more, the copy for the printer. It is not in the manuscript and is apparently lost; it was probably not returned to Thoreau. But this loss does not keep us from following Thoreau's work to the end, for the page proof of *Walden*[11] indicates that the published text represents Thoreau's copy for the printer save for the change of an occasional word or phrase.

With the manuscript versions of *Walden* thus identified and arranged in the order of their writing, we can follow the making of *Walden* in detail, and we gain essential information about Thoreau's career as a writer and a fuller understanding of the place of *Walden* in his life. In the successive versions we see how Thoreau polished his sentences and paragraphs to achieve the clarity, force, and rhythm of the published version. Even more interesting, because rarer, is what we learn of the growth of the material Thoreau used and the reshaping of it that determined the final form of the work. Although the journals made it clear that Thoreau added to *Walden* between 1847 and 1854, and especially after 1850, only the manuscript could reveal to how great an extent *Walden* is the result of a gradual re-creation of his experience rather than simply a recounting of that experience as he had entered it in his journal when it happened. And, further, only the manuscript could show the way in which Thoreau reshaped his material as the image of what he wanted to make became clearer.

Thoreau's way of working is perfectly described in S. Alexander's account of the creative process (the manuscript, for its part, provides just the sort of data which the philosopher found it very hard to come by). The artist works, Alexander wrote, "partly . . . from new images" (images, that is, which his imagination creates and which he seeks to reproduce in his medium), and "partly . . . by what a correspondent calls *tâtonne-*

11. HM 925 in the Huntington Library.

ment [groping], perpetually correcting the product. It may be asked, does not his correction show that the work achieved falls short of his ideal, of some image in his mind of the perfect work. The answer I suggest is that it falls short of his ideal, but not of the alleged image. If he had that image in his mind, his failure could only be a matter of technical unskill. He goes on correcting because his work does not satisfy the impulse which drives him into his work. . . ."[12]

Thoreau did not remodel and enlarge *Walden* as Byron added to *Childe Harold*, after the fashion of many a New England house with wings and ells and sheds added as occasion demanded and circumstances allowed. He did not, on the other hand, as Pope probably did in remaking *The Rape of the Lock*, envisage from the beginning of his reworking a larger and more formal structure, each part of which could be done according to a new plan that he had before him as remodeling began. Thoreau's method of remodeling was more complex than either of these. It was as if, after having built a modest six- or seven-room house and living in it for a time, he found that it was not large enough. First he began by enlarging and remodeling most of the rooms, and then, as he did so, he decided to add new rooms, and still later he found he could improve the proportions and disposition of the various parts of the house. But he did all this work from the inside out, cutting apart and spreading the foundations, walls, and roof wherever necessary to accommodate the changes within, without destroying the fundamental character or any considerable portion of the original.

Even while the manuscript reveals how much more polished, more spacious, and better designed the published *Walden* is than the first and other earlier versions, it also reveals that the essential nature of *Walden* did not change from first to last. Much material was added over the years, but it did not introduce a new element and create a new strain; it was absorbed by and used according to the nature of the original piece.

The manuscript thus gives us information that is essential to a just interpretation of Thoreau's work and life, as well as an insight

12. *Beauty and Other Forms of Value* (London: Macmillan & Co., 1933), pp. 67–68.

into his craft and art. It emphasizes anew the enduring and supreme importance to Thoreau of his Walden experience. We know, as we did not before, how long he dwelt upon his life in the woods, going back to it again and again, solicitous that his story should be fully told, and constantly moved to recapture for his readers more of the delights he had sought and found in living. Desire for a finished piece of work was in part responsible for the labor he undertook. But more important was the desire, as he put it, "to make [*Walden*] a completer & truer account of that portion of the author's life."[13] For it was not only the story of the experience which settled his life for him but also a statement of his beliefs which had flourished under the test of time.

That his beliefs did stand firm and that *Walden* expressed his thoughts and feelings at the time he published it is quite clear from his constant and extensive work on it from 1851 to 1854. It is not a book which he had practically finished in 1849 but did not publish until 1854 because of external circumstances. The full expression of the joy and confidence of *Walden* depended greatly upon the work Thoreau did after 1851. The knowledge of this makes less plausible than ever "the legend," as Canby so aptly named it, of Thoreau growing more frustrated and unhappy in the years after he left Walden Pond, because he lost faith in the life he had chosen and because he was overwhelmed by his ceaseless observing and measuring of the world around him.[14]

It is true that after 1850 he wrote in his journal from time to time of being dissatisfied with himself and his life, of a sense of having lost something he had in his youth: "I think that no experience which I have to-day comes up to, or is comparable with, the experiences of my boyhood. . . . My life was ecstacy. In youth before I lost any of my senses, . . . I was alive . . ." (July 16, 1851). "The youth gets together his materials to build a bridge to the moon . . . and at length the middle-aged man concludes to build a wood-shed with them" (July 14, 1852). "Ah, those youthful days! are they never to return? when the walker does not too curiously observe particulars, but sees, hears, scents,

13. Unpublished preface in manuscript version VII.
14. Canby, *Thoreau*, p. 333.

tastes, and feels only himself,—the phenomena that show themselves to him,—his expanding body, his intellect and heart. No worm or insect, quadruped or bird, confined his view, but the unbounded universe was his. A bird is now become a mote in his eye" (March 30, 1853).

But such feelings are commonplace in the experience of many mature and reflective people who are far from being frustrated and unhappy. If one of them is a poet, he may write an ode on the "Intimations of Immortality"; if he writes an autobiography, he may observe as did Yeats in 1914 at the end of "Reveries over Childhood and Youth": "For some months now I have lived with my own youth and childhood, . . . and I am sorrowful and disturbed . . . when I think of all the books I have read, and of the wise words I have heard spoken, and of the anxiety I have given to parents and grandparents, and of the hopes that I have had, all life weighed in the scales of my own life seems to me a preparation for something that never happens."[15] If he keeps a journal like Thoreau's, in which everything is to be recorded, he will note these moods as they occur. It is a mistake to take them as more than occasional moods and to see in them the reflection of a dominant note at one time or another in the years after Thoreau left the pond.[16]

The evidence of what *Walden* says and of when and how Thoreau wrote it, added to the full record of what he did and thought and felt, makes it clear that the perceptive and balanced judgments of H. S. Canby and J. W. Krutch on Thoreau's life after 1855 hold true also for the years from 1850 to 1855: "Ecstacies were rare with him in these years, nostalgia for his more impressionable youth frequent, but the joy of free observation was constant. . . . For a man of his tastes, his temperament, and his philosophy, life had arranged itself ideally."[17] "Obviously the

15. *The Autobiographies of W. B. Yeats* (New York: Macmillan Co., 1938), p. 94.

16. Mark Van Doren, *Henry David Thoreau* (Boston: Houghton Mifflin Co., 1916), presents Thoreau as unhappy in the last years of his life; Ethel Seybold, *Thoreau: The Quest and the Classics* (New Haven: Yale University Press, 1951), chap. iv, places Thoreau's unhappiness in the period between 1848 and 1852; Sherman Paul, "Resolution at Walden," *Accent*, XII (1953), 101–13, apparently dates the period of what he calls Thoreau's "decay" from 1850 to 1854.

17. Canby, *Thoreau*, p. 333.

moments of happy insight did come less frequently. But at least they never ceased entirely and there is no evidence that Thoreau ever found his life other than rewarding and sweet."[18]

Of course, what Thoreau said in *Walden* in 1854 does not prove what he thought and felt from 1855 to 1862, but it certainly suggests how unlikely was a descent into unhappy frustration in those years. And when we know how long and how late he worked on *Walden* and that he had less than seven years between finishing it and the collapse of his health, the fact that he completed no major work after *Walden* will not lead to the conclusion that his creative powers faded seriously after 1854. Between 1854 and 1862 he published *Slavery in Massachusetts*, four chapters of *Cape Cod*, *Chesuncook*, two papers on John Brown, and *The Succession of Forest Trees;* he partly prepared a number of posthumously published pieces, and there was the unceasing work that made up the last eight volumes of the printed journal as well as much unprinted material.

We must see the collecting of the data that looms so large in these last years of his life for what it was: not a dusty road to an impenetrable swamp but a deeper and satisfying exploration of the world that Thoreau wanted to know. Only one enamored of what Thoreau called the "sublimo-slipshod" appreciation of things can bewail his measuring snow depths, counting tree rings, and studying the temperatures and currents of the rivers. Those who do so do not see at all where Thoreau was going and apparently think that exact knowledge must inevitably rob one of imagination and insight. They fail to appreciate Thoreau's pioneer study of ecology.[19] He could not have written *The Succession of Forest Trees* had he been content to exclaim over fine prospects and nice combinations of light and shade, or to stop on finding tropes and metaphors for man's moral life in natural events. Thoreau knew, though he never found all the right methods, that

18. Joseph Wood Krutch, *Thoreau* (New York: William Sloane Associates, 1948), p. 174.

19. See Philip and Kathryn Whitford, "Thoreau: Pioneer Ecologist and Conservationist," *Scientific Monthly*, LXXIII (1951), 291–96; and Kathryn Whitford, "Thoreau and the Woodlots of Concord," *New England Quarterly*, XXIII (1950), 291–306.

tree rings had to be counted and snow depths measured (as they are today) if he was to learn, as he wanted to, the relation between the Concord environment and Concord men, and to understand what made things happen as they do.[20]

He described his situation in a letter of May 21, 1856, to his friend Blake, who had invited him to lecture in Worcester. Whatever mistakes others may make about his work, Thoreau recognized his raw research notes for what they were: "In fine, what I have is either too scattered or loosely arranged, or too light, or else is too scientific and matter of fact (I run a good deal into that of late) for so hungry a company. I am still a learner, not a teacher, feeding somewhat omnivorously, browsing both stalk and leaves; but I shall perhaps be enabled to speak with the more precision and authority by and by,—if philosophy and sentiment are not buried under a multitude of details."[21] He died before he could join philosophy and sentiment to any great part of the material he had gathered. As Emerson put it: "The scale on which his studies proceeded was so large as to require longevity, and we were the less prepared for his sudden disappearance."[22] There is no evidence that he had lost the ability to deal with the details. What would we have guessed of the scattered and unrefined matter of *Walden?* Certainly not the great crystal Thoreau made.

DESCRIPTION OF THE MANUSCRIPT

Group I. 116 leaves; $9\frac{7}{8}$ by $7\frac{7}{8}$ inches; light-blue paper faintly lined, with a faint margin drawn on most leaves; a round stationer's mark, with a rose on a stem with leaves and a bud, is clearly impressed in the upper left corner of a number of leaves. Only some leaves bear the embossed stationer's mark because the die that made the mark was apparently applied to a number of leaves at one time, and it made a clear impression on only some in each batch; on other leaves only the over-all shape of the mark is discernible; on others there is no trace of it. Crowded in the

20. Canby, *Thoreau,* p. 336.

21. *Familiar Letters,* p. 280.

22. "Biographical Sketch," reprinted in *A Week on the Concord and Merrimack Rivers;* p. xl.

narrow margin at the top of the first page, center, in pencil, is a motto: "Where I have been / There was none seen." To the right of this, in ink: "Walden or Life in / the woods by Henry Thoreau / Addressed to my Townsmen." The handwriting in this version is smaller than that in any of the others; the ink is lighter and of a brownish color.

Many leaves have a faintly penciled number (a few leaves have two numbers) in the upper right corner of the recto. Thoreau numbered most of the odd pages of the first version (and later those of the second and third versions) in two sequences, one for the pages of "Economy" and one for the rest of the material. Owing to the confusion caused by the lack of a number on some pages and the presence of two numbers on others, the significance of the numbers was not clear until the manuscript groups had been established on the basis of other criteria. There is a total of only seventy-three numbers that belong in the sequences for the first version, since quite often Thoreau numbered only every other recto—the first one of a double leaf—and since some of the numbered leaves are lost. The sequence for "Economy" ran from 1 to 51; the sequence for the rest of the material from 1 to 235. There are also twelve leaves in "Economy" which were inserted at several points after the other pages were numbered but which on the basis of handwriting and ink are clearly part of this version. A few leaves have a lightly penciled number in the upper right corner of the recto that does not fit in the original sequences; and a few leaves have a second number there that does not fit in the sequences. These numbers are part of the sequences that resulted when Thoreau renumbered after adding material in versions II and III and inserting the leaves in I. The last extra leaf that belongs in the first version—with the last paragraph of "Economy" on it—is numbered 137. It is not clear whether this is part of a sequence in the manuscript or whether it is simply the number of a page from a notebook—Thoreau frequently numbered the pages of his notebooks and journals.

Group II. 79 leaves; $9\frac{5}{16}$ by $7\frac{5}{16}$ inches; white paper, lined; an oval stationer's mark with a border inclosing "H & E Goodwin" is clearly impressed in the upper left corner of a number of leaves.

The handwriting on most of the leaves is more carefully formed than that in any of the other groups. Many leaves have a faintly penciled number in the upper right corner of the recto; as in version I, one sequence runs for the material of "Economy" and another for the rest of the material. Neither sequence is complete since the leaves here were fitted in with leaves of versions I and III.

Group III. 33 leaves; same paper and stationer's mark as in II. On the top half of page 1, Thoreau wrote: "Walden, / or / Life in the Woods. / Addressed to my Townsmen. / By / Henry D. Thoreau." These pages were written with a blacker ink and a thinner pen point than were those of II; the handwriting is not so carefully formed. Many of the leaves are numbered in sequences with leaves in I and II. In two places, passages of III were begun in blank spaces on pages in II. In one case (at "Economy," 37) the continuation of the new passage consists of material transposed from another place in II. In the other (at "Economy," 60) the continuation runs for two new leaves; although these leaves belong to III, they have been left with the leaves of II in the manuscript as it is now arranged in the Huntington Library, in order that the relations of the material may be clear.[23]

Group IV. 64 leaves; $9\frac{7}{16}$ by $7\frac{9}{16}$ inches; some white and some cream-colored paper, faintly lined; a round stationer's mark, with an anchor surrounded by a border in which is "GOODWIN * HARTFORD," is clearly impressed in the upper left corner of a number of both the white and the cream-colored leaves. The handwriting varies more within this group than within any other, but, in spite of this and the variation in the paper, this group is clearly established by the relation of the contents of its leaves to the contents of preceding and following groups and to the contents of Thoreau's journals. Only a few leaves have one of Thoreau's numbers in the upper right corner of the recto.

Group V. 112 leaves; $9\frac{10}{16}$ by $7\frac{9}{16}$ inches; darker-blue paper than in I, faintly lined; same stationer's mark as in IV. Handwriting is large, free, heavy. Pages are not numbered.

---

23. Four of the leaves included in II may belong to III. The ink and thickness of pen line indicate that they belong to II; the form of the handwriting suggests that they may belong to III.

The Walden *Manuscript*

Group VI. 119 leaves; $9\frac{6}{16}$ by $7\frac{9}{16}$; white paper, very faintly lined; an oval stationer's mark with decorative border inclosing "G & Co" is clearly impressed in the upper left corner of a number of leaves. Handwriting much like that in V. Pages are not numbered.

Group VII. 46 leaves; $9\frac{10}{16}$ by $7\frac{9}{16}$ inches; white paper clearly lined; no stationer's mark. The first leaf of this group has a title page on the recto and a table of contents and a preface on the verso. The title page reads: "Walden, / or / Life in the Woods. / By / Henry D. Thoreau; / Author of 'A Week on the Concord and Merrimack Rivers.' / [Drawing of a crowing cock] / [interlined motto:] I do not propose to write an ode to dejection, but to / brag as lustily as chanticlere in the morning, standing on his roost, / if only to wake my neighbors up. / 'The clouds, wind, moon, sun, and sky, / act in cooperation, that thou / might get thy daily bread, and not / eat it with indifference; all revolve / for thy sake, and are obedient to / command; it must be an equi- / table condition, that thou shalt / be obedient also.' Sadi." Ink is lighter than that in all the other groups but I. Pages are not numbered.

Group VIII. 28 leaves, which contain short pieces written—some in ink, some in pencil—between the seven major groups, are of various sorts of paper, different from the papers used in the major groups, save for four leaves of the light-blue paper of group I. The contents and the handwriting and ink of these four leaves indicate that they were written after Thoreau had completed the first version.[24]

Group IX. 25 leaves of all sorts and sizes, some torn from journals and notebooks. In a few instances, they were partly blank leaves discarded from other pieces of work, which Thoreau used as scratch paper. This group is no doubt a bare fraction of the notes he used in preparing *Walden;* similar pieces are found in gatherings of miscellaneous pieces of Thoreau manuscript in various libraries. (But Thoreau did not, as he is generally reputed to

24. The manuscript (HM 924) in the Huntington Library is distributed in eight envelopes, and the leaves of group VIII are distributed among the envelopes containing groups I–VII, according to the relations of these leaves to the major groups.

have done, use scratch paper of any old sort for his formal com-position. He wrote only a few brief inserts for *Walden* on anything but fresh whole leaves.)[25]

Some leaves are certainly missing from the seven major manu-script groups. According to the gaps in the sequence of page num-bers Thoreau used in the first version, there are thirty-eight leaves missing from it. Thoreau may have destroyed or discarded some of them as they became useless because of revisions; the greatest losses occur at points where he revised his work most radically. Some of the leaves may be extant but scattered and still unidenti-fied—especially in copies of the manuscript edition of Thoreau's writings.[26] One leaf of version I is in the Berg Collection in the New York Public Library, and another was in a gathering of mis-cellaneous Thoreau manuscript leaves in the Huntington Li-brary. Leaves from other groups, too, are scattered; I have lo-cated five leaves belonging to V, one in the Yale University Li-brary, and four in a private collection; part of a leaf of VI in an-other private collection; and a leaf of VIII in still another private collection. Some leaves of the later groups were clearly destroyed; parts of pages of V and VI are pasted together at several points. I do not think, however, that any considerable number of leaves is missing from the groups after I. Only in the last half of *Walden* in II and III is there any remarkable lack of manuscript, and I think that this is owing primarily not to a loss of manuscript leaves but to the fact that Thoreau probably did not do much revision there.

The following outlines of the development of two passages in *Walden* will show how one can follow Thoreau as he canceled, added, revised, and rearranged material in his progress from version to version. The second outline will also help to make clear how he put together the material of the manuscript groups in the various versions of *Walden*. Roman numerals refer to the groups and arabic numerals to the paragraphs of the chapters.

25. In addition to the 622 leaves counted in the nine groups, there are six pieces of paper pasted to leaves in various groups: one in I, one in IV, two in V, one in VI, and one in VII.

26. Six hundred large paper copies of the 1906 edition of Thoreau's writings, each of which had a piece of Thoreau manuscript tipped in.

The Walden *Manuscript*

I. (*a*) 37. Almost all the second half ("It is desirable . . . reverence?") was written on the top two-thirds of the recto of a leaf and was followed on the verso by the beginning of "Economy," 44.

I. (*b*)   Thoreau canceled I(*a*) and wrote the following on the recto and verso of a new leaf and on the bottom third of the page that had the canceled passage on it.

    37. As in I(*a*).

    39. The first two-thirds: "On the whole . . . Cannibal Islands."

    41. All but the last sentence.

    40. First sentence plus another not in text.
        A passage on wornout garments not in text.

II.   Beginning on a new leaf, this is a fair copy of I(*b*), marked for:
Insertion of material to follow 37.
Proper order of 40 and 41.
Cancellation of sentence in 40 that is not in text.
Insertion of additional material in 40.

III.   This begins on what was the blank verso of a leaf in II.

    37. As in preceding versions.
        Beginning of the passage on the ragged ice-cutters which was marked for insertion in II; the rest of the passage was on a leaf that came earlier in II. The passage was ultimately used in "Economy," 105.
        Insertion of beginning of 38 is indicated.

IV.   The following was part of a longer piece of new copy in this version.

    37. Now complete as in text.

    38. First half: "When I ask . . . but they do not." From the journal of 1850 (II, 5).

    39. Last third added, and paragraph is practically complete, but with passage on "worn-out garments" (once in 40) inserted after "Cannibal Islands" and also the sentence on a dog barking at a tramp, which is in "Economy," 35 in the text.

    40. Complete as in text; some of it is from the journal of February 6, 1852.

41. Complete as in text.
    Marked for insertion of material in 38.

VII.   The following was written so as to fit in IV where appropriate lines were canceled.

38. The insertion in 38 includes the rest of 38 as it is in the published text, plus six sentences which are not in the published text. This material is from the journal of January 14, 1854.

39. Greatly expanded by the inclusion, after the sentence on the dog and tramp, of a long description of a countryman's strange and wonderful clothes; this is not in the text.

"THE VILLAGE"

I. Paragraph 1 (with "Economy," 89, within it) is an integral part of the first version; the first sentence of "The Ponds" follows it immediately.

Between I and II Thoreau wrote the first part of paragraph 2 on a separate leaf. It runs from the beginning of the paragraph through "mouth without assistance" and contains material that is not in the final text.

II. On a new double leaf he copied I, paragraph 1, from the beginning through "houses are so arranged as to make" and added five or six lines within it. This was to be followed by I, paragraph 1, from "the most of mankind" through "drowned the voices."
At the same time on another new leaf he copied I, paragraph 1, from "of the Sirens" to the end and rewrote the material of paragraph 2, making it essentially what it is in the text. The beginning of "The Ponds" was to follow.

III. On a new leaf he wrote the first draft of paragraph 3. Later, at two different times, he interlined the third sentence of the paragraph from the journal entry of June, 1850 (II, 40), and the quotations at the end of the paragraph. At this time he also canceled in I the material for "Economy," 89.

V. On a new leaf Thoreau copied paragraph 2 as it stood in II from "and I have thought" to the end of paragraph and canceled these lines in II. Then he rewrote paragraph 3 from the beginning through "to the pond, I suffered no" and canceled these lines in

III. This was to be followed by the rest of paragraph 3 as it stood in III.

VI. On another new double leaf he copied again the last lines of paragraph 2, as it stood, and then he wrote the first draft of the last part of paragraph 2 from the journal entry of March 29, 1853: "Several times when a visitor . . . infinite extent of our relations." He revised this in the copy for the printer.

When Thoreau wrote the copy for the printer, he had the material for all of "The Village" in the following order: paragraph 1 in groups II, I, and II; paragraph 2 in II and VI; paragraph 3 in V and III. Since he had marked all the pieces for joining, he would have had no extraordinary trouble in preparing his final copy. It is more difficult to follow him in other places because the development of many parts of *Walden* was more complicated. Thoreau was a careful workman, however, and always knew where he was.

II

The Successive Versions of Walden

THE immediate beginning of *Walden* was in 1846 when Thoreau learned that the audience at one of his Lyceum lectures —probably the one on Carlyle on February 4, 1846—had expected to hear about his life in the woods. People on the streets and in stores and parlors had asked him, "What's it like there?" "What do you eat?" "Aren't you lonesome?" They seemed incredulous concerning his life; some were clearly bewildered, like the man who came to the hut looking for his dog but was incapable of listening to Thoreau's attempts to help him; he kept repeating, "What do you do here?"[1] Thoreau discovered that all this was more than idle curiosity and that people did want answers and enlightenment if they could be had. Sometime before March 13, 1846, he wrote in his journal in preparation for a lecture, "After I lectured here before, this winter, I heard that some

1. *The Writings of Henry David Thoreau* (20 vols.; Boston: Houghton Mifflin Co., 1906), *Journal*, I, 398; entry is undated; whenever possible, journal entries are referred to by date. Unless otherwise indicated, all references to Thoreau's published writings are to this edition.

of my townsmen had expected of me some account of my life at the pond. This I will endeavor to give to-night."[2]

This was no encouragement for Thoreau to let pass; he wanted to lecture and write for money, and his journal already contained the beginnings of the two major elements in *Walden:* the story of how he lived at the pond, and the comparison of what he lived for with what many people of New England lived for. From the time he went to the pond, he had noted in his journal the events and thoughts of his days, undoubtedly with the idea of using the notes for lectures and essays as he was even then using earlier ones in writing *A Week.* And he was also thinking of a lecture on the mean and sneaking lives led by many people in Concord and New England. Sometime between December 23, 1845, and March 26, 1846, he wrote the opening lines of the lecture in his journal; they consisted of the first sentence of "Economy," 3, and all of "Economy," 7, and they began: "I wish to say something to-night not of and concerning the Chinese and Sandwich-Islanders, but *to* and concerning you who hear me."[3] With the stimulus of his townsmen's questions, he set out to develop and combine the two elements.

His first step in writing the first version was to gather the material which lay everywhere in his journals, not only those written at the pond but also the ones he had kept in earlier years. From notes of 1840 and 1841 he took items for his comments on clothes;[4] and from the journal he had kept while living at William Emerson's on Staten Island in 1843[5] he took the lyrical passage on the

2. I, 485; entry is undated; it precedes by several pages an entry dated March 13, 1846. In slightly revised form it is the second paragraph of the first version. The reference is probably to his lecture on Carlyle, on February 4, 1846, at the Concord Lyceum; see Walter Harding, "A Checklist of Thoreau's Lectures," *Bulletin of the New York Public Library*, LII (1948), 80.

3. I, 395; entry is undated. The journal entry immediately preceding it is dated December 23, 1845, but many pages were torn out between the two entries. The first dated entry after the one quoted is for March 26, 1846; it is considerably farther on in the journal.

4. See transcript of version I, "Economy," 36, 37, and 39, and the journal for July 12, 1840, February 5, and April 5, 1841. He did not use earlier journal items of April 8, 1839, and March 21, 1840, until later versions.

5. HM 13182 in the Huntington Library; printed in *The First and Last Journeys of Thoreau*, ed. F. B. Sanborn (Boston: Bibliophile Society, 1905).

coming of spring, "Spring," 13. He used the material of successive entries or even the parts of a single entry at widely scattered points in the first and later versions of *Walden*. For example, eleven consecutive journal paragraphs written on or near July 16, 1845, dealt with Alek Therien and other visitors, the advantages of a frontier or primitive life, and the mice at Walden; in the first version Thoreau used them in "Visitors," in two places in "Economy," and in the section on animals. Frequently, as a comparison of journal entries and the text shows, he adopted material from the journal with little change. Often, however, a journal entry was only the germ of a longer passage. He developed the following unpublished interlineation as the first draft of "Economy," 56, in I; later he interlined the rest of the paragraph in III: "There is no place in the village for a work of art, or statue for instance if one had come down to us—for our lives our houses furnish no proper pedestal for it. It is more beautiful out of doors where there is no house—no man."[6]

In the cases just given, Thoreau took what he wanted from various journal entries and did not go back to them when he revised his work; in other cases, however, he used only some of the material at hand and later returned for more. In the first version he took over from his journal the material for "Economy," 7, but not until the third version did he take over the first sentence of "Economy," 3, which immediately preceded 7 in the journal.[7] He drew on the following journal entry of his third day at the pond, July 6, 1845, at five different times. He used three items in three widely separated places in the first version, and after writing the second version, he interlined two other items from this entry, again at some distance from one another:

July 6. [Version I. Cf. "Where I Lived," 16:] I wish to meet the facts of life—the vital facts, which are the phenomena or actuality the gods meant to show us—face to face, and so I came down here. Life! who knows what it is, what it does? If I am not quite right here, I am less wrong than before; and now let us see what they will have. [Interlined

6. See the transcript of version I, p. 122, and the manuscript journal, Vol. VII, in the Morgan Library, New York, N.Y.

7. I, 395–96; entry is undated.

in version II. Cf. "Where I Lived," 20:] The preacher, instead of vexing the ears of drowsy farmers on their day of rest, at the end of the week,—for Sunday always seemed to me like a fit conclusion of an ill-spent week and not the fresh and brave beginning of a new one,—with this one other draggletail and postponed affair of a sermon, from thirdly to fifteenthly, should teach them with a thundering voice pause and simplicity. "Stop! Avast! Why so fast?" [At the beginning of "Reading" in version I, but not in text:] In all studies we go not forward but rather backward with redoubled pauses. We always study *antiques* [Thoreau's italics] with silence and reflection. Even time has a depth, and below its surface the waves do not lapse and roar. [Version I, "Economy," 8:] I wonder men can be so frivolous almost as to attend to the gross form of negro slavery, there are so many keen and subtle masters who subject us both. [Interlined in version II, "Economy," 8:] Self-emancipation in the West Indies of a man's thinking and imagining provinces, which should be more than his island territory,—one emancipated heart and intellect! It would knock off the fetters from a million slaves.

He did not always lift separable items and use them in more or less developed form. Sometimes he found suggestions for two or three different points in a single note. An unpublished leaf (HM 924), torn from a journal or notebook, contains a series of brief notes that Thoreau developed in "Visitors," "The Ponds," "House-Warming," and "The Pond in Winter"; one of the notes reads (unless otherwise noted, italics here and in subsequent quotations from manuscripts indicate material interlined by Thoreau):

A place of pines—of forest scenes and events visited by successive nations of men all of whom have successively *admired & *fathomed it— but still its water is green and pellucid, not an intermittent spring— somewhat perennial in it—while the nations pass away *offering its perennial well to the animal nations. A true well—a gem of the first water— which Concord wears in her coronet.
looking blue as amethyst or solidified azure far off as it is drawn through the streets. Green in the deeps—blue in the shallows. Perhaps the grass is a denser deeper heaven.

He used "a place of pines," the "perennial" quality of the spring-well, and the observation on the green and blue of Walden's water in "The Ponds," 5, the color of the ice in "The Pond in Winter," 16, and the major part of the note in "The Ponds."[8]

When he was actually writing out the first version, Thoreau did not simply leaf through his journals and take what he wanted as he found it. He first gathered his material and ordered it. The evidence for this is clear, even though not extensive. In the back of one of his journals of 1845–47 he wrote out a preliminary list of topics for the later part of the first version, and then he numbered the topics in the order in which he first intended to use them in *Walden*.[9] In the margin of the manuscript journal of July, 1845, he marked the order of the items on the advantages of a primitive and frontier life before he copied them in the first version.[10] In other cases, as with the following notes on clothing, he wrote out his material with the intention of working it over later. The phrase at the end indicates that he had previously assembled or written out other material on clothing.

Comparatively speaking tattooing is not necessarily the hideous custom it is described to be. It is the same taste that prints the calico which the wearer put off and on, and the consistent objection is rather to the fashion of the print than to the practice itself. It is not therefore barbarous because it is skin deep. [Compare "Economy," 40.]

When I meet a fine lady or a gentleman dressed at the top of the fashion I wonder what they would do if there should be an earthquake or a fire should suddenly break out; for they appear to have counted on fine weather & a smooth course only. Our dress should to some extent be such as will fit equally well in good & in bad fortune. [Compare "Economy," 37.]

When our garments are worn out we hang them up in the fields to scare crows with, as if the reason why men scare crows was in their clothes. I have often experienced the difficulty of getting within gunshot of a crow. It is not because they smell powder. [This appears in the first and other versions but not in text.]

8. Neither "an intermittent spring" nor "a gem . . . in her coronet" is in "The Ponds," 8, in version I; how much of paragraph 5 was in I is not certain because some of it was on a missing leaf.

9. Volume VI of the manuscript journals in the Morgan Library; see note 1 in Appendix for the details of this list.

10. Compare *Journal*, I, 367–68, undated entry, and the transcript of version I, pp. 121–22.

The Successive Versions of Walden

It is true all costume off a man is grotesque. It is only the serious eye
& the sincere life passed within it, which restrain laughter, and consecrate the costume of any people. Let Harlequin be taken with a fit of
the colic in the midst of his buffoonery, and his trappings will have to
serve that mood too. When the soldier is hit with a cannon ball rags are
as becoming as purple. As soon in short as a man engages to eat walk
work & sit & meet all the contingencies of life therein, his costume is
hallowed, and may be the theme of poetry. [Compare "Economy,"
39.]

I have little hesitation in saying & [in the first version this phrase introduces material that is in "Economy," 41].[11]

In some cases he assembled notes on a topic by tearing pages out
of his journals; hence the mutilation of the early manuscript
journals and the presence of torn-out journal pages in the *Walden*
manuscript and in miscellaneous manuscript gatherings.

As he took over his raw material, Thoreau broke it up, changed
it in detail, developed it, and finally ordered it so that he might
offer his hearers and readers, not the immediate, random, and
intermittent notes of a journal, but a reflected-on and consciously
shaped re-creation of his experience. A torn leaf in the *Walden*
manuscript gives us a glimpse of how he roughed out such a piece
as the story of investigating, wrecking, and removing James
Collins' shanty. He went over it at least twice, for he made one
set of interlineations in ink and another in pencil (here and elsewhere, angle brackets ⟨ ⟩ indicate canceled material in manuscripts):

[Torn; two words not clear] became a dead cat—and buried at last.
Lintel none but perennial passage for hens *under the door board.* I threw
down this dwelling ⟨next day⟩ [pencil:] *this morning*—drawing the nails
—and removed it to the pond side in small cart loads *one early thrush gave
me a note or two by the way—which was encouraging* [second interlining in
pencil:] *as I drove along the woodland path.* Penurious[?] Seeley neighbor
Irishman—as I was informed *by young Patrick treacherously* transferring in
the intervals the still tolerable straight driveable nails—staples spikes to
his pocket—and then stood to look on unconcerned *in the sun* and pass
the time of day. ⟨There by the ponside [*sic*] they bleached—warped⟩
[pencil:] *& then spread the boards on the grass to bleach and warp* back again

11. HM 924, on the verso of a leaf discarded from *A Week.*

in the sun ⟨upon the grass⟩ Seeley *with his spring thoughts* gazing freshly up at the devastation seeking [for "seeing"?] there is a dearth of work—he *there* to represent spectatordom jingling his pockets lowly—a transaction of singular quietness.

Thoreau must have begun to write out the first version of *Walden* late in 1846 or early in 1847. He had finished part of it by February 10 and 17, 1847, when he lectured at the Concord Lyceum on his life at the pond;[12] but he was still at work later in the winter and spring, for in this version he wrote of the ice-cutters of the winter of 1846–47: "This winter [later changed to 'In the winter of 46 & 47'] as you all know there came a hundred men"; and "They have not been able to break up our pond any earlier than usual this year as they expected to—for she has got a thick new garment to replace the old." Speaking of his house-keeping earlier, he had said: "I trust that none of my hearers will be so uncharitable as to look into my house now—after hearing this, at the end of an unusually dirty winter, with critical house-wife's eyes, for I intend to celebrate the first bright & unquestionable spring morning by scrubbing my house with sand until it is as white as a lily—or, at any rate, as the washerwoman said of her clothes, as white as a 'wiolet.' "[13] He wrote these passages with the possibility of reading them in lectures in 1847. They were not written, as were some later additions, merely as if he were at Walden.

There is no conclusive evidence that he completed this version before he left the pond in September, 1847, but since he was writing about the ice-cutters of "The Pond in Winter" by early spring,[14] it seems reasonable to conclude that he would have written the remaining twenty-seven pages of version I by September, or even earlier. The fact that he later interlined "Left Walden Sept. 6, 1847" at the end of this version also suggests that he had finished before that date.

Thoreau's own statements seem to imply that the first version

12. Harding, "A Checklist of Thoreau's Lectures," p. 80.

13. See transcript of version I, pp. 153, 199, 200.

14. On p. 209 of the 236 pages in the second sequence of Thoreau's numbering.

was longer than it actually was. The first draft of the first paragraph of *Walden* (in version III, 1849) begins: "At the time the
following pages were written I lived alone in the woods." Late in
1853 or very early in 1854 he changed this to read as it does in the
published text, "the following pages, or rather the bulk of them."
In the unpublished preface of version VII, 1854, he said: "Nearly
all of this volume was written eight or nine years ago in the scenery & under the circumstances which it describes, and a considerable part was read at that time as lectures before the Concord
Lyceum. In what is now added the object has been chiefly to
make it a completer & truer account of that portion of the author's life." By the phrases "the bulk of them" and "nearly all of
this volume" Thoreau may have meant that he had written more
of *Walden* at the pond than at any other one time; certainly, the
version of *Walden* he wrote at the pond was only about half as long
as the final text.

A detailed description of the first version is given in the Appendix. Its general nature can be suggested here by comparing it
briefly with the final text. The first version has the spirit and the
style of *Walden,* but the spirit is not so strongly developed and the
style is not so finished. Mark Van Doren said of *Walden,* "it was
written in bounding spirits, with eyes twinkling and tongue in
cheek."[15] So it was, and Thoreau wrote with the same joy and
humor and challenging assurance at the beginning. There is a
considerable difference, however, between the first and the last
versions; the flavor is the same, but at the end it is much richer,
since, as time went on, Thoreau added more and more of every
element: for example, by far the greater part of the description of
his immediate surroundings in "The Ponds," all the account of
the friends who came to see him in "Winter Visitors," and the
gay satire and poetry of all of "Conclusion." And he added the
learning and authority of most of his quotations and specific references to earlier writers. Of fifty such items in the first half of
Walden[16] only seven are in the first version; Thoreau added the

15. *Henry David Thoreau,* p. 11.

16. Counting separately the quotations from the Bible in "Economy," 47 and 48;
and those (from Confucius?) in "Solitude," 7, 8, 9. Because of the leaves missing in

others at various times in all the later versions.[17] He also improved the flavor significantly by cutting out the mediocre verse which bulks large in the first version.

The style of this version is recognizably that of the published text—homely and elaborate, witty and humorous, reflective and argumentative, scornful and gentle. And narrative, anecdote, lyric description, character sketch, satire, exposition—all kinds are here. But, understandably enough, in many places the writing does not have the clarity, force, and rhythms that we find in *Walden* itself; only by a long and untiring pursuit was Thoreau to win that perfection. A number of passages in the first version, if taken by themselves, may be superior in some respects to the revisions of them in the final text. The description of his partially finished house, "Where I Lived," 8, and the advice of his "Good Genius," "Baker Farm," 6, for example, have a greater spontaneity and immediacy in the first version. But the later versions of such passages are more in keeping with the movement and tone of the final text. Thoreau inevitably sacrificed some liveliness and directness as he developed his lectures into a book which would give a fuller account of his experience.

Thoreau's quarrel with the ways of his contemporaries and the general outline as well as a large part of his story are in the first version, but it is by no means a "scale model" of *Walden* in either content or form. The major points of his criticism in "Economy" are laid out, but many illustrations and some reflections are missing, and there is little of "Higher Laws" and nothing of "Conclusion." As for his story, this version contains the greater part of his account of what he did in the summer and the description in the earlier chapters of the general quality of his life, but the account of the rest of the year is thin. Various parts of the final

---

the later part of the first version of *Walden*, it is not possible to tell what quotations were in it.

17. In the first half of *Walden* he added quotations and specific references to authorities thus: he interlined two in version I; twelve in II; three in III; he wrote six in IV and interlined one; wrote three in V and interlined three; wrote six in VI and interlined one; wrote three in VII. Three quotations and references are not in the manuscript; either Thoreau added them in the copy for the printer, or they were on leaves missing from versions later than the first.

text are very unevenly represented, and the order and relations of the parts are quite different in many places, particularly in the second half, where the sequence of topics and of the events of the year is by no means so carefully worked out. Much was to be changed by later work.

When Thoreau left Walden Pond and returned to the village in September, 1847, he probably had a draft of *A Week* as well as the first version of *Walden,* and he also had material for several articles. If he was to realize his hopes of a career as a writer, he had to finish some of his pieces and publish them. At first, in the last months of 1847 and well into 1848, he seems to have been engaged on things other than *Walden.* By January 12, 1848, he lectured on the trip he had made to Ktaadn in the summer of 1846, and he sent off the completed essay "Ktaadn" to Horace Greeley by the end of March.[18] He had also prepared at least part of "Civil Disobedience" by January and February, 1848, when he lectured on the relation of the individual to the state.[19] And he worked on *A Week* in the spring and part of the summer of 1848, for in March he told Elliot Cabot that since he had not yet found a publisher for it, he was going to "mend it" and would "look at it again directly" when he had finished some other things; and in May he wrote to Greeley, "My book grows in bulk as I work on it."[20]

In view of all this, Thoreau probably did not return to any extended work on *Walden* until sometime after the middle of 1848. When he did so, he revised the first version in great detail not only to improve it for lectures such as those he gave in 1848–49 in Salem, Portland, and Worcester, as well as in Concord[21] but also with an eye toward publication. He crowded in at the top of the first page of the first version: "Walden or Life in / the woods by Henry Thoreau / Addressed to my Townsmen;" and later he put in a motto: "Where I have been / There was none seen." In

18. *Familiar Letters*, p. 150; *The Maine Woods*, p. ix.
19. Harding, "A Checklist," pp. 80–81.
20. *Familiar Letters*, pp. 156, 172.
21. Harding, "A Checklist," pp. 81–82.

a number of places he changed "lecture" to "book," "audience" to "readers," and "hear" to "read."

Having worked over the first version, Thoreau wrote version II.[22] He revised it and then wrote version III so close upon II that they almost seem one piece. At one point, a passage of II is on one side of a leaf and a passage of III on the other; at a second point, a passage of III that runs for five pages begins on the bottom of a page that has material of II on it. Furthermore, the pagination of the two versions runs in one series where Thoreau fitted the material of III into II. It is certain, however, that there are two versions here and that Thoreau wrote III after II: not only are the ink and handwriting different, but also III contains revisions of parts of II.

Neither version II nor III is much longer than I. The effect and apparent intention of his work in these versions was to tidy up and to increase the clarity and force of the first version, which he had written at the pond. And so he could properly write in III: "At the time the following pages were written I lived alone, in the woods."[23] There is no direct evidence as to when he wrote II and III, but all the circumstances indicate conclusively that he did so in 1848–49 and that he was preparing for early publication. Version II is essentially a fair copy of much of I with its corrections; the handwriting in II is the most carefully formed in the whole manuscript. In III, which consists almost entirely of rewriting of parts of I and II, the first page has in its upper half both title and author written out in a large hand, and it contains the first draft of the explanatory first paragraph of *Walden*.[24] The

22. Thoreau made most of the revisions in version I before writing II and III, but he went over I at later times too; for example, he interlined material from the journal for November 3, 1852, in "Winter Animals," 3, in I.

23. The nature of his additions, cancellations, and rearrangements of material from version to version makes it impossible to give descriptions of the contents of the various versions that would be accurate and at the same time clear. The Table of Additions on pp. 70–73 shows in summary fashion what each new version contributed to the building up of *Walden;* chap. iv gives a full account of the way in which Thoreau made the additions.

24. Thoreau thriftily thought of lectures even as he wrote versions II and III for publication; the manuscript of both versions has "book," "readers," etc.; but at several points it has "lecture" where version I had been revised to read "book." In

external evidence has been mentioned already: early in 1849 Thoreau asked Ticknor and Company about the possibility of their publishing *Walden;* on February 28, 1849, his Aunt Maria wrote that he was preparing *Walden* for the press;[25] and some copies of the first edition of *A Week* included a notice in the advertising pages that *Walden* would be published soon.

In 1849 Thoreau had a version of *Walden*, consisting of material in I, II, and III, which members of his family read and of which he could have made a fair copy; but there is no evidence in the manuscript that he made such a copy, although a letter of February 8, 1849, to Thoreau from Ticknor's might suggest that he had sent the publisher a manuscript of *Walden*. They wrote: "We find on looking over publishing matters that we cannot well undertake anything more at present. If however you feel inclined, we will publish 'Walden or Life in the Woods' on our own a/c, say One Thousand copies, allowing you 10 pr. ct. copyright on the Retail Price on all that are sold. The style of printing & binding to be like Emersons Essays."[26] On the other hand, there is no copy in the *Walden* manuscript that Thoreau could have sent to the publishers at this time; and in view of all that is there, it seems most unlikely that, if there had been such a copy, it would not be in the manuscript.

I think the situation in February, 1849, was this. Thoreau had completed his work on *A Week* and was probably not very far from being able to complete a publishable version of *Walden*. We know that he had finished *A Week* and that he sent a fair copy of it to Ticknor's, for in a letter of February 16, 1849, they told him that they would publish the book at his expense, 1,000 copies in sheets for an estimated $381.24.[27] But it seems likely that he only inquired in advance about the possibility of their publishing *Walden*. Apparently the price quoted for *A Week*, and perhaps the

---

version III in the first sentence of "Economy," 3, Thoreau wrote of his lecture in "this city" (later changed to "town"), probably Portland in March, 1849, or Worcester on April 20, 1849.

25. *The Cost Books of Ticknor and Fields*, ed. W. S. Tryon and William Charvat (New York, 1949), p. 289; Canby, *Thoreau*, p. 248.

26. *The Cost Books*, p. 289.

27. *Ibid.*, p. 289.

terms offered for *Walden*, led Thoreau to seek another publisher, James Munroe, who published *A Week* in May, 1849, and at the same time announced in the advertising pages of *A Week* that *Walden* would "be published soon." But Thoreau never finished preparing *Walden* for publication at this time because *A Week* did not sell.

A publisher would hardly have risked Thoreau's second book immediately, and Thoreau could not put out a second book at his own expense—he did not settle his account with Munroe for publishing *A Week* until November 28, 1853.[28] Even had he had the money, perhaps Thoreau would not have finished *Walden* and published it at this time after seeing the reception given to *A Week*. How much the failure of *A Week* affected the course of Thoreau's life is a matter for conjecture, but the results for *Walden* are plain. William Charvat points out how the work of Poe, Melville, Hawthorne, Emerson, and others benefited in some respects because of "the pressures which contemporary readers and the booktrade exerted upon them."[29] The much-lamented plight of the artist in America may have its good effects. Indirectly, the public's lack of appreciation of *A Week* had a great deal to do with *Walden*'s being the masterpiece it is. The financial failure of *A Week* kept Thoreau from publishing *Walden* when he first wanted to, and when he did publish it five years later, he had enlarged and improved it almost beyond compare.

From 1849 until late 1851 or the beginning of 1852, Thoreau's work on *Walden* consisted only of revisions in the copy of versions I, II, and III. It is not possible to determine exactly when he made various corrections, but it was undoubtedly during 1850–51 that he put in all or most of the quotations from Chinese and Hindu writings that are interlined in II and III, for he commented in the journal for May 6, 1851: "Like some other preachers, I have added my texts—derived from the Chinese and Hindoo scriptures—long after my discourse was written." A few other scattered items in the journals of 1850–51 suggest that he

28. *Journal*, V, 521, see also p. 459.

29. "Literary Economics and Literary History," *English Institute Essays, 1949* (New York: Columbia University Press, 1950), pp. 73–91.

thought of *Walden* from time to time, but it is certain that he did not write any significant amount of new material in the manuscript until January or February of 1852.[30] By January 17, 1852, he was engrossed in *Walden* once more. On that day he wrote in his journal two items on visitors and a short paragraph on the date and manner of his moving to the hut, and he clearly intended to use them in his book.[31] Then in the journal for January 21 he wrote the draft of the battle of the ants which he was soon to add to "Brute Neighbors" in version IV; and more *Walden* material appears frequently in the journals of succeeding weeks and months.

Once Thoreau had taken up his work again, he wrote and rewrote and continually added to his book until he sent the final copy to the printer in 1854. There are four distinct groups of leaves in the manuscript marking four distinct stages of work (the lost copy for the printer was a fifth) between the beginning of 1852 and the late spring of 1854. The period during which Thoreau wrote each version can be determined by the dates of the journal material he used in it and by its relation to the versions preceding and following it, but we cannot tell exactly when he began or stopped working on any of them.

He wrote version IV at various times during 1852. He drew much of the new material for it from his journals for 1850, 1851, and the first half of 1852; there are also a few items from September, October, and November, 1852. He published two considerable pieces of this version in *Sartain's Magazine* of July, 1852: "A Poet Buys a Farm" and "The Iron Horse."[32] Late in 1852 or early in 1853 Thoreau dropped IV and fairly soon afterward began version V. In view of the extent of the new manuscript, Thoreau

30. For example, see journal for November 8, 1850, and "House-Warming," 3 and 4. And such an item as "Economy," 31, on the Indian selling baskets, may have been written up before 1852; it depends on undated journal material of 1850 (II, 84), and Thoreau wrote it out on a separate leaf for inclusion in *Walden*.

31. "Visitors," 15; "Where I Lived," 8. On the same day he also wrote his comment on Madame Pfeiffer's clothes, "Economy," 35, and on January 11 he had written much of the passage on architecture, "Economy," 67, but he was not necessarily thinking of *Walden* as he put these two items in the journal.

32. "Where I Lived," 1, 2, 3, and 5; and "Sounds," 5–13; Thoreau revised both passages before the final text of *Walden*.

must have worked on V well into 1853, but it contains practically no material from the journals of 1853. Late in that year he began VI, and he probably did not complete it until the beginning of 1854. As he finished this version he wrote "The End," but he still had considerable work before him.

He undoubtedly wrote VII in February or March, immediately after finishing VI. The title page, table of contents, and preface in this version might suggest that its leaves were the remnants of a rewriting Thoreau prepared for the printer, but they were not. All the passages in VII are short, and Thoreau fitted them into the earlier groups, most into VI, but others into II, III, IV, and V.

His final draft, which is not in the manuscript and was apparently lost, was the copy for the printer. Thoreau must have sent off some of his copy in late February or early March, for he noted in his journal on March 28, 1854, "Got first proof of 'Walden.' " This referred to the first batch of page proof and not to a first set of proofs of the whole work. In the manuscript of VII, in the midst of a sentence in "Economy," 38, Thoreau noted, "end of 2nd proof"; and on page 64 of the page proof (HM 925) he wrote to the printer, "Will try to make the last part of the Ms. more legible." He sent the copy off in parts and received the page proof in the same way.[33] He probably finished the copy for the printer in late April or May. He wrote of the breaking-up of the ice in 1854, "about the 7th of April," in "Spring," 3; and his observation on how long it took for Walden Pond to rise and fall in "The Ponds," 10, is from the journal entry for April 27, 1854; he first put it in *Walden* on a scrap of paper which he attached to a leaf of version VI.

33. The page proof was the only proof he received; he could not have received anything before it. It was set up with three pages on a sheet. In the first batch of proof Thoreau received five sheets; the first sheet contained the title page and the copyright; each of the other four sheets contained three pages of proof. On the verso of the fifth sheet is written "duplicate proof for the editor." The second batch of proof consisted of four sheets—twelve pages—of proof. The end of the twenty-fourth page of text (the end of the ninth sheet of proof) coincides with the point in the manuscript at which Thoreau wrote "end of 2nd proof." On the verso of the ninth sheet is the direction "Henry D. Thoreau, Concord, Mass." There is no evidence as to the extent of later batches of proof.

The Successive Versions of Walden

Even when the copy for the printer was done, Thoreau could not rest. On March 31, 1854, he had written in the journal: "In criticising your writing, trust your fine instinct. There are many things which we come very near questioning, but do not question. When I have sent off my manuscripts to the printer, certain objectionable sentences or expressions are sure to obtrude themselves on my attention with force, though I had not consciously suspected them before. My critical instinct then at once breaks the ice and comes to the surface." The page proof allowed him one more opportunity to make a number of small changes for the published text.[34]

And when it was too late for the benefit of others, he made a few corrections in his own copy of *Walden*.[35]

34. See below, p. 36, for examples.

35. It is in the Abernethy Library, Middlebury College, Middlebury, Vermont. The corrections in it are given by Reginald L. Cook, "Thoreau's Annotations and Corrections in the First Edition of *Walden*," *Thoreau Society Bulletin*, XLII (1953), 1.

III

Perfecting the Style

THE order of treatment in this and the following chapters—
revisions, additions, and, finally, reordering of material—is
to some extent arbitrary; but this order does reflect the fact that
in his earlier rewriting Thoreau's main concern was polishing
what he had first written, that he made considerable additions
only in the versions after III, and that he made the greatest
changes in the order of his material only after he had begun to
add extensively to his story. It must be kept in mind, however,
that he worked in all three ways in all parts and all versions of
Walden.

Thoreau's care and skill in revising sentences and paragraphs
is most tellingly illustrated by passages from the parts of *Walden*
he wrote in the first version, for he had the opportunity of going
over this material more often than that which he added later. But
he took infinite pains at all points. He was so thorough that, as he
drew near the end, he became weary and wished he could "buy at
the shops some kind of india-rubber that would rub out at once
all that in my writing which it now costs me so many perusals,
so many months if not years, and so much reluctance, to erase."[1]

1. *The Writings of Henry David Thoreau* (20 vols.; Boston: Houghton Mifflin Co.,
1906), *Journal*, VI, 30; December 27, 1853. Unless otherwise indicated, all references
to Thoureau's published writings are to this edition.

Perfecting the Style

The innumerable corrections in the manuscript are of every kind. Those most easily accounted for were demanded by the conversion of lectures to a book. We need only note in passing such elementary ones as the substitution of "readers" for "audience" or the tidying-up in version I of hopelessly disjointed sentences like the second one in "Reading," 6 (see p. 149, below). Other changes, however, depended on Thoreau's judgment that what might be effective when read to an audience might not be so when read in a book. He canceled the following in the first paragraph of "Economy" in I since it demanded oral delivery (the italics are Thoreau's): "Some have not come to my house because I lived *there*—others have come because I *lived* there—and others again because *I* lived there." He interlined in "Economy," 7, "though some of you it must be observed have enough of the brass of impudence of your own to live by," but he later gave it up because it needed the face-to-face delivery of the lecture room. He also omitted two timely references that he had inserted in I, probably for lectures: one to the young men in Melville's *Typee* (1846) who climbed sixty-foot trees and the other to those who went off to California in the gold rush.

Related to these changes, but depending on other considerations also, was his moderating of exaggerated statements which might have been rhetorically effective in lectures but which demanded revision upon further thought. He wrote in "Economy," 45, in both I and II "not more than one man in a hundred owns a shelter"; he changed it later to "not more than half the families." In "Economy," 49, he interlined in II "even 99 in a hundred are sure to fail," and in an addition to "Economy," 56, in III, he wrote: "Are you one of the 99 who fail, or the hundredth who succeeds?" When he rewrote paragraph 49 in IV, he added, "though that appears to me too many," and in preparing the final copy he was overcome by his doubts and changed both ninety-nines to ninety-seven.

The other considerations are summed up in Thoreau's dictum that "the one great rule of composition . . . is to *speak the truth*. This first, this second, this third."[2] Even in the smallest points he

2. *Journal*, XIII, 11; the italics are Thoreau's.

constantly strove to be accurate. For example, he first set down the fare to Fitchburg in "Economy," 74, as a dollar but corrected it in the manuscript to seventy cents, only to change it again in the page proof to ninety cents, for, he noted there, "They have changed the fare within the last week." Here is warranty, if needed, for almost all the other figures in *Walden*, even down to the one cent listed as the cost of chalk.[3] Other changes in the page proof reveal his search for the true, the exact word at the last moment. In "The Ponds," 6, he had twice written, "as I stepped ashore I heaved my axe back on to the ice"; but he changed "heaved" to "tossed" because his act had been careless and comparatively effortless. In "The Ponds," 24, he changed the Iron Horse's "ear-rending whinny" to "neigh"; a whinny might conceivably be "ear-rending" because of its pitch, but it was far less likely than a neigh to have the volume to be "heard throughout the town."

But telling the truth is a more complicated problem than stating fairly simple facts, and Thoreau was well aware of the tentativeness of the search for the right expression. As he was preparing the final copy, he commented in his journal for March 1, 1854: "In correcting my manuscripts, which I do with sufficient phlegm, I find that I invariably turn out much that is good along with the bad, which it is then impossible for me to distinguish—so much for keeping bad company; but after the lapse of time, having purified the main body and thus created a distinct standard for comparison, I can review the rejected sentences and easily detect those which deserve to be readmitted." Perhaps he had just noticed a set of changes like that in "The Ponds," 1. In a blank

---

3. Once at least, however, we find him pursuing his passion for exact figures in so strange a fashion as to make us doubt his word unless we are to imagine him measuring cracks in the frozen ground from year to year. Here, if ever, the argument from silence must be valid: there is no series of such measurements in the journal, so one can seriously question that he ever made them. In the journal entry of November 3, 1852, he wrote: "Or I was startled by the cracking of the ground in the coldest nights, which sounded as if it were my house that cracked, and in the morning I would find a crack in the earth a quarter of an inch wide and a quarter of a mile long." The first time he put this in "Winter Animals," 3, he did not mention the width of the crack; but the second time he gave the width as half an inch; the last correction and the text read "a third of an inch."

space at the end of "The Village," 3 (version III), he wrote four or five sentences on the impossibility of getting the true flavor of fruits by buying them in the market. He obviously intended to use them in "The Ponds," 1. But he did not use them directly when he wrote V, and it was only after several sets of cancellations and interlineations that he worked them into the text.

The following examples of Thoreau's revisions will show how he worked, sometimes to gain greater clarity and force, sometimes for greater coherence and unity, and sometimes for new depth or breadth. The examples cover the various kinds of material—satiric, reflective, descriptive, and narrative—but they can only suggest the extent to which Thoreau revised everywhere in his work. The examples drawn from "Economy" are too numerous for strict proportion, but the material there lends itself to illustrations of reasonable length as most of the text does not.

In the first passage, from "Economy," 3, Thoreau gradually made the satiric comparison more effective as he made it more concrete, and as he extended it to achieve the proper exaggeration; at the same time he developed the movement of the sentence so that it reinforced the meaning of his words (italics indicate interlined material; angle brackets (⟨ ⟩) indicate canceled material):

Journal, I, 426–27[4]	VERSION I
I have travelled some in New England, especially in Concord, and I found that no enterprise was on foot which it would not disgrace a man to take part in. They seemed to be employed everywhere in shops and offices and fields. They seemed, like the Brahmins of the East, to be doing penance in a thousand curious, unheard-of ways, their endurance	I have travelled a good deal in Concord, and everywhere, in shops and offices and fields, the inhabitants have seemed to me to be doing penance in a thousand curious ways. What I have heard of Brahmens ⟨standing on one leg on the tops of pillars⟩, *sitting exposed to four fires* & looking in the face of the sun, ⟨dwelling at the roots of trees,⟩ *or hanging suspended*

4. In this case and one other, "Spring," 13, the original passages in the journals are reproduced for comparison. In the other cases journal passages, even if available, are not given because the inclusion of them would have seriously complicated the printing of parallel columns, and because they would not be particularly useful for the study of Thoreau's methods of revision.

The Making of Walden

surpassing anything I had ever seen or heard of,—Simeon Stylites, Brahmins looking in the face of the sun, standing on one leg, dwelling at the roots of trees, nothing to it; any of the twelve labors of Hercules to be matched,—the Nemean lion, Lernaean hydra, Œnœan stag, Erymanthian boar, Augean stables, Stymphalian birds, Cretan bull, Diomedes' mares, Amazonian girdle, monster Geryon, Hesperian apples, three-headed Cerberus, nothing at all in comparison, being only twelve and having an end. For I could never see that these men ever slew or captured any of their monsters, or finished any of their labors. They have no "friend Iolaus to burn, with a hot iron, the root" of the hydra's head; for as soon as one head is crushed, two spring up.

with their heads downward over flames or looking at the heavens over their shoulders "until it ⟨is⟩ becomes impossible for them to resume their natural position, while, from the twist of the neck, nothing but liquids can pass into the stomach," or dwelling chained for life to the foot of a tree or measuring with their bodies like caterpillars the breadth of a vast empire or of devotees standing on one leg on the tops of pillars—even these forms of conscious penance are not more incredible & astonishing than the scenes which I daily witness. The twelve ⟨even⟩ the twelve labors of Hercules are nothing in comparison *with those which my neighbors have undertaken* for they were only twelve and had an end, but I could never see that these men slew or captured any monster, or finished any labor. They have no "friend Iolas to burn, with a hot iron, the root" of the Hydra's head, but as soon as one head is crushed two spring up.

In writing version I, Thoreau first tightened the hasty style of the journal note by making one sentence of the first two and part of the third, thus bringing together the facts of his own experience and getting rid of the wordiness of the journal. By adding the phrase "What I have *heard* of Brahmens" he emphasized the unbelievable quality of what he had *seen* in New England. The major change is in the comparison that follows. He dropped the list of mere allusions to the labors of Hercules and concentrated on the concrete physical facts of the Brahmans' ascetic practices, retaining only the number of Hercules' labors to stress the comparison of extent. As he revised I, he extended the concrete examples, being careful to choose the most uncomfortable ones.

Perfecting the Style

The practical fact behind the separate additions in I may have been that Thoreau drew from memory when he wrote at the pond, but was able to refer to his source later. The artistic fact is that by extending the examples he developed the suggestion of "a thousand curious ways" and the idea that the tasks of his countrymen were endless. Furthermore, what he says is emphasized by the movement of the lengthened sentence with its "or . . . or . . . or" run out so long that he had to put in "even these forms" and also insert "with those which my neighbors have undertaken," lest the comparison read between Hercules and the Brahmans. In the final copy he increased the note of irony by changing "curious" to "remarkable" in the first sentence.

Another example, the revisions of "Economy," 6, shows how Thoreau added material to make the statement of his reflections more exact by fuller expression and also how he reordered his sentences to gain greater clarity and coherence.

VERSION I	VERSION II
(CF. *Journal*, I, 381–82)	
Most men *even in this comparatively free country* through mere ignorance and mistake are so occupied with the factitious cares and *superfluously* coarse labors of life that its finer fruits cannot be plucked by them. *Their fingers from excessive toil are too clumsy and tremble too much for that.* Actually the laboring man has not leisure for a lofty & *serene* integrity day by day, he cannot afford to sustain the noblest relations. ⟨*We should feed and clothe and recruit him with our cordials before we judge of him.*⟩ His labor would depreciate in the market. He has no time to be anything but a machine. How can he remember well his ignorance, ⟨and this⟩ *which* his growth requires—who has so often to use	Most men, even in this comparatively free country, through mere ignorance and mistake are so occupied with the factitious cares and superfluously coarse labors of life that its finer fruits cannot be plucked by them. Their fingers, from excessive toil, are too clumsy and tremble too much for that. ⟨*The finest qualities of our nature are as difficult to preserve as the down on a peach.*⟩ Actually, the laboring man has not leisure for a ⟨lofty and serene *high*⟩ *true* integrity day by day; he cannot afford to sustain the ⟨*truest* & noblest⟩ *manliest* relations *to men.* His labor would ⟨*be*⟩ depreciate⟨*d*⟩ in the market. He has no time to be anything but a machine. How can he remember well his ignorance—which his

The Making of Walden

VERSION I	VERSION II
his knowledge? *We should feed and clothe and recruit him with our cordials before we judge of him.*	growth requires—who has so often to use his knowledge? We should feed and clothe *him gratuitously sometimes* and recruit him with our cordials before we judge of him. *The finest qualities of our nature, like the bloom on fruits, can be preserved only by the most delicate handling.* ⟨*But*⟩ *Yet we do not treat ourselves nor one another thus tenderly.*

By inserting "even in this comparatively free country" in I, Thoreau helped to keep his scornful attack aimed directly at his readers and at the same time prepared for the charge of slavery which follows in paragraph 8. He added "superfluously" to acknowledge the facts of life, for he was no one to deny the necessity and even the benefits of some coarse labor. His main concern in the revisions in I, however, was to enlarge on men's error in working so needlessly hard and to suggest how they might help to correct the error. With "their fingers from excessive toil . . ." he extended the metaphor of picking fruit, and he suggested a remedy by adding, "We should feed and clothe. . . ." But he later shifted this second addition, for he saw that it belonged, not in the midst of the description of the laboring man's condition, but after it; the remedy should not be prescribed until after the trouble is fully set forth.

When he revised II, Thoreau saw the possibility of further extending the fruit-picking metaphor. He adopted a journal entry which originally read, "Seek to preserve the tenderness of your nature as you would the bloom upon a peach" but which he had changed to "As difficult to preserve is the tenderness of your nature as the bloom upon a peach."[5] At first, he did not use the revised sentence satisfactorily; it hardly does to say that men cannot pluck fruits and then to consider the difficulty they have in handling the plucked fruits tenderly. Furthermore, the relation of

5. The published journal, I, 381 (entry is undated), has the revised sentence which Thoreau interlined in the manuscript journal in the Morgan Library.

the "finer fruits" of life and the "finest qualities of our nature" is confused. But by slightly revising and shifting the new metaphor to the end of the passage, Thoreau used it to develop the treatment of men by men and at the same time made it serve as an effective variation of the fruit-picking metaphor.

The changes of single words illustrate his constant striving for the exact phrase. He replaced the "bloom" of the journal with "down," apparently because "down" would apply specifically to peaches handled by clumsy fingers. Later he restored "bloom" because he made the comparison with fruits in general, and "bloom" suggests even greater delicacy than "down" and therefore the need of even more tender handling. The changes in the modifiers of "integrity" and "relations" illustrate the uncertainty and the interdependence of many changes. Thoreau's final choices are characteristically precise: "true" meaning "certain" or "sure" is to the point as "lofty," "serene," and "high" were not, and "manliest" keeps the emphasis on men's difficulty in being men.

The successive versions of "Spring," 13, show Thoreau exercising the same care in perfecting his descriptive and narrative passages as he did in his satiric and reflective ones. The cancellations and interlineations in the versions are not shown because Thoreau adopted all the changes marked in one version in the next (see pp. 42–45).

In the original journal entry, Thoreau caught much of the music and color of spring and, above all, the stirring of its new life; most of the images, including those of sound and color, suggest motion and action: warblings, tinkled, sing, melting, dissolves, flames, streaming, pushing on, lifting. But the picture did not have the clarity and movement that count so much in producing the exciting effect of the final version. In the successive revisions Thoreau cut out superfluous material and reorganized his sentences so as to gain the cumulative effect of a steady addition of one sign of spring after another; and he made all his images even more concrete and exact. He got rid of the repetitions of flakes and rills and hillsides and the irrelevant comment on reformers and faithless men. He dropped "I have seen where . . ."

The Making of Walden

HM 13182

The first sparrow of spring. The year beginning with younger hope than ever. The faint [first?] silvery warblings heard over the bare dank fields as if the last flakes of winter tinkled. What then are histories, chronologies—traditions, and written revelations. Flakes of warm sunlight fall on the congealed earth—the brooks and rills sing carols and glees for the spring. The marsh hawk already seeks the first slimy life that awakes— The sough of melting snow is heard in the dells of the wood, by the sunny river banks, and the ice dissolves in the seething ponds, evaporating hourly. The earth sends forth as it were an inward green heat and the grass flames up on the warm hill sides like a green spring fire. Methinks the sight of the first sod of fresh grass in the spring would make the reformer reconsider his schemes, the faithless and despairing man revive— The grass blade is a perpetual growth a long green ribbon—streaming from the sod into the summer—checked indeed by the frost—but anon pushing on again lifting its withered hay with fresh life below.—I have seen where early in spring the clumps of grass stood with their three

VERSION I

The first sparrow of spring—the year beginning with younger hope than ever—the faint silvery warblings heard over the bare and moist fields from the song-sparrow —the blue-bird—and the redwing—as if the last flakes of winter tinkled as they fell.—What at such a time are histories—chronologies —traditions, and all written revelations?

The brooks sing carols and glees to the spring—the marsh-hawk— sailing low over the meadow—is already seeking the first slimy life that awakes. The sough of melting snow is heard in all dells and on all hillsides—and by the sunny river banks— and the ice dissolves apace in all ponds. The earth sends forth an inward heat to greet the returning sun—not yellow like the sun— but green is the color of its flame.

The grass flames up on all hillsides like a spring fire. Grass is the symbol of perpetual youth its blade like a long green ribbon— longer than was ever woven in the factories of men—streaming from the sod into the summer—checked indeed by the frost, but anon pushing on again—lifting its last year's spear of withered hay with the fresh life below.—It is as steady a

---

6. HM 13182; this passage and other parts of the manuscript were published in *The First and Last Journeys of Thoreau*, ed. F. B. Sanborn (Boston: Bibliophile Society, 1905), I, 69–71.

Perfecting the Style

The first sparrow of spring—the year beginning with younger hope than ever—the faint silvery warblings heard over the bare and moist fields from the song-sparrow —the blue-bird & the red-wing, as if the last flakes of winter tinkled as they fell—What at such a time are histories—chronologies—traditions and all written revelations? The brooks sing carols and glees to the spring. The marsh hawk sailing low over the meadow is already seeking the first slimy life that awakes. The sough of melting snow is heard in all dells and on all hillsides, and by the sunny river banks—and the ice dissolves apace in all ponds. As if the earth sent forth an inward heat to greet the returning sun, the grass flames up on all hillsides like a spring fire— not yellow but green is the color of earth's flame; the symbol of perpetual youth, its blade, like a long green ribbon streaming from the sod into the summer, checked indeed by the frost, but anon pushing on again—lifting its last year's spear of withered hay with the fresh life below. It grows as steadily as the rill which oozes out of the ground, indeed is almost identical with that, for in the growing days of June when the rills are dry, the grass blades are their channels, and from year to year the herds drink at this perennial green stream, and the mower cuts from

The first sparrow of spring! The year beginning with younger hope than ever! The faint silvery warblings heard over the partially bare and moist fields from the bluebird, the song sparrow, and the red-wing, as if the last flakes of winter tinkled as they fell! What at such a time are histories, chronologies, traditions, and all written revelations? The brooks sing carols and glees to the spring. The marsh hawk, sailing low over the meadow, is already seeking the first slimy life that awakes. The sinking sound of melting snow is heard in all dells, and the ice dissolves apace in the ponds. The grass flames up on the hillsides like a spring fire,—"et primitus oritur herba imbribus primoribus evocata,"—as if the earth sent forth an inward heat to greet the returning sun; not yellow but green is the color of its flame;—the symbol of perpetual youth, the grass-blade, like a long green ribbon, streams from the sod into the summer, checked indeed by the frost, but anon pushing on again, lifting its spear of last year's hay with the fresh life below. It grows as steadily as the rill oozes out of the ground. It is almost identical with that, for in the growing days of June, when the rills are dry, the grass-blades are their channels, and from year to year the herds drink at this perennial green

The Making of Walden

inches of new green upholding their withered spears of the last autumn, and from year to year the herds browse and the mower cuts from this never failing outwelling supply—what their needs require. So the human life but dies down to the surface, but puts forth a green blade to eternity.

The grass blade is as steady a growth as the rill which leaks out of the ground—indeed it is almost identical with that, for in the vigorous fertile days of June when the rills are dry the grass blades are their channel.

growth as the rill which oozes out of the ground, and indeed is almost identical with that—for in the fertile and growing days of June, when the rills are dry—the grass blades are their channels— and from year to year the herds drink at this green stream—and the mower cuts from this outwelling supply—what their several needs require.—So our human life but dies down to the surface of nature—but puts forth its green blade still to eternity.

because it spoiled the sense of the immediate apprehension of *one* spring. Of most effect on the rhythm of the whole was his finding the right order and phrasing for "the grass flames up . . . the grass-blade streams . . . it grows . . . it is. . . ." By doing so, he maintained the succession of direct statements with which he began the description and thus reinforced the sense of an ever increasing flow of life.

This sense of life depends also on the sharpness and exactness of the images. Thoreau carefully modified "bare" with "partially," for not all the snow was yet gone; he substituted "moist" for "dank," which was all wrong in its associations for the freshly opening fields of spring. He also named the birds—colorful, concrete images—and by changing "the marsh hawk seeks" to "the marsh hawk, sailing low over the meadow, is seeking," he caught the action directly. He gave up "sough," for, though more specific than "sinking sound," it was not accurate, and he gave up "seething" because it exaggerated. Near the end of the passage he changed "browse" and "cuts" to "drink" and "draws" to carry out the image of the stream. And, probably remembering George Herbert's "Thy root is ever in its grave," he substituted the fine

Perfecting the Style

VERSION V	PUBLISHED TEXT
this out-welling supply what their several needs require. So our human life but dies down to its root, and still puts forth its green blade to eternity.	stream, and the mower draws from it betimes their winter supply. So our human life but dies down to its root, and still puts forth its green blade to eternity.

and accurate image "dies down to its root" for the vague "to the surface of nature."

Taken singly or in small numbers, corrections like those in this last group would not have had any great effect on *Walden*, but in hundreds or ten hundreds they counted greatly in assuring the unerring flight of Thoreau's shots. We may note one more typical group of them in the revisions in the third draft of "Economy," 8 (see pp. 46–47). Thoreau substituted "that" for "how" because it was the fact that he wondered at and not the question of why it existed; he inserted "I may . . . say" and "servitude called" to avoid any possible ambiguity; and he inserted "but somewhat foreign" to achieve a sarcastic irony in keeping with the tone of the passage that followed.

The most interesting aspect of the revisions of this passage is that they make plain how close the problem of what one says is to that of how he says it. Here Thoreau did not simply refine or expand what he had already done; he had to work out the form and substance together. In "Economy," 6, he had pointed out that men work so hard that they cannot enjoy life or maintain their integrity; in "Economy," 7, he had described their mean and sneaking lives; here in paragraph 8 he went on to assert that they are the slave-drivers of themselves and thus directly responsible for the quality of their lives. From the beginning he wanted to present with scornful irony an example of unthinking, self-imposed slavery. But how he could best do it became clear only after he had tried out many different combinations of material.

In the end he portrayed the teamster's sorry plight by exposing his thoughts and feelings in a series of sarcastic and ironic exclamations and questions which follow one another as rapidly as possible. He cut out "Ancient books and some modern ones" in

The Making of Walden

I sometimes wonder how we can be so frivolous almost as to attend to the gross form of Negro slavery, there are so many keen and subtle masters that enslave both north & south. It is bad to have a southern overseer, it is worse to have a northern one, but worst of all when you are yourself the slave-driver.

Ancient books, and some modern ones, talk of a divinity in man. Look at the teamster on the highway, wending to market by day or night—how much of divinity is there in him? *Is he a son of the morning—fearless because immortal—greeting the sun and stars as his fellows and bounding with youthful & elastic steps over his mother earth.* How God-like, how immortal is he? *Very like a God!* ⟨*He feels so cheap that he could lick the dust under his feet.*⟩ See how he cowers and sneaks, how vaguely and indefinitely all the day he fears—not being immortal nor divine, but the slave and prisoner of his own opinion of himself—a fame won by his own deeds. *He feels so cheap that he could lick the dust under his feet. Public opinion is a weak tyrant compared with private opinion. What a man thinks of himself that it is which determines his fate.*

I sometimes wonder how we can be so frivolous almost as to attend to the gross form of Negro slavery, there are so many keen and subtle masters that *who* enslave both north and south. It is bad to have a southern overseer, it is worse to have a northern one, but worst of all when you are the slave-driver of yourself.

Ancient books, and some modern ones, talk of a divinity in man. Look at the teamster on the highway wending to market by day or night. ⟨Is he a son of the morning —fearless because immortal— greeting the sun and stars as his fellows and bounding with youthful and elastic step over his mother earth? How much of divinity is there in him?⟩ *Does the divinity stir with in him. He rolls out of his cradle into a Tom & Jerry & goes at once to look after his team to fodder and water his horses without standing agape at his position. What are life immortal and the destiny of man compared with the shipping interests? What does he care for his creator doesn't he drive for Squire Make-a-stir?* How god-like, how immortal is he? ⟨*Very like a god! Talk of a divinity in man?*⟩ See how he cowers and sneaks, how vaguely and indefinitely all the day he fears, not being immortal nor divine, but the slave and prisoner of his own opinion of himself —a fame won by his own deeds. Public opinion is a weak tyrant compared with private opinion. What a man thinks of himself, that it is which determines or rather indicates his fate. *Self emancipation even in the W. I. provinces of the fancy and imagination, what Wilberforce is there to bring that about?*

46

Perfecting the Style

VERSION III

I sometimes wonder ⟨how⟩ *that* we can be so frivolous, *I may* almost *say,* as to attend to the gross *but somewhat foreign* form of *servitude called* Negro slavery, there are so many keen and subtle masters that enslave both north & south. It is hard to have a southern overseer, it is worse to have a northern one, but worst of all when you are the slave-driver of yourself. Talk of a divinity in man! Look at the teamster on the highway wending to market by day or night. Does any divinity stir within him? He rolls out of his cradle into a Tom-and-Jerry, and goes at once to look after his team, ⟨*For the most part he knows of no higher duty than*⟩ *His highest duty* to fodder & water his horses ⟨-without standing agape at his position. *He is not half horse, half something more; he is merely a horse & a half to the others.*⟩ What ⟨are⟩ *is* life immortal & ⟨the⟩ *his own* destiny ⟨of man⟩ to him, compared with the shipping interests? ⟨What does he care for his creator? *He does not drive for God but*⟩ Doesn't he drive for Squire Make-a-Stir?—How godlike, how immortal is he? See how he cowers and sneaks, how vaguely ⟨and indefinitely⟩ all the day he fears, not being immortal nor divine, but the slave and prisoner of his own opinion of himself,—a fame won by his own deeds. Public opinion is a weak tyrant compared with *our own* private opinion. What a man thinks of himself, that it is which determines, or rather indicates, his fate. Self-emancipation even in the West Indian

VERSION IV

divinity stir within him? His highest duty to fodder and water his horses! What is his own destiny to him compared with the shipping interests! Does not he drive for Squire Make-a-stir? How godlike, how immortal is he? See how he cowers and sneaks, how vaguely all the day he fears, not being immortal nor divine, but the slave and prisoner of his own opinion of himself, a fame won by his own deeds. Public opinion is a weak tyrant compared with our own private opinion. What a man thinks of himself, that it is which determines, or rather indicates, his fate. Self-emancipation even in the West Indian provinces of the fancy & imagination,—what Wilberforce is there to bring that about? *Think also of* ⟨And⟩ the ladies of the land, weaving toilet cushions against the last day, not to betray too green an interest in their fates! As if you could kill time without injuring eternity.

47

order to begin with an exclamation, and he dropped the question "Is he a son . . . ?" because it did not help to expose the teamster's feelings directly; he finally omitted the picture of the teamster's early morning routine because it broke the unity and weakened the force of the series of comments on his thoughts and feelings. He had left out "He feels so cheap . . ." because it stated that the teamster knew his condition for what it was, whereas Thoreau's point is that men don't know the state they are in. He saw too that "merely a horse and a half" was sheer name-calling that had no place here. Earlier, he had returned to the figure of slavery by adding "self-emancipation"; and then, by adding still later the reference to the weavers of toilet cushions, he extended his remarks to women as well as to men, to the quietly domestic as well as to hard laborers. With humor aforethought he prepared for the statement in "Economy," 9, that men lead lives of *quiet* desperation.

Often Thoreau's revision of a passage consisted primarily of additions of details to a picture or story, or of brief comment or reflection suggested by the reconsideration of his material. The first part of the story of building the hut ("Economy," 60) developed in this way (see opposite page).

The details he added about the scene of his work not only set it more clearly but also expressed more fully the pleasure he had had in his labor. The reflections on borrowing and on men's low condition are characteristic additions. From the time he began to write *Walden* Thoreau continually reflected on his experience and on its relation to men's life in general. As he rewrote, he was forever seeing new points, or, as here, better ones. In preparing the copy for the printer he radically changed the reflection on borrowing. The tone of the comment he first added was too solemn, whereas the defense of borrowing in the final text humorously forestalls any charge of improvidence: "perhaps it is the most generous course thus to permit your fellowmen to have an interest in your enterprise."

Another instance of revision by addition of reflection and comment is in "Where I Lived," 12. Thoreau first wrote a simple description of part of his surroundings. Upon later reflection he

Perfecting the Style

Near the end of March 1845 I borrowed an axe and went down to the woods *by Walden Pond* nearest to where I intended to build my house ⟨*I told you that I should put in the I*⟩ and began to cut down some tall arrowy pines still in their youth for timber. *It is difficult not to begin with borrowing—Our very life borrowed and must be returned with interest to him who lent it—the man of whom I borrowed the axe said it was the apple of his eye* ⟨*but*⟩ *however I returned it sharper than I found it. It was a pleasant hillside where I worked, covered with pine woods, through which I looked out on the pond or on a small clearing in the woods now growing up to pines and hickories. The ice in the pond &* The ice in the pond . . . I saw a striped snake run into the water—and he lay on the bottom apparently without inconvenience as long as I stayed there, which was more than 15 minutes, and I know not how much longer he remained there.

Near the end of March 1845 I borrowed an axe, and went down to the woods by Walden Pond, nearest to where I intended to build my house, and began to cut down some tall arrowy *white* pines still in their youth for timber. It is difficult to begin without borrowing. Our very life is *in one sense* borrowed and must be returned with interest to him who lent it. *In my case* ⟨The man of whom I borrowed⟩ *the owner of* the axe, *as he relaxed his hold on it* said that it was the apple of his eye;—but I returned it sharper than I found it. It was a pleasant hillside where I worked, covered with pine woods, through which I looked out on the pond, and on a small open field in the woods *where pines & hickories were springing up.* The ice in the pond . . . I saw a striped snake run into the water, and he lay on the bottom, apparently without inconvenience, as long as I stayed there, which was more than ⟨fifteen minutes, and I know not how much longer he remained there.⟩ *a quarter of an hour, perhaps because he had not yet come fairly out of the torpid state. It appeared to me that for a like reason men remain in their present low condition and are able to live as it were in* ⟨*a*⟩ *this gross* ⟨*element*⟩ *atmosphere; but if they should feel the influence of the spring of Springs arousing them, they would be compelled to rise to a more ethereal element.*

made the description serve as the occasion for describing further the intangible quality of his life in the woods.

VERSION I	VERSION VI
Over the south shore of the pond which was a low hill ⟨covered⟩ *fringed* with shrub oaks & scattered pines which seemed to rise to an illimitable tableland—I seemed to look toward the country of ⟨*some*⟩ a ⟨*new*⟩ *ideal race of* ⟨the⟩ Tartars, where tribes of men dwelt in tents.	⟨But⟩ Though the view from my door was *still more* contracted, *I did not feel myself crowded or confined in the least but there was pasture enough for my fancy & imagination.* ⟨nevertheless, I imagined that⟩ the low shrub oak plateau to which the opposite shore arose stretched away ⟨boundless as the prairies, pampas, and plains of Tartary⟩ *toward the prairies of the West & the steppes of Tartary,* affording ample room for all the roving families of men. "There are none happy in the world but beings who enjoy freely a vast horizon," ⟨So⟩ said Damodara when his herds required new & larger pastures.

These revisions show also how Thoreau was led at times to rewrite passages because of other changes. In version VI he added paragraph 11 (as it is in the published text) in which he described the wider view he enjoyed from a nearby hilltop. This suggested the comment which he added here at the beginning of paragraph 12 and also led to his adding the quotation at the end of the paragraph; with it he re-emphasized the pleasure of the free, imaginative life he enjoyed because of the location of his hut.

It is not feasible to illustrate in detail how Thoreau revised longer pieces such as the portrait of Therien, the description of Walden Pond, or the account of the ice-cutters; but a comparison of the portrait of Therien in version I (see pp. 169 ff.) with that in the published text will show how extensively he reordered the parts of his sketch so as to achieve the unobtrusive but calculated order of the final text. In version I the portrait is alive because of the vivid concrete details, but because of its random order it presents neither the outward facts about Therien nor Thoreau's analysis and judgment of his character and abilities so clearly as the final version. The excellence of the latter depends in part on material Thoreau added in II, III, V, and the copy for the printer, but the clarity and force of the whole depend largely on the fact that part follows part easily and naturally, with Therien's various elements so set forth as to reveal both Thoreau's liking and respect for him and also his dissatisfaction with Therien's limited aim.

In the first two paragraphs of the published text, "Visitors," 8 and 9, Thoreau introduces Therien as he called at the hut one morning and gives a thumbnail sketch of him: occupation, age, place of birth, appearance, diet (important because different from Thoreau's), his easy ways, and his skill in work. There is nothing remarkable in all this, so Thoreau explains why he was interested enough in Therien to single him out for his readers: in many respects he was a man after Thoreau's own heart, "quiet and solitary and so happy"; and Thoreau recounts some of his gay antics. He goes on to describe him more fully, telling first of his physical strength, then contrasting this with his intellectual and spiritual immaturity, which lead in turn to a recital of his unsophistication and humility. Following naturally on these points is the description of Therien's simple and cheerful acceptance of the world as it is and then Thoreau's comment on his difficulty in reading aright the combination of wisdom and ignorance that underlay Therien's happiness. In the remainder of the sketch Thoreau develops further the puzzling contrasts in Therien: his simple learning but his ability to deal in a thoroughly practical way with complex and abstract questions; his clear-headed comments on men and life but his inability to conceive of a higher spiritual life for himself; his original and independent thought which was worthy of expression but which was never brought to light because he lived too low.

In revising individual paragraphs and passages Thoreau cut out material as well as adding it. One may regret the loss here and there of a particular comment or vivid picture, and sometimes the omission may appear to be a debatable question of proportion and extent. But even if one is not quite willing to say of *Walden*,

"None ever wished it longer than it is," Thoreau's revisions must be judged in terms of the whole, and certainly *Walden* and all its parts are rich enough. And generally there are sound reasons for his excisions. He dropped the fine homely comparison, "Its [life's] dish consists almost entirely of fixings & very little of the chicken's meat," from "Where I Lived," 17, in I; he may have rejected it as too homely, but probably because it did not follow logically after "Our life is frittered away by detail." He cut out the suggestive passage on New England heroes and symbols that precedes "Sounds," 4, in I (see p. 157); it was not pertinent once the material of "Where I Lived" had been removed from between "Sounds," 3 and 4. Often, of course, he rejected what was obviously poor. For example, when he first added the story of Hugh Quoil, "Former Inhabitants," 11, he wrote, "All I know of him is tragic," and then commented, "I have noticed that there is always something pathetic in the sedentary life of men who have travelled." He soon struck out this bit of bathos.

As a last example, there are the revisions of "Economy," 9. Here Thoreau sacrificed a vivid satiric anecdote because it was somewhat irrelevant and broke into his argument; he also completely reordered his argument to strengthen its force. He did not think to use this paragraph and its famous opening sentence on "lives of quiet desperation" at least until after he had written version II and more probably not until he returned to work on *Walden* in 1851–52. He originally wrote part of the paragraph in connection with a tale he intended to use in *A Week*. He later dropped both the tale and comment from *A Week;* then he put both in *Walden* but finally dropped the tale and kept only the comment.

The first draft of the comment on despair in the *Walden* manuscript appears in the following fashion on pages written originally for *A Week*. After mentioning the astonishment of his brother and himself at meeting an organ-grinder "away up here in New Hampshire," Thoreau went on for over two pages: "Here also was a poor wretch asking for lodging, whom it was almost no pleasure to befriend he was so helpless. He said that he came from New York and was seeking work . . . he was a desperate man. . . . He had traveled 250 miles from New York . . . with desperate steps. . . . And so he would go on if his constitution held out to the Gulf of St. Lawrence, where he would probably jump in." He continued: "It is the sum of all wisdom not to do desperate things. The great mass of mankind lead lives of quiet desperation. What is called resignation is confirmed desperation —From the desperate city you go into the desperate country and have to console yourself with the bravery of minks and muskrats." There followed here Sadi's statement as to who may travel, which Thoreau used in *A Week* (pp. 324–25) after canceling all the preceding material.

When he decided to incorporate the tale in *Walden,* Thoreau cut out the reference to the organ-grinder and shifted the locale of the meeting with the desperate man from New Hampshire to "this town," that is, Concord. He also interlined the following to precede the tale:

> It is worth the while to remember always that whether we are well or sick rich or poor virtuous or vicious, we are equally and continuously invited to pursue the only right way—& that this is always glorious beyond conception—Indeed to forget this to lose our faith is really the greatest misfortune that can befall us.
>
> How much stereotyped & what is worst of all unconscious despair is concealed under what are called the games & amusements of mankind. [Undecipherable words] have given up or indeed have never taken up or been taken up by Hope—They not only [undecipherable words] but they have the slenderest expectations on the future. They are moral bankrupts.

Thoreau marked this material for insertion after "Economy," 8, in the manuscript of II. In the revision in IV he condensed the interlined material just quoted to read: "A stereotyped but unconscious despair is concealed under what are called the games and amusements of mankind. There is no play in them, for this comes after work." He also shortened the tale, but left the comment on "the sum of wisdom" at the end unchanged.

He made the last revisions when he was preparing the final copy of *Walden* for the printer. He dropped the tale, for he did not need more concrete illustrations at this point, and the folly of a poor itinerant was not particularly relevant for the readers Thoreau could expect. But more important is the new and effective order he gave to his comment:

VERSION IV	FINAL TEXT
A stereotyped but unconscious despair is concealed under what are called the games and amusements of mankind. There is no play in them for this comes after work.	The mass of men lead lives of quiet desperation. What is called resignation is confirmed desperation. From the desperate city you go into the desperate country, and have to console yourself with the bravery of minks and muskrats. A stereotyped but unconscious despair is concealed even under what are called the games and amusements of mankind. There is no play in them, for this comes after work. But it is a characteristic of wisdom not to do desperate things.
[canceled tale]	
It is the sum of all wisdom not to do desperate things. The mass of mankind lead lives of quiet desperation. What is called resignation is confirmed desperation. From the desperate city you go into the desperate country, and have to console yourself with the bravery of minks and muskrats.	

In the final text he began with "The mass of men lead lives of quiet desperation" because it asserts a general proposition that follows effectively on the description of the slavish state of men in "Economy," 8, and "men" replaces "mankind" to keep the sense of individuals. "What is called resignation is confirmed desperation" forestalls a possible "religious" answer and maintains the force of the assertion which Thoreau repeats with a variation in the next sentence. With "A stereotyped but unconscious despair . . ." he forestalls another possible objection to the inclusiveness of his charge. And in the last sentence he prepares for the next paragraphs, in which he considers those who claim to possess some wisdom—those who hold by the catechism, or older people, or the scientific farmer whose powers of observation and reasoning are weak. By changing "It is the sum of wisdom not to do desperate things" to "But it is a characteristic of wisdom . . . ," Thoreau not only avoided rhetorical exaggeration but also saved himself from a statement that would have made anything he had yet to say superfluous.

IV

Completing the Story

IN THE unpublished Preface of version VII, Thoreau explained that he had added to what he had written at the pond in order to give "a completer & truer account" of his experience. He had, in fact, doubled the length of his book. Full of detail though the first version was, it lacked much that was essential to the complete story, and the version that Thoreau might have published in 1849 was not significantly fuller. It would have been a good book; Thoreau did well what he first set out to do. He made clear his quarrel with the life his fellow men lived, and he described the qualities in living that he thought were worth seeking. He also answered the question of how he had lived at the pond, laying out his daily routine of morning work and afternoon rambles and something of his evening pleasures, and also suggesting the variety in his pleasures and interests the changing seasons brought. But on none of these points would the *Walden* of 1849 have had the richness and depth that help to make the published book great.

The manuscript lets us see how *Walden* grew and the way in which Thoreau worked to fill out the account of his life in the woods. A comparison of the versions of 1847–49 with the later ones emphasizes immediately how essential time is for seeing experience clear and whole and for understanding it in such a way that one can re-create it completely for others. In the first place, the versions written by 1849 depended almost entirely on the journals of Thoreau's days at the pond, and they, by the nature of things, were incomplete. What Thoreau said of *A Week* was also true of *Walden* as it was in 1849: "Unfortunately many things have been omitted which should have been recorded in our journal; for though we made it a rule to set down all our experiences therein, yet such a resolution is very hard to keep, for the important experience rarely allows us to remember such obligations, and so indifferent things get recorded, while that is frequently neglected. It is not easy to write in a journal what interests us at any time, because to write it is not what interests us."[1]

Since we do not have the complete journal for July, 1845, to September, 1847,[2] we cannot tell exactly how much of what finally appeared in *Walden* Thoreau wrote in his journal at the pond. But we know that not until later did he have a great deal of the material he added to his book after 1849. Ellery Channing wrote in his copy of *Walden:* "This book . . . is written from his journals and I recognize the sentences. Not writ specially at Walden."[3] Bradford Torrey marked the passages in Thoreau's journals which he found in *Walden,* and the passages so marked after 1849 and others I have noted after that date run to well over sixty pages in the 1906 edition; this total counts only the lines of journal material more or less directly taken over into *Walden* and does not count the expansion and added comment.

In the second place, even if Thoreau had had all the material for *Walden* in 1847–49, he could not have used it then as well as he was able to do later. There is a good deal of material in the pub-

---

1. *The Writings of Henry David Thoreau* (20 vols.; Boston: Houghton Mifflin Co., 1906), *A Week,* p. 354. Unless otherwise indicated, all references to Thoreau's published writings are to this edition.

2. Thoreau tore great numbers of pages out of his journal as he prepared to write *Walden* in 1847. A portion of the journal, in private hands, remains unpublished; it contains "much material afterward used in *The Maine Woods*" (Canby, *Thoreau,* p. 472). It is undoubtedly about Thoreau's trip to Ktaadn in the summer of 1846.

3. Manuscript note in Channing's copy of *Walden,* which is in the Berg Collection in the New York Public Library.

lished text that he had in the journals before 1849 or in work-
sheets of *A Week* but that he did not think of using or did not see
how to use in 1847–49: for example, the material on men's desperation, "Economy," 9; the dialogue at the beginning of "Brute
Neighbors"; and the first paragraph of "Conclusion."[4] In other
words, it was not simply that he had not been able to write down
all that was important as he lived at the pond; there was also the
fact that at first he could not recall and re-create his experience
fully and clearly enough; the significance of many things was
blurred or missed entirely.

Time had to pass before he could achieve the right focus. It is
a commonplace that in many an autobiography the early years
stand out clear and rich and coherent while the later ones are
often thin or confused. In the journal for March 28, 1857, Thoreau commented on his own writings: "Often I can give the truest
and most interesting account of any adventure I have had after
years have elapsed, for then I am not confused, only the most significant facts surviving in my memory. Indeed, all that continues
to interest me after such a lapse of time is sure to be pertinent, and
I may safely record all that I remember." Here he was thinking
primarily of time sifting out superfluous and irrelevant material.
But it is also true that as time sifts out some things it brings to
light others that have been buried. Time may also have the effect
of moving the writer farther from the trees of his experience so
that he is able to see the whole wood and the relation of its parts
to one another. Finally, time gives the writer leisure in which to
reflect on his experience, and it brings new experiences that may
clarify or deepen the significance of earlier ones.

Although a comparison of version I with the final text shows
that the second half of *Walden* grew far more than the first half,
this does not mean that one element or another of the book developed at the expense of others. Thoreau did add somewhat more
to the account of his life in the woods than to his criticism of contemporary ways, for he found his story particularly incomplete.
But on the whole he enlarged every aspect of *Walden* by the work

4. The first was with material used in *A Week;* the second in a notebook that
antedated *A Week;* the third in the journal for March 21, 1840.

he did between 1851 and 1854. He added considerably to the criticism of his contemporaries' desires and ways of fulfilling them: much of the material in "Economy," for example, on men's foolish notions about clothing, on their methods of paying or not paying for their houses, and on the burden of their furniture. He criticized men's domestic arrangements in "House-Warming" in passages added in later versions; and in "Conclusion" he laughed at men's supposed great doings and so-called virtues.

He enlarged even more on the qualities he wanted in living. In one sense, of course, he did this whenever he described more fully the satisfying life he led at the pond; but even limiting ourselves to the explicit exposition of his ideals we find great additions. One of the finest is the first six paragraphs of "Where I Lived," on buying a farm, in which Thoreau told more not only of his attitude toward possessions but also of what he sought from the countryside he knew and loved so well. In "House-Warming" he reiterated the value of men's getting the necessaries of life for themselves, and in "Conclusion" he spoke again for living one's own life with leisure, simplicity, and faith. He most obviously enlarged on the ideals he sought when he added extensively to "Higher Laws." In describing his diet in "Economy," Thoreau suggested the simple life he led, but he might have adopted it on the grounds of economy alone. In "Higher Laws" he made clear that his slender fare was only one of the means to be used in his and all men's attempt to achieve purity, to bring their senses under control in order that they might live finely and nobly.

Most of all, Thoreau extended his account of how he had lived in the woods and of the pleasures he had had. By 1849 he had written very little, for example, of his long and loving description of the pond, which is the product of much work in 1852 and 1853. And he added everywhere, but more in the second half of *Walden* than in the first, such items about his surroundings as those on the hooting owl in "Sounds," the battle of the ants in "Brute Neighbors," the ice-fishermen in "The Pond in Winter," and the thawing of the sand banks and the melting of Walden in "Spring." He also filled out the story of what he did with the accounts of talks with simple-minded visitors from the nearby almshouse, of his pursuit of a loon on Walden, of gathering and cutting wood for his fire, of visits by his friends in the winter, and of chopping through the ice for his water.

Finally, he enriched what he had written earlier with additional information and comment: by way of information, such items as the anecdote of the Indian selling baskets, "Economy," 31; the story of Hugh Quoil, "Former Inhabitants," 11; and the historical evidence of the wild animals that used to be around Concord, "Winter Animals," 11; by way of comment, "Economy," 75, on the universal law which governs the cost of everything; "Solitude," 11, on the doubleness of one's experience; and "The Pond in Winter," 6 and 7, on the errors of the imagination unchecked by observable fact.

Thoreau took much of the new material from his journals and notebooks in very much the same way as he had taken the material for his first version. Often he incorporated journal entries with only slight changes: for example, the story of the simple-minded pauper, "Visitors," 15, and the passage on Gilpin's error in describing Loch Fyne, "The Pond in Winter," 7.[5] At other times he drew together notes he had entered in his journal at various times for various reasons. A most interesting example is the making of the long paragraph on White Pond, "The Ponds," 32. All but a sentence or two of the paragraph is in a group of leaves that are the remains of a notebook or journal of 1848–50;[6] Thoreau did not use this material in *Walden*, however, until 1852–53 in version V.

On page 145 of the notebook he entered the Sudbury man's account of getting the pine tree out of White Pond ten or fifteen years earlier; it constitutes the last half of "The Ponds," 32. Because the preceding leaf of the notebook is missing, the context of the entry is lost, but probably Thoreau entered it as a matter of local information of the sort he was constantly gathering. On page 180 of the notebook he made the following note as part of a cata-

5. See the journal for January 17, 1852, and September 1, 1852.
6. HM 13182 in the Huntington Library.

logue of the countryside's natural objects: "For ponds Walden—Flint's or Sandy White [in pencil:] v 145. Now, since the railroad & the Irish have prophaned Walden—the most beautiful of all our lakes—a gem or crystal—(v tree story) It deserves a better name—One has suggested God's drop—another Yellow pine lake another Hygae's Water and another [The rest is lost.] [Added later:] To be sure its stones are white & I used to gather its sand in my youth to make sandpaper with." (Two interesting changes in the text are the addition of himself to the list of those who had profaned Walden, and the transfer of "God's drop" to Walden Pond at the end of "The Ponds," 26.) On page 338 of the notebook he entered the quotation from *Topographical Description of the Town of Concord*, thus adding local history to verify local lore. When he put the quotation in *Walden*, he omitted this sentence: "The water of this pond has a remarkable crystalline appearance, from which circumstance it takes its name"; but he used its content in the first sentence of paragraph 32.

All these notes lay scattered until Thoreau decided to add the description of White Pond to that of Walden; this was the point which drew together material that came from his inveterate questioning of those he met,[7] from his long study of the Concord scene, and from his constant reading of local histories. And still later he added another item resulting from his ceaseless noting of even the minutest changes in his physical surroundings. When he went to White Pond on the "sultry dogdayish afternoon" of June 23, 1853, he remarked a change in the color of the water; sometime later he inserted the fact as the fifth sentence of the paragraph.

Very often it took more than one writing to bring the proper

7. See, for example, *Journal*, II, 40: "It is astonishing how much information is to be got out of very unpromising witnesses. A wise man will avail himself of the observation of all. Every boy and simpleton has been an observer in some field,—so many more senses they are, differently located. Will inquire of eyes what they have seen, of ears what they have heard, of hands what they have done, of feet where they have been." He questioned not only Emersons and Channings, but woodchoppers, fishermen, Indians, and even brush-burners. In *Cape Cod*, p. 40, he wrote: "We conversed with the boy we have mentioned, who might have been eight years old . . . for we thought it as important to know what life on the Cape was to a boy as to a man." When Channing expressed surprise at Thoreau's persistent search for knowledge, Thoreau answered, "What else is there in life?" (W. E. Channing, *Thoreau the Poet-Naturalist* [Boston: C. E. Goodspeed, 1902], p. 10).

material together. Late in 1853 Thoreau went back to his journal
of March 21, 1840, for the first paragraph of "Conclusion," but,
just as he had done with material for the first version, he put this
paragraph in piecemeal on two occasions. When he rewrote and
rearranged the material for "The Ponds" in versions V and VI,
he found material faster than he could use it. In addition to what
was in the first version, "The Ponds," 5, contains material from
nine different days spread from January, 1852, to January, 1853;[8]
the drafts of the paragraph in versions V and VI are extensively
corrected and interlined. At a few points he rewrote passages
twice in one or the other version.

One may ask whether Thoreau worked mainly by studying
what he had previously written in *Walden* and then going to his
journal whenever he could for what he wanted to add; or
whether, as he continued to enter his adventures, observations,
and thoughts in his journal, he was reminded of events of 1845–47
and of places in *Walden* where this or that item would be relevant
and helpful. I think his work depended on an inextricable combination of both methods. On the one hand, as he re-created his
life in the woods more fully in his imagination, he could see what
was lacking in the account before him. At the same time, he
would have been turning over his journals and the indexes to
them; he was therefore able to tell what he could get from the
journal and to set about preparing it for inclusion in *Walden*.
Thoreau could have written the long additions we find in V and
VI only after gathering and carefully planning how to work his
new material in with the old.

On the other hand, the new material that he daily put into his
journal would have constantly suggested its relation to what he
had already written or reminded him of previously forgotten
events of 1845–47. There are many items from the journal, such
as interlined quotations or brief reflective comments, that Thoreau undoubtedly inserted as they reminded him of his text.
There are also accounts of events in his daily life during 1851–54
that he obviously added separately as they recalled events of his

8. January 24, April 28, June 28, August 27, September 1, October 15 and 26,
November 2, 1852; January 3, 1853.

Walden days. The passage on the hooting owl in "Sounds," 19 and 20, depends on two occasions when Thoreau heard one: November 18, 1851, and July 5, 1852; after the second occasion he put his two journal entries together and inserted them in the manuscript of version II. Part of the description of Alcott and the account of how he and Thoreau sat and whittled in the hut, "Former Inhabitants; and Winter Visitors," 21 and 22, depend upon the fact that Thoreau spent the better part of May 9, 1853, sauntering and talking with Alcott. After writing up this day in his journal, he rewrote the Alcott material on a separate leaf for insertion in the text of V; then he rewrote the whole passage in VI.

Thoreau's use of these incidents serves to emphasize the nature of his work; from the time he first wrote at the pond, *Walden* was an imaginative re-creation and not an attempt to give a literal account of his life in the woods. Not only did he make a story of one year from the experiences of two years; he also used the accounts of experiences of other times, so long as they were true to the nature and tenor of his days at the pond. He took a journal note of May 27, 1841, "I sit in my boat on Walden, playing the flute this evening . . . ," and used it in "The Ponds," 3, beginning, "In warm evenings I frequently sat in the boat playing the flute." He adapted events of later years in the same way. On October 8, 1852, he chased a loon on Walden Pond, and four days later he watched a flight of ducks there; on February 5, 1853, he saw the rude methods of an ice-fisherman there. He wrote of the first two events in "Brute Neighbors" and of the third in "The Pond in Winter" as if they had occurred while he lived at the pond.[9]

Perhaps the most telling example is "Spring," 13, 14, and 15.

9. The journal entries are obviously about things that happened on the days on which Thoreau entered them, days on which he had been to Walden Pond. They begin, IV, 379: "As I was paddling along the north shore"; IV, 383: "Paddled on Walden . . . Scared up ducks"; and IV, 488: "Somebody has been fishing in a rude way." The passages in *Walden* begin, "Brute Neighbors," 17: "As I was paddling along the north shore one very calm afternoon"; "Brute Neighbors," 18: "For hours, in fall days, I watched the ducks"; "The Pond in Winter," 4: "When I strolled around the pond in misty weather."

Completing the Story

Paragraph 13 (the stirring of new life) depends on a journal entry which Thoreau made at Staten Island on September 29, 1843; paragraph 14 (Walden "melting apace") depends on what he saw and heard and wrote in his journal some ten years later on March 20 and 21 and April 1, 1853. The excitement and beauty of the events of 1843 and 1853 were characteristic of his springs at the pond, and so he used them with paragraph 15 ("the change from storm and winter"), which depends on the evening of March 26, 1846. He was careful to add about the melting of Walden, "But this spring it broke up more steadily, as I have said." "This spring" was in fact the spring of 1847, after the great ice-cutting venture of 1846–47. But the artistic reference is to the spring of the one year that he was re-creating for his reader.

The table of additions at the end of this chapter indicates that all parts of *Walden* grew over the years as Thoreau added to them at various stages. He did not do one sort of work at one time and another at another, but all sorts—critical, expository, narrative, descriptive—at all times. For example, the first version contains less than half of a passage on clothing, "Economy," 37 through 41, and of the chapter "The Village." Thoreau reworked both of these pieces five times (see chapter i), and he added comment and anecdote to the passage on clothing in versions III, IV, and VII, and to "The Village" in versions II, III, and VI.

Passages which are not represented at all in the earlier versions grew in similar fashion. There is nothing in I, II, or III, of "Economy," 88 through 95, on the burden of furniture and other household goods. In IV, Thoreau wrote the long paragraph on furniture, 88, and then added another paragraph, not in the published text, on a poor Irish family that lived in a miserable shanty with little furniture or food. In V he added paragraphs 91–93 and 95 on how the Muclasse Indians burned their possessions every year; later he interlined here paragraph 94 on the Mexicans. After January 27, 1854, he wrote up the story of the auction of the deacon's effects and marked it to follow the paragraph on the poor Irish family. In version VII he put paragraph 89, on window curtains and door mat, in its place after 88. The paragraph on the Irish family then followed, but, in preparing the copy for the printer, Thoreau dropped this last item since it described the family's poverty primarily in terms of shelter and food rather than of furniture.

Whole chapters or great parts of them also grew piece by piece. In almost all cases the facts are so complicated as to preclude a clear description, or missing leaves make an exact account impossible, but one reasonably brief example besides that of "The Village" is possible; for, except where a leaf is missing, all the additions to "Brute Neighbors" are clear. In version I Thoreau wrote only about the field mouse, 9; the robin and the phoebe, and possibly the partridge (on the missing leaf), 10; other animals of the woods, 11; and the hunting of the loon, 16. In IV, he added the battle of the ants, 12 and 13, and later he inserted in IV the information on ant battles from Kirby and Spence, 14. In V he rewrote all this material and added the dialogue of the hermit and the poet, 1–7, a paragraph on a ground-bird's nest, his pursuit of a loon, 17, and his watching the ducks on Walden, 18. Later, he interlined paragraph 8 in V and canceled the paragraph on the ground-bird's nest. Not until he wrote VII did he put the material on the dogs and cats in paragraph 15; in VI it had been variously combined with "House-Warming," 18, and "Winter Animals," 12, 13, and 14.

Thoreau's additions cannot be charted or classified according to the kind of material he used at any particular time or in any particular part of *Walden*, nor can we characterize the various versions by what he added in each of them. He drew new material from every kind of occasion: a letter from Horatio Greenough to Emerson about architectural ornament, the auction of a deacon's effects, hoot owls heard at sunset, an afternoon's sport with a loon on Walden, or a day spent talking with Alcott.[10] And he added all sorts of material at all times in all parts of *Walden*. He wrote the story of his almost buying the Hollowell farm in IV;

10. In order, with references to the journal and *Walden:* January 11, 1852—"Economy," 67; January 27, 1854—"Economy," 90; November 18, 1851, and July 5, 1852—"Sounds," 19 and 20; October 8, 1852—"Brute Neighbors," 17; May 9, 1853—"Former Inhabitants; and Winter Visitors," 21 and 22.

one anecdote about Therien in V, and another interlined there later; and the story of the two men lost in the wood, "The Village," 2, in VI. He added material from his reading in the same fashion: for example, from Ovid in "Economy," 5, in III, and in "Spring," 18 and 21, in IV; from Bartram in "Economy," 91–93, in V; from Evelyn and Kenelm Digby in "The Bean-Field," 11, in VI; from Johnson's *Wonder-Working Providence* in "Economy," 57, in VII; and all the quotations from Cato and Varro as he wrote VII or the copy for the printer.

He also added comment and further reflection as they occurred to him over the years. Sometime after June 21, 1850, he interlined in III in the story of his being jailed, "The Village," 3, "But wherever a man goes men will pursue & paw him with their dirty institutions. If they could [they] would constrain [him] to belong to their desperate odd-fellow society." The rest of the comment, on running "amok" against society, he interlined in V. In "Higher Laws," 14, he interlined the first draft of the first sentence in V: "Every man is the builder of a temple called his body, to the god he worships after a style neither Egyptian nor Grecian, nor Gothic—but purely his own—nor can he get off by hammering marble instead." He recopied this in VII and later interlined the first draft of the rest of the paragraph: "Who can doubt the influence of the character on the bodily features? We are all sculptors and painters & our material is our own flesh and blood & bones. Any nobleness begins at once to refine a man's features, any meanness or sensuality to imbrute them." He added "Higher Laws," 10, on the constant moral tension of life, in VI; he only began the elaborate metaphor of the soundings of the pond and a man's character, "The Pond in Winter," 13, in V; he extended it in VI and again in VII.

The way in which Thoreau added to *Walden* raises a question as to whether he knew what he wanted to do and how he was going to do it after he went back to work on his book in 1851–52. Certainly at first he did not have a clear view of what *Walden* was finally to be, nor did he have a plan for developing the account of his life in the woods which we can follow as he carried it out.

The Making of Walden

What he had, as he began, was a memory of his experience and a sense of its significance which were not satisfied by the *Walden* of 1849. He achieved the imaginative re-creation, upon which the final, satisfying account of his experience depended, only gradually and through long care to recollect his experience as richly as possible.

The growth of *Walden* might be compared to that of a living organism that grows continuously and imperceptibly by absorbing new material into its tissue and structure, so that there is no distinguishing between new and old, or first and last. The final size and proportions of *Walden* were potentially, but not necessarily, in its beginning; we cannot see them there any more than we can see the size and proportions of a man in a child, or those of a great oak in a sapling. As the man and the oak grow, we can, on the basis of innumerable examples, speak of fairly distinguishable stages of growth: infancy, childhood, and adolescence, or first-year growth, second-year growth, and on to maturity. But *Walden* is unique, and we cannot distinguish stages of its growth in general terms with any accuracy at all.

We can, however, understand something about its growth by studying Thoreau's progress from version IV to V, and then on to VI and VII and the final copy. When he made version IV, he went over his previous copy and rewrote here and there, and added, besides many short bits, such considerable pieces as those on houses and architecture in "Economy," on his almost buying the Hollowell farm, on visitors at the pond, and on purity in "Higher Laws." He obviously intended to enlarge *Walden* to an extent far beyond what he had done in II and III, but still he added only here and there in IV, and I do not believe that, when he began this version, he looked forward to going as far as he ultimately did in later ones. As he worked on IV, however, and thought more about his life at the pond and accumulated more material related to it in his journal, he saw that he could do much more to make his book a better account of his experience. He therefore gave up IV late in 1852.

Sometime afterward, possibly immediately but in any case by early 1853, he began version V; his work on it indicates without question that as he had been writing IV the conception of *Walden* had grown tremendously. In V he added much more to the description of Walden Pond and thus more adequately represented the fact that it had been an inescapable part of his daily life, which he had never tired of studying in all weathers and in all its moods. He also greatly extended his comments on the conflict between the spiritual and the animal in men and thus more adequately represented the moral and spiritual problems he had sought to settle by his way of life.

The greatest growth in Thoreau's conception of *Walden* resulted, however, from his seeing how he might fill out his account of the progress of the seasons and describe the changes they had brought in his daily affairs and thoughts; by doing so, he would express more adequately the richness and the completeness of his experience. He had to develop particularly the fall and part of the winter. He did so by greatly enlarging "Brute Neighbors," by developing "House-Warming" for the first time, and by completing "Winter Visitors"; he also made significant though smaller additions to "Winter Animals" and "The Pond in Winter." There was so much new material in version V that Thoreau was not able simply to insert it in previous copy as he had done with most of the new material in IV. He had to make fresh copy of practically all of "The Ponds," "Higher Laws," "Brute Neighbors," "House-Warming," "Former Inhabitants; and Winter Visitors," and "The Pond in Winter."

By these additions Thoreau developed the later parts of *Walden* so that they were in proportion with the earlier parts. He was therefore able to mark off chapters in his work. When he decided to make chapters is not ascertainable; he might have thought of them as early as the writing of version IV; but I believe that it was not until he was working on V. In any case he did not put in the titles until he had written V.[11] Even as he put them in, Thoreau undoubtedly knew that he was not finished and that he was

11. At first glance, a reference to chapters in the journal for January 17, 1852, might appear to be related to *Walden:* "Methinks there might be a chapter, when I speak of hens in the thawy days and spring weather on the chips, called 'Chickweed' or 'Plantain.' " But I believe he was thinking here, not of *Walden*, but of the book on

stopping only temporarily. While writing V, he had once more accumulated new material for *Walden* in his journal, and as he looked over V, he saw that he had to redo particularly the last four chapters in it, and at the same time he saw how he could complete the argument of his book.

He therefore began version VI late in 1853. The greater part of this version is a rewriting of earlier work; and two-thirds of it was devoted to a fresh draft of "Former Inhabitants; and Winter Visitors," "Winter Animals," "The Pond in Winter," and "Spring," and the first draft of "Conclusion" (though Thoreau had begun accumulating parts of "Conclusion" when he wrote the fourth version). In the first half of *Walden* he rewrote and added very little; in the second half, besides "Conclusion," he added extensively to "The Ponds" and "House-Warming," and significant amounts to "The Pond in Winter" and "Spring." Altogether Thoreau added a significant portion of new material in VI, but the growth here did not result, as did that in V, in a completely new set of dimensions and proportions. It might be said that Thoreau extended the structure in IV and V and that in VI he filled the gaps he had left; or that *Walden* shot up in its adolescence in IV and V and filled out in its maturity in VI. But both figures are unsatisfactory, for neither adequately suggests the fact that as Thoreau restudied V and began VI, he had to re-create his experience imaginatively again, fuller and clearer than it was in V, and then to discover how he could portray it in VI.

With the completion of VI, Thoreau had told his story. He made a few brief additions in VII, and one or two as he prepared the copy for the printer, but he was no longer working primarily to fill out his tale. In fact, he cut out a considerable amount of material as he wrote VII and the final copy. He was cleaning up his work, and he put in only a few items as they occurred to him: for example, the fine comment on village auctions and what happens to the stuff bought at them, "Economy," 90, and the de-

---

the seasons which he never had time to write. On January 13, 1852, he had written: "Would not snow-drifts be a good study,—their philosophy and poetry? Are they not worthy of a chapter?"

scription of Walden "melting apace," "Spring," 14. *Walden* would not be essentially different without most of what he added at these times. One group of items, however, added a minor but valuable touch of ancient use and authority to his way of living. He was reading the Roman writers on agriculture in 1854,[12] and he added all the quotations from Cato and Varro as he wrote VII or the copy for the printer.[13]

12. See Ethel Seybold, *Thoreau: The Quest and the Classics* (New Haven, 1952), pp. 70–76.

13. The quotations in "Economy," 84, and "House-Warming," 6 and 13, are in VII; that in "Where I Lived," 6, was added in V in the ink and hand of VII; and those at the end of "The Bean-Field," 16, were added in VI, the one from Varro in the ink and hand of VII, that from Cato in pencil; the brief phrase in "The Bean-Field," 13, was apparently added in the copy for the printer.

The Making of Walden

The table on pages 72–73 is designed to provide, with such accuracy as is possible, a summary of Thoreau's additions to *Walden* in the various versions. It is not, however, as precise as such an array of numbers is likely to suggest it is. The contents, the order of the contents of the paragraphs, and the order of the paragraphs themselves were not always from the beginning what they are in the final text. And, in many places, parts of paragraphs were added at various times, and only such indefinite qualifiers as "most," "part," and "begin" could be used to indicate what part was added in a given version. Furthermore, the loss of leaves from the manuscript may well have led to unavoidable errors. Places where leaves are missing are clear in the first version, and it is possible in most cases to make a reasonable judgment as to what material was lost; but in the later versions, although it is certain that some leaves are missing, it is not always clear what ones or how many there may be. Hence, some material may be attributed here to version VI that might have been in version V on a leaf that has been destroyed or lost. And some passages that I have conjectured to have been on leaves obviously missing from V and that I have therefore attributed to V might not have been there in their entirety. But errors of this sort could not be many, for the date of material in the journal and the way in which Thoreau incorporated it in *Walden* give a check on most of the additions.

"Half 105" indicates the first half of paragraph 105; "105 half" indicates the second half; "part," "begin," "end," and other qualifiers explain themselves. The numbers refer, of course, to the paragraphs of the chapters.

Much material appears in the manuscript for the first time in interlineations or inserts in blank spaces, but it is recorded here as having been added in the version in which it was first written out fair and full. In a number of cases, however, the interlined material does not appear written out fair and full anywhere in the manuscript. In these cases, when the material runs to more than a sentence or two, it is listed in the version in which it was interlined and the entry is inclosed in parentheses:

(82) indicates that all of the paragraph was interlined.

(end 82) indicates that the end of the paragraph was interlined.

82 (end) indicates that most of the paragraph was added and written out full and fair, but that the end was interlined.

Material which was probably or possibly on missing leaves in version I and which appears for the first time in the manuscript in a later version is listed in the version in which it first appears, but the paragraph number is inclosed in square brackets ([ ]).

Attributions for which the evidence is quite uncertain are followed by an asterisk (*).

Material written between two major groups (see p. 13) is attributed to the later of the groups.

There is no material in the manuscript for the following paragraphs; it is fairly certain that most of it was on missing leaves:

> Reading: first half of 2, 8, most of 9, 12
> Sounds: most of 12, beginning of 13
> The Bean-Field: second half of 7, 8, 9
> The Ponds: 24, 27, most of 29, 30, 31, most of 32
> Baker Farm: most of 3, 4, 7, 9
> Brute Neighbors: 4, 5
> Spring: most of 7

VERSION

	II	III	IV
Economy	11, 13 half, 19 half, 70 half, (98), 100, be-gin 102, half 105.	1, begin 3, (5 two-thirds), begin 42, 43, (part 56), 68, half 70, (begin 75), 77, begin 78, end 79, (part 81), most 82, two-thirds 85 (part), end 103.	9, (10 end), (14), 35 half, begin 3? half 38, 39 third, half, (part 44), n 46, 47, 48, most most 53, 54 half, [64, 65], 66, 67, n 78, (part 86), 87
Where I Lived	part 19, 20 (part), part 21, part 22.		1, 2, 3, 5.
Reading			
Sounds	(begin 9), most 11, [begin 12, 14, 17, part 21 and 22].*		part 4, [10],* 19, ?
Solitude	2, (end 4), 5 two-thirds, 6, part 10.		7, 8, 9, end 10, 11.
Visitors	part 11.	part 12, end 14.	15, 16, 17.*
Bean-Field			
Village	half 2.	3 (end).	
Ponds			parts of 5 and 7 an? and 10 and 16, three-fifths 18, ? 26, 34.
Baker Farm			2 three-fourths.
Higher Laws			most 11, half 12, 1? 15.
Brute Neighbors			12, 13.
House-Warming			
Former Inhabitants			
Winter Animals			
Pond in Winter			most 7.
Spring	most 23.		18, [19], (20), 21 (part).
Conclusion			half 12, most 13, 1? 15.

V	VI	VII
two-fifths, most 75, (part 82), 83, 88, 91, 92, 93, (94), 95, 104, 106, much 107 and 108 and 109.	96 half.*	38 half, 57, 58 (part), end 84, 90, 105 half, begin 109.
	7 (part), part 9, begin 10, 11, end 13, part 14.	4, 6 (interlined in V).
d 5, (most 6), 16.	[most 13],* most 15.	
	begin 5.	part 5.
d 7, 9, (end 13), most 14, (18). last fourth.	11 two-thirds, part 16 and 17. 2 half.	
rt 1, most 2 and 3 and 5, 12, 13, half 15, part 16, 18 two-fifths, 19, 20, 21 (end), 23, 29, 32, (33). (begin 2).	part 1, part 5, end 10, 11, 14, 15 half, (17), 22. begin 2.	
ch 1, 2, most 3 and 5, 6, 8, 9, 12 half. 2, 3, 4, 5, 6, 7, (8), [10],* 14, 17, 18.	4, 10. part 15 (part).	14 (part). begin 15.
1, 2 (in "The Ponds," 16), 3, 4, 7, 12, two-thirds 13, 14, 15, 16 three-fourths, 17, 19. 3, 4, 5, 6, 7, 8, 9], 11, most 15, 16, 17, 18, part 19, 20, much 21 and 22, 23, 24. [9, 10].	5 (some once in "Economy"), three-fourths 6, 8, 9, 10 (some once in "Economy"), 11. 1,* end 21, begin 22.	end 6, end 13, begin 16, 18 (first half probably in I).
rt 6, begin 7, [9, 10, 11, begin 13, 14, 15],* much 18 and 19. st 2.	1,* [7], part 11, 12. 1, most 2, 4, 5, part 6,* 12, most 13. most 1, 6, begin 7, most 8, half 9, 10, [17].	(part 11). part 2, part 13. (end 2), part 6, part 8, 9 half, 14.
11, 16,* most 18.	1 (part), 2 (part), 3, 4, first third 6, 7, 8, 9, 10, end 12, end 13, 17,* begin 18, 19.	6 two-thirds.

V

Developing the Structure

I~N SOME~ respects the most valuable insight we gain from the manuscript is that which it gives us into the structure of *Walden*. We would know something of Thoreau's revising and adding to his material simply from a comparison of his journals with the published text, but without the manuscript we would know nothing of the way in which he found out how he could best organize his material.

Furthermore, although I do not believe that we must have the information that the manuscript gives us in order to recognize the nice disposition and relations of the parts of *Walden* or that this information proves that the final structure of *Walden* is satisfying, the changes the manuscript reveals often emphasize important points in the organization of the book, and thus they may help to show the whole design to some who might not otherwise see it. This is important, for many critics have denied Thoreau's success in achieving an artistically satisfying organization of his material. James Russell Lowell, for example, declared that Thoreau "had no artistic power such as controls a great work to the serene balance of completeness, but exquisite mechanical skill in the shaping of sentences and paragraphs."[1] Sanborn presumed to "improve" the order of *Walden* in the preposterous edition of the Bibliophile Society; and even a judicious critic and editor commented in 1934 that in "the matter of organization in its larger aspects, one may concede Thoreau's weakness yet offer in extenuation the desultory and casual nature of the author's own plan."[2]

These critics might point for support to Thoreau's judgment on his writing when he was working on *A Week* at the pond: "From all points of the compass, from the earth beneath and the heavens above, have come these inspirations and been entered daily in the order of their arrival in the journal. Thereafter, when the time arrived, they were winnowed into lectures, and again, in due time, from lectures into essays. And at last they stand, like the cubes of Pythagoras, firmly on either basis; like statues on their pedestals, but the statues rarely take hold of their hands. There is only such connection and series as is attainable in galleries. And this affects their immediate practical and popular influence."[3] This describes his characteristic progress from journal notes to publication, and it is a fair comment on the lack of coherence of *A Week*, but it is far from an adequate judgment on the unity of *Walden*, as the appreciation and analyses of F. O. Matthiessen and J. W. Krutch have more recently begun to make clear.[4]

Many readers have failed to appreciate the structure of *Walden*, possibly because they looked for something different from what is there, something at once more simple and more obvious. *Walden* is not a dated chronicle of Thoreau's two years in the woods; nor is it a handbook on how to live alone at little expense, organized according to sharply defined and separated topics; nor a rigor-

1. *My Study Windows* (Boston: J. R. Osgood & Co., 1871), p. 200.

2. Bartholow V. Crawford (ed.), *Henry David Thoreau: Representative Selections* (New York: American Book Co., 1934), p. 1.

3. *The Writings of Henry David Thoreau* (20 vols.; Boston: Houghton Mifflin Co., 1906), *Journal*, I, 413; entry is undated. Unless otherwise indicated, all references to Thoreau's published writings are to this edition.

4. Matthiessen, *The American Renaissance* (New York: Oxford University Press, 1946), pp. 166–75; Krutch, *Thoreau*, pp. 95 ff. See also Sherman Paul, "Resolution at *Walden*," *Accent*, XII (1953), 101–13, and John C. Broderick, "Imagery in *Walden*," *University of Texas Studies in English*, XXXIII (1954), 80–89.

ously constructed argument designed to prove that he was right and others wrong. It is rather a unique combination of all three kinds—chronicle, topical essay, and persuasive argument.

To understand how Thoreau put these together, it is necessary first to see in some detail what the final structure of *Walden* is in the order and the relation of its parts. This structure was determined for the most part by the fact that the book was an autobiographical narrative that Thoreau wrote to answer those who had asked him what his life in the woods was like and what he did there. It was also determined, however, by the fact that in addition to answering his townsmen's questions, Thoreau wanted to point out how wrong were their assumptions about living and, as a result, how poor their lives were. This second theme provided the frame in which he set his story.

He began *Walden* with his argument, saying, in effect, in "Economy": "Your lives are mean because you do not know what is worth having in life, or how to get it. I have better notions of how to live and I have tried them out. Let me tell you what I did." Then, from the beginning of "Where I Lived" through "Spring" he described his experience in such a way as to show how satisfying and joyful it was. But as he did this, he frequently reverted to his criticism of the life of most people and to his own ideals, and thus kept his argument up, not in such a manner as to prove it logically, but rather to keep reminding his readers of the contrast between their sorry pleasures and the profoundly rewarding ones he had had. For example, in "Solitude" he compared the companionship he found in the things around him with his contemporaries' loneliness in crowds; in "Baker Farm," he portrayed John Field as an example of their slavery to things and set this off against his sense of freedom; in "Brute Neighbors" he showed that the hunters of the loon did not enjoy their short-lived sport as he enjoyed his pursuit of the bird; in "House-Warming" he compared the pleasures of his simple house with the lack of real pleasure in more elegant ones. When he had finished his story, he added in "Conclusion": "Now this shows you what can be done. You don't have to waste your lives and cower despairingly before what you think are the facts of life. You too can live freely and richly; everything lies before you if you will only have faith." With "Conclusion" Thoreau rounded out Walden most fittingly: it completed his argument, and in it he returned to speaking directly to the condition of his readers just as he had done at the beginning.

Within this frame, Thoreau ordered the story of his experiment in three ways: by topics, describing various qualities and aspects of his life; by the cycle of the day, telling of the events and occupations of typical days; and by the cycle of the year, narrating the changes in his surroundings and his doings that the progress of the seasons brought about. These factors do not operate separately, but together or in turns. Thoreau's transitions from part to part are deliberately casual; the movement is not rigorous. It is conceivable that he might have arranged some of his topics in different order, but their order and relations as they stand raise no questions, cause no jars, but create the sense of an easy and natural progress through his experiences. The order Thoreau established is absolutely proper to his aim. The proof of the excellence of his life in the woods and the strength of his answers to the incredulous and the scornful did not depend on some particular predetermined scheme or on irrefutable logic but on the creation of a living sense of what his days and months had been like.

At the start he ordered and related his material primarily by topics. First he had to describe his house and its location; in "Economy" he had told only of building it. He began "Where I Lived" with an anecdote that emphasized his uncommon taste for retired and unimproved property and also restated his very uncommon attitude toward possessions. Then he launched into the description of living in his simple, unfinished hut and of the pleasures of its site and its distance from the rest of the world. Since he went to live where he did in order to live as he wanted to, he continued in this chapter by setting forth the qualities he sought in his life.

These implied study and contemplation as opposed to hurry and acquisition, and Thoreau therefore next wrote "Reading," in which he extolled the riches to be gained from the study of the classics of all peoples and contrasted the nourishment to be had from them with the thin fare with which most of his contemporaries were content. "Reading" has a place in his story on other grounds too, for Thoreau went to the pond to write and study, and he wrote *Walden* in part at least for others who wanted to do the same. It is the one part of the book, however, that may be criticized for not being completely of a piece with the rest. Not because it is not fitted in properly, for it is, but because its material seems to have a slightly different flavor from that of the other parts; it does not appear to depend directly on his days and nights at the pond; it does not smell of the woods, as does everything else in his story.

Of course, as he pointed out in both "Reading" and "Sounds," Thoreau spent much of his time in his first summer hoeing beans. But he did not tell about that at the very beginning; from "Where I Lived" through "Visitors" he was primarily concerned with describing certain general aspects of his life before telling what he did in the different seasons as they followed one another. After "Reading," then, he wrote in "Sounds" of his study of and absorption in the sights and sounds around him. Sometimes he did nothing but sit "rapt in a revery"; at other times he watched the life about the pond, or the trains on the Fitchburg Railroad, or listened to everything that spoke around him, the bells of Acton and Bedford, the cows in distant pastures, and the whippoorwills and owls and frogs. We should note, too, that Thoreau placed and ordered this material by more than its topical relations. He carefully marked the time as summer when he sat on his doorstep or swept his house or listened to the sounds of the day and night. This is important in the total effect of summer which the early chapters develop. In addition, he took great pains to arrange the cycle of the day from morning to afternoon to evening to night throughout the chapter (see p. 86 below).

In "Solitude" he further described his enjoyment of and sympathy with his surroundings and answered directly the questions about the loneliness of his life, as well as emphasizing again how he gained the things he wanted. The answer was that he wasn't lonely even when alone. Moreover, not being a hermit in fact or in taste, he did see people; he had visitors, and in the next chapter, "Visitors," he told of his simple provisions for hospitality and described with charitable humor the pleasure he took in the simple and sometimes simple-minded company he found in the woods.

Through "Visitors" Thoreau had been answering primarily the question of what it was like to live as he had. With "The Bean-Field" he turned to answering "But what do you do there?" (This distinction is, of course, one of emphasis; he was answering both questions in all parts.) From the beginning of this chapter to the end of "Baker Farm," Thoreau ordered his material to show how he spent his summer days—morning, afternoon, and evening —at the pond. He began "The Bean-Field," "Meanwhile my beans . . . were impatient to be hoed," and thereby related his culture of beans to all that he had already written of; he had been caring for his beans ever since, and even before, he had moved into his hut in July. After describing the major morning task of his first summer in this chapter, he turned to telling of his afternoons and evenings in "The Village," "The Ponds," and "Baker Farm." He began "The Village," "After hoeing, or perhaps reading and writing, in the forenoon, I usually bathed . . . and for the afternoon was absolutely free" and continued, "Every day or two I strolled to the village . . . it was very pleasant, when I stayed late in town, to launch myself into the night. . . . One afternoon, near the end of the first summer"; and in "The Ponds," "Sometimes . . . I rambled still farther westward [to gather berries on the hills]. . . . Occasionally, after my hoeing . . . I joined [a fisherman] . . . in warm evenings I frequently sat in the boat playing the flute. . . . Sometimes, after staying [late] in a village parlor I . . . spent the hours of midnight fishing . . . a walk through the woods [to other ponds] was often my recreation"; and in "Baker Farm," "Sometimes I rambled to pine groves . . . to particular trees. . . . I set out one afternoon to go a-fishing to Fair Haven." The long description of Walden Pond and the shorter ones of Flint's and White Pond break into the recital of his doings; but, as Thoreau said, they were his "lake country," and the wealth of details he supplied about it suggested the many afternoons he spent in it.

The Making of Walden

When he had finished telling what he did in his summer days, Thoreau was led on from the account of his fishing in "Baker Farm" to reflect, in "Higher Laws," on the conflict between his theories and practices in regard to fishing and eating and then to the never-ending conflict in all life between virtue and vice. At first glance this chapter might seem a serious break in his story, but the reflections in it are an important part of Thoreau's comment on life and his description of the qualities he sought in living; and in addition these reflections recall and pick up not only "What I Lived For" but also the argument he began in "Economy." Moreover, the pause here in his story is rhetorically sound; with "Baker Farm" Thoreau had finished one part, the account of his daily occupations in the summer, and he started afresh with new interest for his reader in "Brute Neighbors."

He used the comic interlude of the Hermit and the Poet to begin "Brute Neighbors," probably because he felt the need of some such descent from the level of "Higher Laws." In telling of the animals who were the neighbors he saw all the time, he took up again both the description of what living in the woods was like and the recital of what he did. But the major factor in organizing and relating the material from here to the end of "Spring" is the passage of the months and seasons. Thoreau arranged "Brute Neighbors" with great care to run from the time when he was building his house, to June, through summer, and on to October. Thus he made the transition from the summer months of the earlier chapters and began to stress the cycle of the year. "Brute Neighbors" and "House-Warming" carry him from summer to the fall and early winter; "Former Inhabitants; and Winter Visitors" and "Winter Animals" are the deep middle of winter; "The Pond in Winter" takes him almost to the end of winter; finally there is "Spring."

But Thoreau also treated his material topically in these later chapters, and there is an interesting repetition with variation of earlier topics: parts of "House-Warming" recall the description of his hut in "Economy" and "Where I Lived"; "Former Inhabitants; and Winter Visitors" reminds us of "Solitude" and "Visitors"; in "Winter Animals" we have the "Sounds" and

Developing the Structure

"Brute Neighbors" of winter; and "The Pond in Winter" recalls the earlier observations on "The Ponds."

At the beginning of "House-Warming," Thoreau returned to telling of his daily occupations, going a-graping and gathering wild apples and nuts for the winter. He noted very specially that he did these things in October, and in the rest of the chapter he noted the time of year at every point. He marked the passage of fall in the succession of September foliage, the numbed wasps of October, and the last warmth of the sun in November; and then, as he told of sitting before his fire and plastering his house and gathering wood, he marked the advance of winter: "the north wind had already begun to cool the pond. . . . I did not begin to plaster until it was freezing weather. . . . The pond had in the meanwhile skimmed over . . . at length the winter set in in good earnest." In "Former Inhabitants; and Winter Visitors" he told more of "cheerful winter evenings" by the fire when the snows were deep and the village farther away than ever; at such times he had to conjure up the former inhabitants of the neighboring woods for company. But he added that even "in the deepest snows" of winter he walked about the countryside, and from time to time three or four choice friends made their way to visit him "through snow and rain and dark."

He began "Winter Animals" with "When the ponds were firmly frozen," and described the changes in his surroundings that deep winter brought: new paths across country, new sights, new sounds, and new aspects of his animal neighbors. The activities and events of "The Pond in Winter"—cutting the ice to get water, ice-fishing, the survey of the pond through the ice, and the tale of the great ice harvest—these quite naturally followed the firm freezing of the ponds. And although robbing Walden of its coat of ice did not cause the spring breakup to come any earlier than usual, it did suggest the day when the pond would once more be a clear mirror; and so Thoreau went on to his delighted description of the coming and flourishing of spring and the advance of the year to summer again, when his first year in the woods was completed. Then, he turned back to speak directly to his readers in "Conclusion," and the gay and triumphant tone of

"Spring" is continued in Thoreau's challenge to others to live with the faith his experience justified.

Much of this organization of the published *Walden* is discernible in the first version. The sequence and relations of topics, the scheme of describing his typical summer occupations, and the chronology beginning with the summer and ending with the spring—all three factors helped to organize the first version. But *Walden* was very incomplete and uncertain at many points in the first version, and it did not have the careful order and the nice articulation of parts that give the final text its complete and satisfying structure.

The changes Thoreau made in reshaping *Walden* can best be dealt with according to whether he made them to gain clarity and coherence of topics or to establish the cycle of the day or the cycle of the year. Sometimes more than one consideration dictated a change, since at a number of points the organization of the material depended upon more than one of the factors that determined the order of his story. Examples of minor changes in organization that resulted from the revisions of single paragraphs or of passages such as the sketch of Therien have already been considered. They will not be repeated here, for, although very important in the whole effect of *Walden*, they were not controlled by the demands of the over-all structure.

The first considerable change by which Thoreau achieved greater topical unity was taking the material of "Where I Lived, and What I Lived For," 18, 19, 21, and 22,[5] from its position in the first version (after "Sounds," 1, 2, and 3) and putting it, in version II, where it is in the final text. Since the passage asserts the value of living quietly and deliberately, it was not completely out of place when it followed the account of his morning meditation in "Sounds"; but Thoreau saw at his first rewriting that it

5. They were not in this order in I, but when Thoreau moved them, he added paragraph 20 and ordered all the material essentially as it is in the final text: the questions of hurry and waste, with the excuse of work to be done, led to Thoreau's satire on men's desire for news and on the post office and newspapers. Following the suggestion that the preacher should cry out to men to slow down, he proposed that men should live more deliberately so that they might observe realities steadily and see things as they are.

was essentially an extension of his remarks on the qualities that he lived for. He gained in a second respect too, for, by removing this passage from its original place within "Sounds," he brought together the passages in "Sounds" that describe his morning meditation as he sat on his doorstep and his afternoon enjoyment of sights and sounds while he sat at his window. There is no evidence to prove that Thoreau thought of one of these improvements before the other, except that he wrote the new version of "Where I Lived, and What I Lived For" before he wrote the new one of "Sounds"; he may well have seen both improvements at once.

Thoreau did not always solve the problem of the proper place for many items so soon or so directly. In version I he had introduced his boasting of his lack of window curtains, "Economy," 89, in the middle of "The Village," 1, with: "I would observe, in a parenthesis." When he wrote version III, he decided that the passage was too parenthetical, and so he canceled it in I and copied it on a new leaf. But he does not seem to have found the place for it until version VII, when he saw that he could use it to contrast his attitude toward furniture with that of those who were trapped by theirs (see p. 63).

He was still later in settling on the right place for some of the material in "The Bean-Field." Not until he wrote the copy for the printer did he take the material on the sounds of the guns on gala days and the hum of the "trainers" out of "Sounds" and make them paragraph 7 of "The Bean-Field." They belong there rather than in "Sounds" because they were not regular daily sounds that he heard as he sat at his hut, but ones that he heard only a few times when he was "away there" in his beanfield. And not until the copy for the printer did he put his detailed farm accounts in "The Bean-Field," 12 and 13. In the first version and again in version V he wrote them out in "Economy" with his other accounts; later in V he penciled this note: "Here or under beans." In the end he transferred them to "The Bean-Field" where they belong, for they are an important item in the description of his cash-crop venture; furthermore, when they were with his other accounts in "Economy," there were too many figures together.

The Making of Walden

Even these few examples suggest that no matter where in *Walden* Thoreau might be working at any time, he strove to keep the whole piece in mind. The shift of one small item at three different times adds further evidence of this. In version II in a paragraph following "Economy," 21, he added the anecdote of the ragged Irishman who fell into the pond while cutting ice, by way of proof that the rich do not know how to use their money: he pointed out that the poor ice-cutter was more warmly dressed than his readers would be in their "fashionable garments." In version III he used the anecdote following "Economy," 37, as evidence that adequate clothing is not expensive. In V he put it in "The Pond in Winter," 18, which was at that time a more elaborate description of the ice-cutters at work than it is in the final text. In version VII and the final text, the anecdote is in "Economy," 105, where it serves as an illustration of how people often err in the pity and help that they extend to others who are supposedly worse off than themselves.

Besides the moving of items from one chapter to another, the manuscript also shows how Thoreau reorganized material within chapters and how he changed the chapter divisions themselves in order to make his topics clear and coherent. The first of these points can be illustrated only briefly here, for the changes in most chapters are too complicated to be described. The simple case of "Visitors" will have to serve. The transcription of version I shows the order of the chapter at the beginning (see pp. 169–77). Here and in version II the transition from the material of "Solitude" was: "As for men, they will hardly fail one anywhere," and then the description of Therien and the other individuals whom Thoreau talked with preceded the general remarks on his domestic arrangements for hospitality. But when he wrote version IV, he took from amid the material of "Solitude" the paragraph that serves as the introduction of "Visitors" in the final text: "I think that I love society as much as most. . . ." Sometime later (there is no evidence as to exactly when), he put the rest of his general remarks on visiting here at the beginning of the chapter in order to make his topic clear and to provide a better contrast to the preceding account of the pleasures of living alone in his house in the woods.

Developing the Structure

In two other cases he gained greatly by changing the points at which he had made chapter divisions. He first wrote the title of "Baker Farm" at the end of what is paragraph 2; the chapter then included only the story of his afternoon visit to Baker Farm and Fair Haven Bay. But he soon saw that "The Ponds" must end with the tribute to Walden and White ponds in paragraph 34; anything added after "Talk of heaven! ye disgrace the earth" would have been a hopeless anticlimax, and, besides, the beginning of "Baker Farm" serves to introduce the third in a series about his afternoon walks: "Sometimes I rambled to pine groves . . . or to the cedar wood . . . or to swamps. . . ."[6] He shifted the title of "House-Warming" in much the same way and for similar reasons. At first, in version V, he entitled the chapter "Fire," which he wrote at the top of a blank page, the fourth of a folio; the immediately preceding paragraph told of his sitting in the November sunshine, "House-Warming," 4. Later he wrote "House-Warming" above what is paragraph 1; the last paragraph of "Brute Neighbors" is clearly the end of the account of the animals, and "House-Warming," 1, "In October, I went a-graping . . . ," begins the description of his fall occupations.[7]

The change of name here is one of a number that Thoreau made; they too reflect his care in defining his topics. He originally wrote "Society" before the first paragraph of "Visitors," in contrast, of course, to the preceding title "Solitude." But "Visitors" is more concrete and indicates the nature of the content of the chapter more accurately. He changed "Beans" to "The Bean-Field," "Animal Food" to "Higher Laws," and "Fire" to "House-Warming" because in each case the first title was too

6. Originally there was a brief paragraph (canceled in the manuscript) preceding what is now paragraph 1 of "Baker Farm." The manuscript does not reveal for certain whether Thoreau canceled this paragraph before or after he moved the title "Baker Farm." The paragraph would have served the same function as the present first paragraph, but not so well; it began: "I also visited many a nameless little rill. . . ."

7. He also effected a change when he made one chapter of "Former Inhabitants" and "Winter Visitors." At first they were separate. Perhaps they seemed too short to stand separately, but the main reason for bringing them together could well have been that they both dealt with people as compared with "Winter Animals" and "The Pond in Winter" which preceded and followed them until Thoreau reordered his chapters at the very last (see p. 88).

narrow. "Fire," for example, did not cover the chimney-building, plastering, wood-gathering, and other items as does "House-Warming." "Brute Neighbors" was first entitled "Fall Animals"; since the chapter includes animals of the spring and summer, Thoreau later struck out "Fall." Finally, he wrote "Brute Neighbors," which is better than "Animals" because it suggests Thoreau's attitude toward the animals around him. "Winter Animals" was originally "Animals"; when "Fall Animals" was changed to "Animals," Thoreau added "Winter" to the title of the later chapter to distinguish it; it is a better title because more specific, and it is in keeping with "Winter Visitors" and "The Pond in Winter."

The changes Thoreau had to make in order to maintain the cycle of the day were few. As he put new material in "The Village," "The Ponds," and "Baker Farm," he did so in such a way as to keep the sequences of afternoon and evening and night with which he began. But the way in which he reordered "Sounds," 14 to 22, is a good example of his careful reworking. By the shift in version II of material from between "Sounds," 3 and 4, to "Where I Lived" (see p. 82), he had brought together in "Sounds" the events of a summer morning and a summer afternoon. But the order of the last part of the chapter was poor: the sound of cockcrow preceded the bells, and the frogs came between the whippoorwills and the screech owls. He did not work out the firm but unobtrusive progress of the final text—from afternoon through evening and finally to dawn of the next day—until the copy for the printer (or possibly version VI; the manuscript evidence is incomplete). In place of the scattered order of the earlier versions, the final text has: the rattle of a carriage or team in the afternoon, or the bells on Sundays; then at evening the distant lowing of some cow still in pasture; at "half-past seven" came the whippoorwills; later, "when other birds are still" he heard the owls; and also "late in the evening" he might hear wagons again or a cow now in a distant barnyard; "in the meanwhile" the frogs had begun their revels, which they kept up until the sun dispersed the morning mist. And so the night ended with dawn, and Thoreau went on to his remarks on cockcrowing;

these led to others on his lack of the usual domestic sounds and surroundings, and so on to "Solitude."

The most extensive changes that Thoreau made in the order and relations of his material were those by which he completed the cycle of the seasons. These changes were essentially of two sorts. The first were directed to filling out the account of the seasons; they depended upon great additions, especially in version V and to a lesser extent in IV and VI. The second were directed to recording the individual events in the proper months and seasons; these depended for the most part on shifts of material that Thoreau made in the versions after V. The general effect of the changes can best be seen from a summary comparison of the contents and the order of the contents in the later parts of *Walden* in versions I and V and the published text (there were no chapter titles, of course, in I):

VERSION I	VERSION V	PUBLISHED TEXT
Brute Neighbors	Brute Neighbors	Brute Neighbors
Winter Animals	House-Warming	House-Warming
Former Inhabitants	Winter Animals	Former Inhabitants;
The Pond in Winter	Former Inhabitants	and Winter Visitors
Spring	Winter Visitors	Winter Animals
	The Pond in Winter	The Pond in Winter
	Spring	Spring
		Conclusion

In the early versions the months of fall and early winter were treated very briefly, and deep winter followed close upon the summer; it was as if Thoreau had been carried hastily into winter as he told the whole story of the animals in the woods in one long section. Details of his winter life were also missing.

Between versions IV and V, he wrote out much of the section on winter visitors. Perhaps he had not thought to include any account of his particular friends when he was preparing for lectures; but as he later reconstructed his life in the woods, he would have remembered his talks with those who were especially important as visitors when casual passers-by were few. When he wrote version V, he developed these notes into a separate whole piece, "Winter Visitors."

He made an even greater change by filling in the hitherto neglected season between the hunting of the loon and the ice-and-snow-bound world of mid-winter. He began by adding the pursuit of the loon and the flight of the ducks at the end of "Brute Neighbors"; he then made the great addition of almost all of "House-Warming" in versions V, VI, and VII. He told of his varied activities in late fall and early winter: going a-graping and nutting, building his chimney, plastering his house, gathering wood for fuel; and he described the changes in his surroundings as winter closed in. He also added a few details and comments to complete the picture of winter in "Winter Animals" and "The Pond in Winter."

When he had added the material that was necessary to fill out the cycle of the seasons, Thoreau had also to make sure that the various parts were related properly and that events of each season were in their right places. This involved the shift of material at a number of points. The major change of this sort was the reversal of the order of "Winter Animals" and "Former Inhabitants; and Winter Visitors"; he made it as he wrote the copy for the printer. The changing relations of the material in this part of *Walden* re-emphasize the fact that the topical and the cyclic organizations are interwoven in the book and also that, while Thoreau's progress to his final form was constant in force, it was often tentative and complicated. In version I the sequence had been from all the material on the animals to "Former Inhabitants" to "The Pond in Winter." Topical considerations apparently influenced the placing of the material on the animals, and the cycle of the day influenced the relation of the material that followed: before Thoreau added "Winter Visitors" and "The Pond in Winter," 1 and 2, the transition was from "And with such thoughts as these I lulled myself asleep" ("Former Inhabitants," 16) to "Early in the morning" ("The Pond in Winter," 3).

After the additions, there was only a verbal transition from the allusion to "eventide" in the quotation from the Vishnu Purana ("Former Inhabitants; and Winter Visitors," 24) to the new beginning of "The Pond in Winter": "After a still winter night I awoke." But with "Winter Animals" placed after "Former Inhabitants; and Winter Visitors," there is a new transition from evening to morning, since at the end of "Winter Animals" Thoreau describes how he watched the rabbits in the evening, and then comes the morning at the beginning of "The Pond in Winter." This, however, would not have been the only or the major reason for the change; there were several others. First, the description of his cheery winter evenings by the fire in "Former Inhabitants" follows the talk of chimney, fuel, and fire in "House-Warming" better than did the beginning of "Winter Animals": "When the ponds were firmly frozen." Second, the change brought this freezing of the ponds in "Winter Animals" immediately before the ice-bound world of "The Pond in Winter." Finally, by separating "Brute Neighbors" and "Winter Animals" more widely, it produced a better distribution of the material on the animals.

At no other point did Thoreau shift or change so extensive a piece; but the very briefness of some items indicates the care with which he worked to arrange the details as well as to construct the outline of the seasons. Changes were necessary in every season. In versions I and II in "Sounds," 2, he wrote, "Sometimes in a spring morning . . . or later in the summer." In version VI and possibly in IV on a missing page, he dropped the reference to "spring," and the final text reads: "Sometimes, in a summer morning." He undoubtedly did sit on his doorstep in the spring too, but at this point he wanted to establish the fact that he was beginning his story with summer.

For the fall and winter he had a number of changes to make, and, as was the case with several "topical" items, he did not always find the right answer at once. Sometime after writing version IV, he wrote nine or ten lines on the beauty of the turning maples in September and inserted them in a blank space after the first part of "The Ponds," 18, which is a description of the surface of Walden Pond on a calm September afternoon. They were not relevant at this point, and in version V Thoreau moved these lines on September foliage to "The Ponds," 16, in which he comments on the happy juxtaposition of water and wooded hills. But once again these new lines broke the unity of the passage to which they had been added; the emphasis on the fact that it was "September" and that there was daily changing foliage was out of place here.

When he wrote version VI, however, Thoreau was exquisitely successful in his search for the right place. In "House-Warming," 3, he had already described the numbed wasps that gathered in his house in October, and in paragraph 4 he had told how he sought the late sunshine of November on the northeast shore of the pond. Now he saw that the lines on the beauty of the September foliage would serve perfectly as the first of a three-part ode on autumn and the dying of the year, and he made them paragraph 2 of "House-Warming."

There is another interesting series of shifts of material for "House-Warming." In version VI Thoreau took the accounts of building his chimney and plastering his house from "Economy" and put them in "House-Warming" as a consecutive piece. In the copy for the printer, however, he separated them, using the passage on the chimney in "House-Warming," 5, and that on plastering in paragraph 10. He thus brought the building of the chimney into the story when he "began to have a fire at evening" in the fall, but he did not plaster his house "till it was freezing weather" in November.

It is impossible to know all the changes he made in some of the "winter" chapters and in "Spring" because of the leaves missing from version I. Certainly he moved material on the freezing and thawing of the ponds and rivers, but most details are lost. There are also a number of complicated moves of material on animals that are not fully describable. But the general nature and effect of what Thoreau did can be adequately seen from a few more items. He transferred the mice's girdling of the pitch pines from "Brute Neighbors" to "Winter Animals," 13, since they did this in the winter at the same time as they raided his store of nuts.[8] And, to put the events of spring in their proper places, he moved the spring racketing of the squirrels under his house from "Winter

---

8. He also moved the paragraph on the moles from "Winter Animals" to "House Warming," 18, and the passage on "Bose" and the cats to "Brute Neighbors," 15, for "topical" reasons.

Animals" to "Spring," 12, and details on the breaking-up of the ice on Walden Pond from both "The Ponds," 13, and "The Pond in Winter," 16, to "Spring," 1.

As a last example, there is the change Thoreau made to mark the end of the cycle of the seasons. In version I he had described in "Brute Neighbors" how a phoebe had sometimes come and looked in at his house while he was building it in the spring months (see p. 191). Quite late in all his rewriting he wrote a revision of the passage on the last page of version I and marked it for insertion in "Spring," 25, leaving only the mere mention of the phoebe in "Brute Neighbors," 10.[9] In its new position at the end of "Spring" the passage begins: "The phoebe had already come once more and looked in at my door and window." The "once more" marks the full turn of the seasons, and thus Thoreau completed the story of his first year's life in the woods.

9. The manuscript offers no evidence as to the exact time of this change; it was certainly after version V.

APPENDIX

A Comparison of the First Version with the Published Text of Walden

ALTHOUGH one or more leaves are missing at nineteen points in the manuscript of the first version, there is very little question about its contents, length, and organization and the ways in which it differs in these respects from the published text of *Walden*. Where leaves are missing, detailed knowledge of its contents is impossible, but at most points reasonable conjectures are possible as to what material is missing—on the basis of the material that precedes and follows the lost material in the manuscript, or on the evidence of what was available in Thoreau's journal by 1846–47, or on both.

The first version is only about half as long as the published text. According to the gaps in the sequences of page numbers in the first version, there are thirty-eight leaves, or approximately seventy-six pages of writing, missing. There is no certainty that both sides of every leaf were used; on the other hand, it is conceivable that a few more than thirty-eight leaves are missing, since there might have been some leaves lost that were not in the numbered sequences. It does not seem probable, however, that the total of lost pages of writing was significantly more or less than seventy-six. The pages we have plus seventy-six more would run to approximately half the length of the published *Walden*.

This version represents various parts of *Walden* very unevenly. It contains approximately 70 per cent of the first half—"Economy" through "The Bean-Field"; a little less than 30 per cent of "The Village" through "Higher Laws"; less than 50 per cent of "Brute Neighbors" through "Spring"; and none of "Conclusion." The organization of the material through "Higher Laws" is, in general, the same as that of the published text, though it varies considerably within "chapters." (There were no chapter divisions in version I, but it is necessary to use the chapter titles of the final text in order to identify material in the manuscript.) First, there is the comparison of his contemporaries' ideas on living with his own ideas, and then in succession the description of where and how he lived, and the account of what he did in the summer, first in the mornings and then in the afternoons. From "Brute Neighbors" to "Spring" the organization is quite different: the full and carefully arranged story of the seasons of the year in the final text is by no means laid out here.

From the beginning through paragraph 34, "Economy" is fairly complete, though the famous "lives of quiet desperation," 9, is not here. Thoreau states why, what, and for whom he speaks, describes the troubles of his hearers, comments on their mistaken notions concerning the necessaries of life, and tells why he went down to the pond to live. In the next sixty-one paragraphs of the final text Thoreau tells how he managed to live at Walden and comments on the methods of others as compared with his. Version I lacks many of his observations and illustrations on clothing and shelter and also passages on education by doing, organic architecture, modern improvements, barns and monuments, and furniture. His summary of the reasonableness of his way for himself and *some* others and his insistence that this is an individual problem (96–100) and finally his refutation of the charge of selfishness by comparing philanthropy with the striving for self-perfection (101–9)—these passages he later enlarged, and the second he revised very considerably. The final paragraph is only slightly different. Thoreau may have added this later; it is impossible to be certain.

In "Where I Lived and What I Lived For," he wrote nothing of prospecting for and almost buying the Hollowell farm, 1–6, and the description of his hut and its situation is briefer. He described quite fully the qualities he sought in life, but in different order; not until after the account of his morning meditations in "Sounds" did he use the material of paragraphs 18, 19, 21, and 22, on hurry, waste, news, and shams, over against deliberateness and reality.

Although three leaves are missing from "Reading," it is fairly safe to assume that it was practically in its final form here; only the criticism of the town's failure to provide adequate mental and spiritual nourishment, paragraph 12, and small portions of other paragraphs were certainly not in this version; and paragraph 7 follows 11.

In "Sounds" a total of seven leaves are missing, a group of four, one of two, and a single leaf. The general content was apparently the same as that of the final text, but the order was significantly different at several points. Paragraphs 6 and 10 and most of 11 (on the railroad) and 19 and 20 (on the hooting owl) were certainly added later, and perhaps other material on the railroad was also added. As for the order, the first part of the chapter had within it not only material of "Where I Lived and What I Lived For," but also "The Bean-Field," 7, on the sounds of the gala-day guns and the "trainers," and possibly paragraphs 8 and 9. The second part of the chapter, from paragraph 14 to the end, was in very different order, and the material on the cock included a good deal that Thoreau dropped before the final text.

Most of "Solitude" is in version I; Thoreau extended it later by adding his remarks on the visitors and passers-by whom he did not see, 2, and by expanding his appreciation of the pleasures and value of solitude, 5–11. The movement from "Solitude" to "Visitors" and the order of "Visitors" are quite different. The first paragraph of "Visitors," which serves as a transition and introduction in the text, was between paragraphs 4 and 12 in "Solitude"; a comparatively rough portrait of Therien begins the section on "Visitors"; then comes a long and friendly account of other visitors, particularly the railroad workers; and the general description of his hospitality, paragraphs 2–6, ends the chapter instead of beginning it.

Of "The Bean-Field" we have the fine picture of him at work in paragraphs 1 through 6, 10, and the first half of 11. His advice on how to raise beans, 14, and his ideas on the spiritual seeds that one might sow, 15, follow paragraph 11 in something very like their final form; the financial statement in 12 and 13 is with his other accounts in "Economy." The comparison of ancient and modern husbandry, 16, is longer here than in the final text, with numerous mythological allusions that Thoreau dropped later; the last paragraph is complete save for the etymologies which first appear in VI, 1853–54.

In "The Village," 1, Thoreau turned from his morning work to his afternoon walks and recreation; at this point, the discrepancy between version I and the final text begins to be great. At first, the difference is simply in extent. The beginning of "The Village" is the mid-point of the published *Walden*, but here it is two-thirds of the way to the end; this version contains approximately only two-fifths of the material of the second half of *Walden*. Thoreau had by no means worked out the later details of his life in the woods, his comment on it, or, as is evident farther on, the organization of his material. "The Village," "The Ponds," "Baker Farm," and "Higher Laws" developed from a section in version I that is a comparatively brief account, with a few comments, of where he walked and fished in the afternoon. There were fourteen manuscript leaves, the equivalent of little more than eighteen of the sixty-three printed pages in these chapters in the *Walden* of *The Writings of Henry David Thoreau* (1906): about two and a half pages of "The Village," five and a half of "The Ponds," six of "Baker Farm," and four of "Higher Laws." Six of the leaves are missing, but most of their contents can be fairly safely conjectured on the basis of context and material in Thoreau's journal.

Of "The Village," Thoreau wrote only paragraph 1, the account of his frequent afternoon visits to the town, with the material on curtains, "Economy," 89, in it. He continued immediately with other afternoon pastimes: walks into the fields, fishing in Walden, walks to Flint's Pond (parts of "The Ponds," 1, 2, 4, 28), and a very brief description of Walden Pond (parts of 5, 6, 7, 8). He then went on to other afternoon rambles, his visit at John Field's hut at Baker Farm, the message of his "Good Genius," and his fishing in Fair Haven Pond. Three leaves are missing at the end of the description of Walden Pond and the beginning of the story of Thoreau's visit to Baker Farm; they undoubtedly contained the beginning of the visit; the material for the missing paragraphs, 3 and 4, is in the journal, I, 383 ff. A leaf is also missing at the end of "Baker Farm" and the beginning of "Higher Laws"; it probably contained "Baker Farm," 9, and some of "Higher Laws," 1. Then there is a leaf with passages from "Higher Laws," 1, 3, and 5, and then another leaf is missing before we go on to "Higher Laws," 7, and to "Brute Neighbors"; it is clear that the reflections on fishing and hunting and on food and other sensual pleasures were very brief compared with the extended treatment in the published text.

For the material beginning with "Brute Neighbors" and extending through "Spring," there were 40 manuscript leaves, the equivalent of only some 50 of the 106 printed pages in the 1906 *Walden*. Twenty of the manuscript leaves are missing; and in several places it is not at all clear what is missing. But there is no question about the great difference between the first version and the final text, in organization as well as in content, from this point on. The order of the material is quite different in several respects. The transition from "Higher Laws" to "Brute Neighbors" reads: "Generally I was the friend and defender of such of the brute creation as were my neighbors. Walden was formerly a place of eagles—and the woods are still extensive and various. I amused myself with watching what life still remains—my only companions." Thoreau then wrote a long account of the animals, including some of "Brute Neighbors," a very large part of "Winter Animals," and one or two items of "House-Warming"; he did not develop a significant portion of "House-Warming" until version V, 1852–53. Following the material on animals he began the account of the ice-cutters, "The Pond in Winter," 16, but he canceled this and wrote most of "Former Inhabitants." From his closing his door and going to sleep, "Former Inhabitants," 15, he continued with his waking "early in the morning" in "The Pond in Winter," 3. There was none of "Winter Visitors." "Spring" followed "The Pond in Winter" as it does in the text.

Of "Brute Neighbors" there is only the phoebe and robin, 10, the mice, 9, the variety of animals in the woods, 11, possibly on a missing leaf the partridge, 10, and the townsmen's hunting of the loon, 16, with the girdling of the pitch pines by the mice, "Winter Animals," 13, between "Brute Neighbors," 9 and 11. Five leaves are missing between the hunting of the loon, "Brute Neighbors," 16, and the cat owl's voice, "Winter Animals," 2, and another leaf is missing between "Winter Animals," 6 and 14. On the evidence of a preliminary outline for the later parts of the first version, which Thoreau wrote on the inside back cover of journal volume VI in the Morgan Library (see note 1 below), the contents of the missing leaves quite probably included the first half of "House-Warming," 18, and "Winter Animals," 7, 9, and 10. There is no evidence for the order of the material here, but the whole section was far from the order of the final text; Thoreau was thinking more of a full account of his brute neighbors than of a carefully worked-out and articulated description of his seasonal life.

Having completed the description of the animals around him, he first intended to go on to the story of the ice-cutters, and at least began "The Pond in Winter," 16, but he canceled whatever he had written and instead went on with "Former Inhabitants." Three leaves are missing here in the manuscript, but quite probably the missing material consisted of much of "Former Inhabitants," 2 through 9; the material for these paragraphs is in the journal written at Walden but not represented in the leaves we have. The manuscript picks up in paragraph 10, and continues with 12, 13, 14, and 15. Thoreau proceeded from the closing of his door and going to sleep, "Former Inhabitants," 15, to "Early in the morning, while all things were crisp with frost,"

Appendix

"The Pond in Winter," 3. Following the first half of this paragraph four leaves are missing; the manuscript resumes in the midst of a passage on the temperature of the water. Probably the rest of paragraph 3 was in the four missing leaves, and a number of points suggest that a good part of the missing pages contained material on the freezing, melting, and other conditions of Walden and neighboring waters: the presence here of material on temperatures from both "Spring," 1, and "The Ponds," 13; the item numbered 13, "Freezing of pond & qualities of ice," in the list of topics in the manuscript journal VI, and the item "Walden 194" in another list on another journal or notebook cover (see note 2 below). Thoreau's survey of the pond follows; but after a sentence of "The Pond in Winter," 6, and most of 8, there is a gap of three leaves; they probably contained material from paragraphs 9 through 15 and undoubtedly the beginning of 16; the phrase "qualities of ice" in the list of topics would seem to refer to material for paragraphs 14 and 15. The manuscript picks up near the beginning of 16, and the ice-cutting and Thoreau's thoughts on the destinations of the ice follow; the ice-cutting was enlarged later.

"Spring" begins with the melting of the ice, paragraph 3; much of the final text follows. The major additions that Thoreau made later were in paragraphs 1 and 2, in the description of the sand foliage, 6–10, and the quotations in paragraphs 18, 20, and 21. The order of the material in this version is: 3, 4, 11, 5, a few lines on sand foliage, 13, 15, 16, possibly 17 and part of 19 on one missing leaf (part of 19 was added in a later version), 22, part of 23, 24, most of 25, and finally "Thus was my first year's life in the woods completed."

Note 1. Except for part of "Winter Animals," 9, which is in the printed journal, none of the material of "House-Warming," 18, and "Winter Animals," 7, 9, and 10, is in either the manuscript journal or the printed journal or the manuscript of version I. But originally the material for these paragraphs was certainly in the manuscript journal (on leaves Thoreau probably tore out as he prepared to write version I); and almost without doubt it was also in version I on the missing leaves. The evidence is that the material is referred to in a list of topics that Thoreau drew up on the inside back cover of Volume VI of the manuscript journal in the Morgan Library. The list is obviously a preliminary outline for the later part of version I. After each item Thoreau noted the volume and the page or pages of the journal where the material was to be found. He later numbered the items, but neither the original order of the list nor the numbered order corresponds to the order of the material in version I. The list, with the references to the journal omitted (most of them are illegible), is as follows (the place of each item in the published version is given in square brackets with as much definiteness as is possible):

	1. beans	[The Bean-Field]
	3. Field mouse Pewee & Robin	[Brute Neighbors, 9, 10; Win-
	& [illegible word] & Jays	ter Animals, 6]
21.	4. Geese & ducks [illegible words]	[Spring, 16]
	2. Walden place of eagles	[Not in text; in version I]
	7. ground nuts	[House-Warming, 1]
	6. bread	[The Bean-Field, 15; House-Warming, 1?]
	8. nuts	[House-Warming, 1]
	5. Racoon loon	[Brute Neighbors, 11, 16]
	9. Flints goose Fair Haven ponds	[The Ponds]
	10. John Field	[Baker Farm, 3, 4, 5, 9]
	11. savage life &	[Higher Laws, 1]
	13. Freezing of pond & qualities of ice	[The Ponds, 13; House-Warming, 1; Winter Animals, 1; The Pond in Winter, 14, 15; Spring, 1, 3]
	14. Winter sounds	[Winter Animals, 2, 3]
	15. Fox hunter	[Winter Animals, 9, 10]
	16. Foxes	[Winter Animals, 4]
	18. chickadees	[Winter Animals, 7]
	19. ice men Fishermen	[Pond in Winter, 3, 16, 18, 20]
	17. moles	[House-Warming, 18]
	12. old inhabitants	[Former Inhabitants]
	20. survey of Pond	[Pond in Winter, 6, 8]
21.	Spring	[Spring]

Appendix

Note 2. On the inside front cover of another journal or notebook (only the covers are in the Morgan Library) Thoreau wrote a list of thirty-two items in the order of their appearance in the first version of *Walden*. All but three of the items are followed or preceded by a number or numbers; the numbers indicate the pages of the first version (according to Thoreau's numbering) on which the items appear; in one or two cases there is a slight discrepancy. The list is not an outline of all that Thoreau wrote in the first version from "Reading" through "Spring," nor is it a note for revisions in a later version. It may be a list of topics and items that he intended to use in the lectures he gave in 1848–49 on his Walden experience. He could not have made the list until after he had completed the first version in the late spring or summer of 1847, and he must have made it before he wrote version II in 1848–49, since the numbers refer to the pagination of version I. The starred items help to identify material that was on missing pages in version I. (The list is in one column in the manuscript with a line drawn across the page after "beans 111 to 128.")

Through verses on 19 then
Most all of read.
How spent morn & housework 39 to 43
Reality 46–8–9
Priest of Isis hears whistle
Cock-crow 67
On down [?], sounds 70
Bells 71
trainer Music 72
Frogs & owls
Visitors 80
81 society & loneliness
Therien 94
chairs visitors in small room [?] 105
beans 111 to 128

The village 129
Fishing at night 134
*Ground nut 138
John Field 141
Eating fish & flesh 150
red-bellied field mouse 157
loon 161
owls in winter night 171
The squirrel 175
The hair 182
ancient inhabitants 185
*Walden 194
ice-cutters 208
grass in spring 225
change from winter to spring 226
merlin 231
Dead horse & 233

The First Version of Walden

The First Version of Walden

WHAT follows is a transcript from Huntington Manuscript 924 of the version of *Walden* that Thoreau wrote in 1846–47. It reproduces only a very few of the many corrections and interlineations in the manuscript—only those which, on the evidence of handwriting and ink and context, Thoreau certainly made as he was writing this version. The few interlineations that have been included are printed in italics; any material Thoreau canceled when he made one of these interlineations is given in a footnote. The reasons for not including any other changes are: Thoreau made them at various times; in many cases they were by no means the final ones; and they are only a small portion of the innumerable changes between the first version and the final text of 1854. In other words, a transcript that included them would not represent any one definite stage of *Walden.*

Save for the few exceptions noted below, I have transcribed the manuscript literatim, in order to keep the flavor of Thoreau's actual work. I have not marked his slips (they include one in addition in his accounts) with "*sic.*"

Spelling and grammar are as in the manuscript, save that apostrophes have been supplied if missing in possessives and verbal contractions. Capitalization is as in the manuscript, though at many points Thoreau's intention is doubtful. Punctuation is as in the manuscript, save that periods have been supplied at the ends of sentences which lacked any other mark and quotation marks have been supplied where Thoreau inadvertently omitted them at the end of a quotation. Single words or very brief phrases that Thoreau inadvertently omitted at first have been inclosed in square brackets ([ ]); at one time or another he inserted all the words and phrases himself. Slips of the pen such as "brinks" for "bring" or "the the" have been corrected, but the manuscript reading is given in a note. The abbreviation "Ind" for "Indian" has been expanded silently in four places, and "Jan" for "January" in one.

The order of the leaves and pages of the extant manuscript is indicated by numbers followed by "r" (recto) or "v" (verso) and inclosed in brackets. Often there is a second number outside the brackets; this number is one of Thoreau's original page numbers; for example, "[23r] 39." indicates that the material following it is on the recto of the twenty-third leaf of the manuscript of this version, and that the recto was marked as the thirty-ninth page by Thoreau when he numbered the pages of the first version. (His renumbering after versions II and III is not reproduced.) A system of numbering in addition to Thoreau's original one is necessary since some leaves are missing, since he used two series of numbers for the pages of the first version—one series for the material of "Economy" and a second for the rest of the material—and since he added extra leaves after he had numbered the pages of "Economy." The extra leaves are marked by an asterisk, for example, [1r*].

Editorial comment on missing leaves and their probable contents is placed within brackets between sections of the text whenever necessary.

References to chapter and paragraph of the published text are given in the outside margin; there were no chapter headings or divisions in this version.

THE TEXT

[1r*] I should not presume to talk so much about myself and *Economy* my affairs as I shall in this lecture if very particular and personal 2 inquiries had not been made concerning my mode of life,—what some would call impertinent, but they are by no means imperti-

Economy nent to me, but on the contrary very natural and pertinent, con-
  2 sidering the circumstances. Some have wished to know what I got
to eat—If I didn't feel kind o' lonesome—If I wasn't afraid—
What I should do if I were taken sick—and the like. Others have
been inquisitive to know what portion of my income I devoted to
charitable purposes,—some who have large families, how many
poor children I maintained. Some have not come to my house
because I lived *there*—Others have come because I *lived* there—
and others again, because *I*[1] lived there.

    After I lectured here last winter[2] I heard that some had ex-
pected that I would answer some of these questions in my lecture—So I must ask all strangers, and all who have little or no
interest in me in this [1v*] audience to pardon me, if I undertake
to answer them in part now. In most lectures or stories the I, or
first person is omitted; in this it will be inserted, that is the main
difference. We are not apt to remember that it is after all always
the first person that is speaking. Perhaps this lecture is more particularly addressed to the class of poor students; as for the rest of
my audience, they will accept such portions as apply to them. I
trust that none will stretch the seams in putting on the coat, for it
may be of good service to him whom it fits.

  3   I have travelled a good deal in Concord, and everywhere, in
shops and offices and fields, the inhabitants have seemed to me to
be doing penance in a thousand curious ways. What I had heard
of Brahmens standing on one leg on the tops of pillars, looking in
the face of the sun, dwelling at the roots of trees,—even the twelve
labors of Hercules are nothing in comparison, for they were only
twelve and had an end, but I [2r*] could never see that these men
slew or captured any monster, or finished any labor. They have
no "friend Iolas to burn, with a hot iron, the root" of the Hydra's
head, but as soon as one head is crushed two spring up.

  4   I see young men, my townsmen, whose misfortune it is to have
inherited farms, houses, barns, cattle, and farming tools, for these
are easier acquired than got rid of. Better if they had been born in

---

1. All Thoreau's italics.

2. Probably a reference to his lecture on Carlyle, at the Concord Lyceum, February 4, 1846.

the open pasture and suckled by a wolf, that they might have seen *Economy*
with clear eye what field they were called to labor in. Who made *4*
them serfs of the soil? Why should they eat their sixty acres, when
man is condemned to eat only his peck of dirt? Why should they
begin digging their graves as soon as they are born? They have got
to live a man's life pushing all these things before them, and get
on as well as they can. The portionless, who struggle with no such
inherited incumbrances, find it labor enough to subdue and cultivate a few cubic feet of flesh.

But men labor under a mistake. [2v*]³   *5*

[3r] 3. But men labor under a mistake. The better part of the
man is soon plowed into the soil for compost. By an apparent fate,
soon called necessity, they are employed, as it says in an old book,
laying up treasures which moth and rust will corrupt and thieves
break through and steal.

It is a fool's life, as they will find when they get to the end of it.

Most men through mere ignorance and mistake are so occupied *6*
with the factitious cares and coarse labors of life that its finer fruits
cannot be plucked by them. Actually the laboring man has not
leisure for a lofty integrity day by day, he cannot afford to sustain
the noblest relations. His labor would depreciate in the market.
He has no time to be anything but a machine. How can he remember well his ignorance, and this his growth requires—who
has so often to use his knowledge?

Some of you who hear me we all know are poor, find it hard to *7*
live, are sometimes, as it were, gasping for breath. I have no doubt
that some of you [3v] who are here tonight are unable to pay for
all the dinners you have actually eaten, or for the coats and shoes
which are fast wearing or already worn out, and have come here
to spend borrowed time, robbing your creditors of an hour.

3. 2 v was originally blank; in view of both the repetition of "But men labor under
a mistake" and the page number "3" on 3r, I believe that these first two leaves replaced an original single leaf. On 2v Thoreau later wrote this note, probably in 1849:
"To show how little men have considered what is the true end of life—or the nature
of this living which they have to get—I need only remind you how many have within
the last month started for California with the muck rake on their shoulders. According to the precepts of the received catechism—as if our life were a farce and God had
cast down one of his handfuls of true believing [?] on to the mountains of California
for men to scramble for."

The Making of Walden

Economy
7

It is very evident what mean and sneaking lives many of you live, always on the limits, trying to get into business and trying to get out of debt, a very ancient slough, called by the Latins *aes alienum*⁴ another's brass, for some of their coins were made of brass, still living and dying and buried by this other's brass. Always promising to pay—promising to pay—to-morrow—and dying to-day insolvent.—Seeking to curry favor, to get custom by how many modes only not state prison offences—lying, flattering, voting, contracting yourselves into a nutshell of civility, or dilating into an atmosphere of thin and vaporous [4r] 5. generosity, that you may persuade your neighbor to let you make his shoes or his hat or his coat or his carriage or import his groceries for him. Making yourselves sick that you may lay up something against a sick day—something to be tuckt away in an old chest, or in a stocking behind the plastering, or more safely in the brick bank— no matter where, no matter how much or how little.

8

I sometimes wonder how we can be so frivolous almost as to attend to the gross form of Negro slavery, there are so many keen and subtle masters that enslave both north & south. It is bad to have a southern overseer, it is worse to have a northern one, but worst of all when you are yourself the slave-driver.

Ancient books, and some modern ones, talk of a divinity in man. Look at the teamster on the highway, wending to market by day or night,—how much of divinity is there in him? How godlike, how immortal is he? [4v] See how he cowers and sneaks, how vaguely and indefinitely all the day he fears—not being immortal nor divine, but the slave and prisoner of his own opinion of himself—a fame won by his own deeds.

10

When we consider, in the words of the Catechism, what is the chief end of man, and the necessaries & the means of life, it appears as if men had deliberately chosen this mode of living, preferring it; but not so, they really think that there is no choice left.— But it is not necessarily, it was not always so; alert and healthy natures remember that the sun rose clear.

It is never too late to give up our prejudices. No way of doing or thinking, however ancient, can be trusted. What every body

4. Thoreau's italics.

echoes, or in silence passes by as true today, may turn out to be *Economy* sheer falsehood tomorrow, mere smoke of opinion falling back in *10* cinders, which some had trusted for a cloud [5r] 7.⁵ that would sprinkle fertile rain upon their fields—What old people say you can't do, you try and find that you can,—Age seems no better hardly so well qualified for an instructor as youth, for it has not profited so much as it has lost.

Men have left off rum safely and imprisoning for debt, and chattel slavery in some places, and several other things, but they are not inclined to leave off hanging men because they have not got accustomed to that way of thinking.

The whole ground of human life seems to some to have been *12* gone over before us by our predecessors, both the heights & the valleys. Hippocrates has even left directions how we should cut our nails i. e. even with the ends of the fingers, neither longer nor shorter. The very tedium and ennui which presumes to have exhausted the variety & the joys of life is as old as Adam.

But man's capacities have never been measured, nor are we to judge of what he can do by any precedent, so little has been tried.

[5v] We might try our lives by a thousand simple tests greatly *13* to our advantage—by any natural fact—by this, for instance, that the same sun that ripens my beans illumines at once a system of worlds like this. If I had known this it would have prevented some mistakes. This was not the light in which I hoed them.

The stars are the apexes of what singular triangles, what distant and various natures are perhaps beholding the same one at the same moment! The departing and the arriving spirit—the joyful & the sad—the innocent and happy child & the melancholy suicide, the northern farmer & the southern slave. These are trivial instances.

I think we may safely *trust*⁶ a good deal more than we do. We *15* may waive just so much care of ourselves as we devote elsewhere.

5. At this point the manuscript contains a torn leaf of version I paper that has on its recto a revised version of the first half of the material on this page; on its verso it has "Economy," 11, the last clause of "Economy," 82, a sentence not in the text, and the last half of "Economy," 13. I believe Thoreau wrote all this after he had finished I.

6. Thoreau's italics.

The Making of Walden

Economy   Suppose we choose the better part & fail,—whose failure is it?
15   Nature is after all as well adapted to our weaknesses, as to our talents. The incessant anxiety & strain of some persons is a well nigh incurable form of disease. We are made to [6r] 9. exaggerate the importance of what work we do and yet how much is not done by us, or what if we had been taken sick?—How vigilant we are? Determined not to live by faith if we can avoid it—all the day long on the alert, at night we unwillingly say our prayers and commit ourselves to uncertainties. So thoroughly and sincerely are we compelled to live, reverencing our life, and denying the possibility of change. This is the only way, we say; but there are as many ways as there can be drawn radii from one center. All change is a miracle to contemplate, but it is a miracle which is taking place every instant.

16   Let us consider for a moment what all this trouble and anxiety is about—what are the gross necessaries of life. I imagine it would be some advantage to live a primitive and frontier life, though in the midst of an outward civilization, if only to know what are after all the necessaries of life, and what methods society has taken [6v] to supply them. Even to look over the old Day Books of the merchants to see what it was that men most commonly bought at the stores—what are the grossest groceries. All the improvements of the ages do not carry a man backward or forward in relation to the great facts of his existence. As our skeletons are not to be distinguished from those of our ancestors.

17   To many creatures there is only one necessary of life—*food*.[7] To the bison of the prairie it is a few inches of palatable grass—unless he seeks the *shelter*[8] of the forest or the mountain's shadow. None of the brute creation require more than food and shelter.

For man, in this climate, the necessaries of life may be distributed under the several heads of Food Shelter Clothing and Fuel—for he has invented clothes and cooked food, and probably from the accidental discovery of the warmth of fire, at first a luxury, arose the present necessity to sit by it. We observe cats and dogs acquiring the same second nature.

7. Thoreau's italics.

8. Thoreau's italics.

[7r] 11. By Shelter & Clothing we legitimately retain our own *Economy* internal heat, but with Fuel or an external heat greater than our *17* own internal, cookery may properly be said to begin. From this list it appears that the expression "animal heat" is nearly syno[ny]mous with "animal life," for Shelter Clothing and Fuel warm us, so to speak from without, Food from within. The New Hollander who goes naked while the European shivers in his clothes, warms his whole body simply by putting his extremities closer to the fire than the former can bear. According to Liebig, man's body is a box stove, and food the fuel which keeps up the internal combustion in the lungs. In cold weather we eat more in warm less. The animal heat is in fact the result of a slow combustion, and disease & death take place when this is too rapid, or for want of fuel—or from some defect in the draught, the fire goes out.

The grand necessity then for our bodies is to keep warm—to *18* keep the vital heat in us. What pains accordingly do we take with our beds, which are our night clothes, robbing the nests of birds [7v] and their breasts, to prepare this shelter within a shelter, as the mole has its bed of grass and leaves at the end of its burrow.

The summer makes possible a sort of Elysian life to man. Fuel, except to cook his food, is then unnecessary. The sun is his fire, and many of the fruits are sufficiently cooked by its rays, while food generally is more various and more easily obtained, and clothing and shelter are half dispensed with even in our climate.

At the present day and in this country, a few implements, a knife—an axe—a spade—a wheelbarrow—&c and with the studious light stationary, and access to a few books rank next to necessaries, and can all be obtained at a trifling cost.

To the elevation and ennoblement of mankind what are called *19* the luxuries & many of the comforts of life are not only not indispensable, but positive hindrances. With [8r] respect to luxuries and comforts the wisest have ever lived a more simple and meagre life than[9] the poor. The ancient philosophers were a class of men than whom none were poorer in respect to outward riches, none so rich in respect to inward. We know not much about them. It is astonishing that *we*[10] can know as much as we do. None can be

9. MS: "than than."   10. Thoreau's italics.

Economy an impartial or wise observer of human life but from the vantage
19 ground of what *we*[11] should call voluntary poverty. Of a life of
luxury the fruit is luxury, whether in agriculture or commerce, or
literature, or art.

20   When a man is warmed by the several modes I have described,
what more does he want? Not surely more warmth of the same
kind, or more and richer food, larger and more splendid houses,
finer and more abundant clothing, more numerous, incessant,
and hotter fires, and the like, but to adventure on life now, his
vacation having commenced. The soil, it seems, is suited to the
seed, and it may germinate at length. Why has he rooted himself
thus firmly in the earth but that he may rise in the same proportion
into the heavens above, for the nobler plants bear their fruit at
last in the air and light, [8v] far from the ground, and are not like
the[12] humbler esculents, continually cut down at top that[13] they
may make more root.

21   I do not mean to prescribe rules to strong and valiant natures,
which will mind their own affairs in heaven or hell indifferently,
and build more magnificently and spend more lavishly than
Croesus, without ever impoverishing themselves, not knowing
how they live—nor to those, if there are any, who find their
encouragement and inspiration in precisely the present condition of society, and cherish it with the fondness and enthusiasm
of lovers—not to those who are well employed under whatever
circumstances, and they will know whether they are well employed or not—but to the mass of men who are discontented and
idly complaining of the hardness of their lot and of the times,
when they might improve them.—Why! there are some who
complain most energetically of all because, as they say, they are
doing their duty.—And to that seemingly wealthy, but most ter-
ribly impoverished class of all, who have accumulated dross but
know not how to spend it, and thus have forged their own golden
or silver fetters.

22   If I should undertake to tell how I have desired to spend my
life in years past I [9r] 15. should probably only startle you who
are somewhat acquainted with its actual history.

11. Thoreau's italics.   12. MS: "the the."   13. MS: "that that."

I will only hint at some of the enterprises I have cherished.   *Economy*
In any weather at any hour of the day or night, I have been 23
anxious to improve the nick of time & notch it on my stick too—
to stand on the meeting of two eternities, the past & future, which
is precisely the present time—to toe that line. You will pardon
some obscurities—for I believe there are more secrets in my trade
than in most men's, and yet not voluntary ones either, but in-
separable from its very nature. I would gladly tell all I know
about it, & never paint "No Admittance" on my gate.

I long ago lost a hound—and a turtle dove and a bay horse— 24
and am still on their trail. Many's the traveller I have spoken concerning them—describing their tracks and what calls they answered to. I have met one or two who had heard the hound, and
the tramp of the horse, and even seen the dove disappear behind
a cloud, and they seemed as anxious to recover them as if they had
lost them themselves.

[9v] To anticipate not the sunrise & the dawn merely, but if 25
possible nature herself. How many mornings summer & winter
before yet any man was stirring about his business I have been
about mine. No doubt some of my hearers have met me returning
from this enterprise, farmers starting for Boston in the twilight, or
woodchoppers going to their work. To be sure I never assisted the
sun materially in his rising—but be sure it was of the last importance only to be present at it.

So many autumn aye & wintry days spent outside the town, 26
trying to hear what was in the wind, to hear and carry it express.
I well nigh sunk all my capital in it, and lost my own breath into
the bargain, running in the face of it. If it had concerned either of
the parties depend upon it it would have appeared in the Gazette
with the earliest intelligence—

At other times watching from the observatory of the Cliffs or
some tree—to telegraph any new arrival.

For a long time I was reporter to a journal of no very wide cir- 27
culation, and, as is too common, I got only my pains for my labor.
[10r] 17. Literary contracts are little binding.

For many years I was self appointed inspector of snow storms & 28
rain storms, and did my duty faithfully—Surveyor if not of high-

Economy
28 ways then of forest paths, and all across lot routes, keeping them open and ravines bridged & passable at all seasons, where the public-heel had testified to their utility.

29 I have looked after the wild stock of the town, which pastures in common which as everyone knows give you a good deal of trouble in the way of leaping fences—and have had an eye to the unfre- quented nooks and corners of the farm—Though I did not always know whether Jonas or Solomon, worked in a particular field to- day—that was none of my business.

I have watered the red huckleberry—the sand-cherry & the nettle tree, the cornel, the white grape & the yellow violet—which might have withered else in dry seasons.

30 In short, I went on for a long time, I may say it without boast- ing, faithfully minding my business, [10v] till it became more and more evident that my townsmen would not after all admit me into the list of town officers, nor make my place a sinecure, with a moderate allowance.

My accounts indeed, which I can swear to have been faithfully kept, I have never got audited, still less accepted, still less paid
32 and settled. However I haven't set my heart on that.—I found in short that they were not likely to offer me any office in the Court House—any curacy or living anywhere else—but I must shift for myself.

So I turned my face more exclusively than ever to the woods where I was better known;—I determined to go into business at once, without waiting to acquire capital.[14]

33 Strict business habits I have always endeavored to acquire. They are indispensable to every man. If your trade is with the Celestial empire, then some small counting house on the coast, in some Salem harbor, will be fixture enough.

You will export such articles as the country affords, purely native products [11r] 19. much ice, and pine timber, and a little

14. Marked for insertion at this point was a scrap of version I paper which con- tains: "using such slender means as I had already got. [This phrase was probably added later.] My object in going to Walden Pond was not to live cheaply nor to live dearly there, but to transact some private business with the fewest obstacles—a busi- ness to be prevented from accomplishing which for want of a little common sense, a little enterprise and business talent, seemed not so sad as foolish."

granite, always in native bottoms. These will be good ventures. *Economy*
    To oversee all the details yourself in person, to be at once pilot *33*
& captain and owner & underwriter, to buy and sell and keep the
accounts,—to read every letter received and write or read every
letter sent—to superintend the discharge of imports night & day
—to be upon many parts of the coast almost at the same time.—
Often the richest freight will be discharged upon a Jersey shore—
To be your own telegraph unweariedly sweeping the horizon,
speaking all passing vessels bound coast wise,—to keep up a
steady dispatch of commodities—for the supply of such a distant
& exorbitant market—to keep informed of the state of the markets—prospects of war and peace everywhere, and anticipate the
tendencies of trade & civilization—taking advantage of the results, of all exploring expeditions—using new passages and all improvements in navigation. Charts to be studied, the [11v] position
of reefs and new lights and buoys to be ascertained—and ever and
ever the logarithmic tables to be corrected—for by the error of
some calculator the vessel often splits upon a rock that should
have reached a friendly pier—There is the untold fate of La
Perouse—Universal science to be kept pace with—studying the
lives of all great discoverers and navigators—great adventurers
and merchants from Hanno and the Phoenicians down to our
days. In fine account of stock to be taken from time to time, to
know how you stand—It is a labor to task the faculties of a man—
Such problems of profit & loss—of interest, of tare and tret, and
gaugeing of all kinds in it—as demand a universal knowledge.
    I have thought that Walden Pond would be a good place for *34*
business, not solely on account of the railroad and the ice-trade.
It offers advantages which it may not [12r] 21. be good policy to
divulge. It is a good port and a good foundation. No Neva
marshes to be filled—though I suppose you must everywhere
build on piles of your own driving. It is said that a flood tide with
a westerly wind and ice in the Neva would sweep St. Petersburg
from the face of the earth.
    As this business was to be entered on without the usual capital, *35*
it may not be easy to conjecture where those means that will still
be indispensable to every undertaking where to be obtained.

The Making of Walden

As for Clothing, perhaps we are oftener led by the love of novelty and a regard for the opinions of men in procuring it, than by a true utility. It was no doubt the strongest argument against the faith of the Millerites, that most of them continued to build and accumulate property so as to be prepared in case the world should not come to an end—But let him who has work to do reflect that the object of clothing is first [12v] to retain the animal heat—and secondly in this state of society to cover nakedness—*and how much of any important and necessary work might be accomplished without making any addition to his wardrobe!*[15]

The bank bill that is torn in two will pass if you save the pieces, if you have only got the essential piece with the signatures. Lowell & Manchester think you will let their broadcloth currency go when it is torn, but hold on, have an eye to the signature, clout the back of it, or if it is a transmittendum endorse the name of him from whom you received it.—No man ever stood the lower in my estimation for having a patch in his clothes. But there is certainly greater anxiety to have clean and whole clothes, than to have a sound conscience—though even if the rent is not patched perhaps the worst vice betrayed is improvidence.

Kings & Queens who wear a suit but once, though made by some tailor or dressmaker to their majesties, cannot know the [13r] 23. comfort of wearing a suit that fits. They are no better than wooden horses to hang the clean clothes on. Every day our garments become more assimilated to us, and receive the impress of the wearer's character. We know after all but few men, a great many coats and breeches. Dress a scarecrow in your last shift, you standing shiftless by, who would not soonest salute the scarecrow?

Above all, clothes brought in sewing a kind of work you may call endless.

36 A man who has at length found out something important to do will not have to get a new suit to do it in,—for him the old will do, that has lain dusty in the garret for an indefinite period. Old shoes will serve a hero longer than they have served his valet. Bare feet

---

15. Canceled: "and there will be found old clothes enough in everybody's garret to last till the millenium if he only has faith in *that*." Thoreau had underlined "that."

are the oldest of shoes, and he can make them do. Only they who
go to soirees and legislative halls must have new coats, coats to
turn as often as the man turns in them.

Who ever saw his old shoes, his old coat actually worn out, re-
solved into its primitive elements, so that it was [13v] not a deed of
charity to bestow them on some poorer boy, by him to be be-
stowed on some poorer still, or shall we say richer, who can do
with less?

I should say beware of all enterprises that require new clothes,
and not rather a new wearer of clothes. If there is not a new man
how can there be a new suit, and not rather a new miss-fit & non-
suit—

If you have any enterprise before you, I say, try it in your old
clothes.

All men want not something to do *with*,[16] but something to *do*[17]
—or rather something to *be*.[18]

Once more I should advise never to procure a new suit of
clothes however ragged or dirty the old, until you have so con-
ducted, so enterprised or sailed in some way, that you feel like a
new man in the old, and that to retain them would be keeping
new wine in old bottles—thus the snake casts its slough—and the
caterpillar its wormy coat by an internal industry and expansion.
—Otherwise you would be found sailing under false colors.

[14r*][19] It is desirable that a man be clad so simply that he can *37*
lay his hands on himself in the dark, and live in all respects so
compactly and prepared that if an enemy should take the city, he
can, like the old philosopher, walk out the gate empty handed,
without anxiety.

While one thick garment is as good as three thin ones, and
cheap clothing can be obtained at prices really to suit customers,
while cowhide boots can be bought for 8 shillings a pair, a summer hat for 25 cents, and a winter cap for 5 shillings, or a better

16. Thoreau's italics.

17. Thoreau's italics.   18. Thoreau's italics.

19. According to the page numbers—23 on 13r and 25 on 15r—this is an extra
leaf. Thoreau apparently put it in after canceling the first two paragraphs on 15r.
He recopied them here on 14r, then continued on 14v and on the bottom of 15r, the
top of which contained the two canceled paragraphs.

Economy may be homemade at a nominal cost, where is he so poor that
37   clad in such a suit *of his own earning*[20] there will not be found wise
men to do him reverence.

39   Clothing has not in this country or any where in modern times
risen to the dignity of an art. At present men make shift to wear
what they can get. Like shipwrecked sailors they put on what they
can find on the beach, and at a little distance laugh at each other's
masquerade. Every generation laughs at the old [14v*] fashions,
but follows religiously the new. We are amused at the pictures of
Henry VIII and Queen Elizabeth, as much as if they were the
41   King & Queen of the cannibal islands.—I have little hesitation in
saying that our factory system is not the best mode by which men
may be clothed, and the condition of the operatives is becoming
every day more and more like that of the English.—And it cannot
be wondered at, since, as far as I have *heard or* observed the prin-
cipal object is not that mankind may be well and worthily clad,
but unquestionably that the corporation may be enriched. In the
long run mankind hit only what they aim at.

40   The savage and childish taste of men and women for new prints
& patterns keeps how many men shaking and squinting through
kaleidoscopes that they may discover the particular figure which
the skin deep taste of this generation requires today.—As if, after
all, the Ethiopian could change his skin, or the leopard his spots.

When our garments are worn out we hang them up in the fields
[15r] 25. to scare crows with, as if the reason why men scare crows
was in their clothes. I have often experienced the difficulty of getting within gunshot of a crow.—It isn't because they smell powder.

44   [15v] *As for a Shelter,* If any one designs to construct a dwelling
house, it behoves him to exercise a little Yankee shrewdness &
care lest after all he find himself in a workhouse—a labyrinth—a
museum—an almshouse—a prison—or a splendid Mausoleum
instead.

42   Man does not live long in this world without finding out the
comfort there is in a house—the domestic comforts—which phrase
originally signified the satisfactions of the house more than of the

20. Thoreau's italics.

family. Though these must be extremely partial & transitory in those climates where the house is associated with winter or the rainy season chiefly, and for $\frac{2}{3}$ of the year, except for a parasol, is dispensed with. In our climate, in the summer season, the house was formerly only a covering at night. In the Indian gazettes the wigwam was the symbol of a day's march, and a row of them cut or painted on the bark of a tree signified that so many times they had camped.

Man was not made so large- [16r] 27. limbed and tough, but that he must seek to narrow his world, and wall in a space such as fits him. He found himself all bare and out of doors (and divested of prejudice, out of doors he is still, though that is a country we do not inhabit)—Though this was pleasant enough in serene & warm weather, by day-light the rainy season and the winter would perhaps have nipped his race in the bud, if he had not made haste to clothe himself with the shelter of a house. Adam and Eve according to the fable wore the bower before other clothes. Man sought a home, a place of warmth, first of physical warmth, then the warmth of the affections.

A tolerable house for a rude and hardy race that lived much out 44 of doors was once made here almost entirely of such materials as nature furnished ready to their hands. According to the testimony of the first settlers of New England, an Indian wigwam was as comfortable in winter as an English house with all its wainscot-ting. It was sometimes 40 feet long, and carpeted and lined within & covered without with [16v] well-wrought embroidered mats & furnished with various utensils. They had advanced so far as to regulate the effect of the wind by a mat suspended over the hole *in the roof* which was moved by a string. Such a lodge was in the first instance constructed in a day or two, and taken down & put up in a few hours, and every family owned one.

In the savage state every man owns a shelter as good as the best, 45 and sufficient for his ruder and simpler wants—but though the birds of the air have their nests, and the foxes their holes, in mod-ern civilized society not more than one man in a hundred owns a shelter. The 99 pay an annual tax for this outside garment of all— indispensable summer & winter—which would buy a village of

Economy Indian wigwams, but now contributes to keep them poor as long
45   as they live.

But, answers one, by simply paying this tax, the poorest man
secures an abode which is a palace compared [17r] 29. with the
Indian's. An annual rent of from 20 to a hundred dollars entitles
him to the benefit of all the improvements of centuries—Rumford
fire-place—backplastering—Venetian blinds—copper-pump—
spring-lock &c.

52   But while civilization has been improving our houses she has
not equally improved the men who were to inhabit them. She has
created palaces, but it was not so easy to create noblemen & kings.

53 Just in proportion as some have been placed in outward circumstances above the Indian—others have been degraded below it—
The millions who built the pyramids for the tombs of the Pha-
raohs fed on garlic, and perhaps were left unburied themselves.—
The mason who finishes the cornice of the palace returns at night
52 perchance to a hut not so good as a wigwam. And if the civilized
man's pursuits are no worthier than the Indian's, if he is employed the greater part of his life in obtaining gross necessaries
and comforts merely, why should he have a better dwelling [17v]
than the former?

45   If civilization claims to have made a real advance in the welfare
of man, she must show that she has produced better dwellings,
without making them more costly—and the cost of a thing it will
be remembered is the amount of life it requires to be exchanged
for it—immediately or in the long run. An average house costs
perhaps 1000 dollars, and to lay up this sum will require from 10
to 15 years of the laborer's life, even if he is not encumbered with
a family. So that he must have spent more than half his life commonly before his wigwam will be earned. If we suppose him to
pay a rent instead, this is but a doubtful choice of evils.

Would the savage have been wise to exchange his wigwam for
a palace on these terms?

46   It will be perceived that I set down the whole advantage of
holding this superflous value as a fund in store against the future
—as far as the individual is concerned, to the score of funeral
expenses merely.

The First Version of Walden

[18r] 31. When I consider my neighbors the farmers of Con- *Economy* cord who are at least as well off as the other classes, I find that for *49* the most part they have been toiling for 10—20—or 30 years to pay for their farms, and we may set down one half of that toil to the cost of their houses—and commonly they have not paid for them yet. They are endeavoring to solve the problem of a liveli- *50* hood by a formula more complicated than the problem itself. To get his shoe strings the farmer speculates in herds of cattle. This is the reason he is poor—With exquisite skill he has set his traps with hair springs to catch comfort & independence—and then as he turned away got his own leg into them—This is the reason he is poor—And for a similar reason we are all poor in respect to a thousand savage comforts, though surrounded by luxuries.

Most men do not know what a house is (which is not to be won- *54* dered at for I am not sure that there is one in the country) and they are actually though needlessly poor all their lives [18v] be- cause they think they must have such a one as their neighbors. As if one were to wear any sort of coat the tailor might cut out for him, or gradually leaving off palm-leaf hat or cap of wood chuck's skin, complain of hard times because he could not afford to buy him a crown.

Shall the respectable citizen thus gravely teach by precept and example the necessity of the young man's providing himself with a certain number of superfluous glow shoes & umbrellas, and empty guest chambers for empty guests, before he dies?

There is no reason why our furniture should not be as simple as the Arab's or the Indian's. At present our houses are cluttered and defiled with it, and a good housewife would sweep out the greater part into the dust hole, or leave her morning's work undone.

At first the thoughtful [&] wandering man plucked in haste the *56* fruits which the boughs extended to him, and found in the sticks and stones around him [19r] 33. his implements ready—to crack the nut and build his shelter with, and he was still a sojourner in nature. When he was refreshed with food and sleep he contem- plated his journey again. He dwelt in a tent in this world—and was either threading the vallies, or crossing the plains, or climbing the mountain tops.

Economy   But lo! men have become the tools of their tools—the man who
56   independently plucked the fruits when he was hungry, is become
a farmer. Now the best works of art even, serve comparatively but
to dissipate the mind, for they themselves represent transitionary
and paroxismal not free & absolute thoughts. There is actually no
place in this village for a work of art, a statue, for instance, if any
had come down to us, to stand, for our lives, our houses & streets,
furnish no proper pedestal for it. There is not a nail to hang a picture on, nor a shelf to receive the bust of a hero. When we consider
how our houses are built and paid for, and their internal economy
[19v] managed and sustained, who does not wonder that the floor
does not give way under the visitor while he is admiring the gew-
gaws upon the mantel and let him through into the cellar—to
some solid and honest, though earthy, foundation! Before we can
adorn our houses with beautiful objects—the walls must be stript
—and our lives must be stript, and beautiful housekeeping and
beautiful living be laid for a foundation. Now what we call taste
for the beautiful is most cultivated out of doors, where there is no
house, and no housekeeper.

Compare   [20r*]²¹ I have often been struck by that fable of Momus.
51   Momus was the god of pleasantry among the ancients. He
was Jupiter's jester or fool, and many a time he set the gods in
a roar. "He was continually employed in satirizing the gods, and
whatever they did was freely turned to ridicule." Neptune—
Minerva and Vulcan had a trial of skill. The first made a Bull;—
the second a House; the third a Man. "Momus found fault with
them all. He disliked the Bull because his horns were not placed
before his eyes that he might give a surer blow." "He censured the
House which Minerva had made because she had not made it
moveable, by which means a bad neighborhood might be
avoided." "With regard to Vulcan's Man, he said he ought to
have made a window in his breast." "Venus herself was exposed

21. Originally 19v was followed by 21r (page 35 in Thoreau's numbering), which
was only half filled at first. Sometime later, Thoreau filled the bottom half of 21r
with a rough draft of the story of Momus. Then on the new leaf, 20r and 20v, he rewrote this story and copied, with very slight changes, the material of "Economy,"
59, which was in the last eight lines of 19v and the first eleven lines of 21r. He canceled the last eight lines of 19v and all of 21r.

to his satire; and when the sneering god found no fault in the body *Economy*
of the naked goddess, he observed, as she retired, that the noise of *Compare*
her feet was too loud, and greatly improper in the goddess of *51*
beauty. These reflections were the cause that Momus was driven
from heaven." What, think [20v*] you would Momus say if he
were living in our day? And I am not sure but what he is.

Though we are not so degenerate but that we might possibly *59*
live in a cave or a wigwam, or wear skins today, it is certainly
better to accept the advantages, though so dearly bought, which
the invention and industry of mankind offer. In such a neighborhood as this, boards and shingles, lime and bricks, are cheaper
and more easily come at, than suitable caves, or whole logs, or
bark in sufficient quantities, or even well-tempered clay and flat
stones. I speak understandingly on this subject, for I have gone
into it both theoretically and practically.

With a little more wit we might use these materials so as to become richer than the richest now are, and make our civilization a
blessing.

But to make haste to my own experiment. [21r] 35. [See note
to 20r.]

[21v] Near the end of March 1845 [I borrowed an axe] and *60*
went down to the woods nearest to where I intended to build my
house, and began to cut down some tall arrowy pines still in their
youth for timber. The ice in the pond was not yet dissolved,
though there were some open spaces, but it was all dark-colored
and saturated with water. There were some slight flurries of snow
during the days that I worked there, though when I came out
upon the rail-road on my way home its yellow sand-heap
stretched away gleaming in the hazy atmosphere, and the rails
shone in the spring sun, & I heard the woodpecker & vireo &
other birds already come to commence another year with us.

They were pleasant spring days in which the winter of man's
discontent was thawing as well as the earth, and the life that had
lain torpid began to stretch itself. I remember that one day when
my axe had come off, and I had cut a green hickory for a wedge,
driving it with a stone and the handle, and had placed it [22r] 37.
to soak in a pond hole in order to swell it, I saw a striped snake

Economy
60
run into the water—and he lay on the bottom apparently without inconvenience as long as I stayed there, which was more than 15 minutes, and I know not how much longer he remained there. I had previously seen them on frosty mornings in my path—with a portion of their bodies still numb & inflexible, waiting for the sun to thaw them.

On the first of April it rained and melted the ice in the pond, and in the early part of the day which was very foggy I heard a stray goose groping about over the pond & cackling as if lost— like the spirit of the fog.

61   So I went on for some days cutting and hewing timber, and also studs and rafters, all with my borrowed axe, not having many communicable or scholar-like thoughts—singing to myself—

> Men say they know many things
> But lo! they have taken wings,
> The arts & sciences,
> And a thousand appliances—
> The wind that blows
> Is all that anybody knows.

[22v] My days were not very long ones but I usually carried my dinner of bread & butter and read the newspaper in which it was wrapped at noon, sitting amid the green pine boughs, and to my bread was imparted some of their fragrance for my hands were covered with a thick coat of pitch. Before I had done I was more the friend than the foe of the pine tree, having become better acquainted with it, though I had cut down some of them. Sometimes a rambler of the wood was attracted by the sound of my axe, and we chatted pleasantly over the chips I had made.

62   By the middle of April for I made no haste in my work—but rather made the most of it—my house was framed and ready for the raising.

I had already bought the shanty of James Collins Irishman, for boards.—James Collins' shanty was considered an extra fine one. When I called to visit he was not at home, I walked about the outside, at first unobserved from [23r] 39. within, the window was so deep & high. The dirt was raised 5 feet all around as if it were

124

a compost heap. The roof was the soundest part, though a good *Economy* deal warped and made brittle by the sun. Door sill there was *62* none, but a perennial passage for hens under the door-board. Mrs. C came to the door & asked me to view it from the inside. The hens were driven in by my approach. It was dark, of small compass—peaked cottage roof, dirt floor mostly—dank—& aguish, here a board and there a board which would not bear removal. She lighted a lamp to show me the ceiling and the sides, and also that the board floor extended under the bed—warning me not to step into the cellar, a sort of dust hole 2 feet deep. In her own words they were "good boards overhead—good boards all around, good window" of two squares *originally*—only the cat passed out that way lately. There was a stove, a bed, & a place to sit— an infant in the house where it was born—a silk parasol—gilt-framed looking glass, and patent new coffee mill nailed to an [23v] oak sapling—all told. The bargain was soon concluded, for James had returned. I to pay $4.25 tonight, he to vacate at 5 tomorrow morning—selling to nobody else meanwhile—I to take possession at six. It were well he said to be there early and anticipate certain indistinct but wholly unjust claims on the score of ground rent and fuel,—this he assured me was the only incumbrance. At six I passed him and his family on the road. One large bundle held their all—bed—coffee mill—looking glass—hens— all but the cat, she took to the woods & became a wild cat, and, as I learned afterward, trod in a trap set for woodchucks and so became a dead cat at last.

I threw down the dwelling the same morning, drawing the nails *63* and removed it to the pond side, by small cart loads, spreading the boards on the grass there, to bleach and warp back again in the sun. One early thrush gave me a note or two as I drove along the woodland path.

I was informed treacherously,

[One leaf missing; it probably contained the rest of 63 and some of 64 and 65.]

[24r] 43. answered the same purpose as the Iliad. *65*

When I came to build my chimney—my bricks were old ones

and had to be cleaned with a trowel—so that I learned more than is usual of the manufacture of bricks & trowels—I filled the spaces between the bricks about the fire place with stones from the pond shore, and also made my mortar with the white sand from the

10 same place. Some whiter and cleaner sand for plastering I brought over from the opposite shore in a boat several cartloads at once with my spade and barrow, and I was very glad to avail myself of this sort of conveyance—a highway that never needs to be mended—and over which you pass with the heaviest loads without a jar or a scar.

I have a house 10 feet by 15—& 8 feet high—with a garrett & a closet, a large window on each side—two trap doors, one door at the end, and a fire place opposite.

The exact cost of my house, when completed, paying the usual price for the materials, but not counting the work, all of which was done [24v] by myself—was as follows

Boards	8.03½
Refuse shingles for roof & sides	4.00
Laths	1.25
2 2ⁿᵈ hand windows with glass	2.43
1000 old brick	4.00
2 casks of lime	2.40
Hair	.31
Mantle-tree iron	.15
Nails	3.90
Hinges & Screws	.14
Latch	.10
Chalk	1
Transportation	1.40
	———
in all	$28.12½

[There followed here on the lower half of the page the beginning of paragraph 76, but Thoreau canceled it when he inserted the following two leaves with material of paragraphs 71, and 72, 73, and 74; he then copied the beginning of 76 on the verso of the second extra leaf; he had added one sentence to 76: "One farmer said it was good for nothing but to raise chipping squirrels on."]

[25r*] I intend to build me a house which will surpass any on *Economy* the maine street in grandeur and luxury as soon as it pleases me as *71* much and will cost me no more than my present one.

In Cambridge College the mere rent of a student's room, which *72* is no better than my own, is 30 dollars each year, though the corporation had the advantage of building 32 side by side and under one roof, and the occupant has the inconvenience of many and noisy neighbors, and a residence perhaps in the 4th story. If the college and the students had more wit in these respects the expense of getting an education would not only for the most part vanish, but less education would be needed, because more would already have been acquired. Just those conveniences which the student requires at Cambridge cost him or somebody else 10 times as great a sacrifice of life as they would with proper management on both sides.

The mode of founding a college is [25v*] to get up a subscription of dollars and cents and then employ Irishmen *or other operatives* actually to lay the foundations—to call in a contractor to make this a subject of speculation—while the students that are to be are *fitting themselves for*[22] it—and for these oversights succeeding generations have to pay, I think that it would undoubtedly be better for the students or those who desire to be benefitted by it, to lay the foundation themselves.

And so with a hundred modern improvements—there is an il- *73* lusion about them. There is no positive advance. The devil goes on exacting compound interest to the last for his early interest and numerous investments in them. Men are in great haste to construct a magnetic telegraph from Maine to Louisiana—but Maine and Louisiana have nothing to communicate. I don't remember anything that Louisiana ever said. She is in such a predicament as the gentleman who was earnest to be introduced to a distinguished deaf woman, but when he was presented and *one end of* the ear trumpet put into his hand—had nothing to say.

[26r*] Men are mad to tunnel under the Atlantic, and bring the Old World some weeks nearer to the new—and perchance the first news that will leak through into the broad flapping American

22. Thoreau's italics.

Economy ear will be that the princess Adelaide has the whooping cough.

74 One says to me I wonder you don't lay up money—you love to travel—you might take the cars and go to Fitchburg today—and see the country. But I am wiser than that. I have learned that the swiftest traveller is he that goes afoot.—I say to my friend suppose we try, who will get there first—The fare is a dollar—that's a day's wages—I start now on foot and get there before night, you will in the meanwhile have earned your fare and get there sometime tomorrow. And so if the railroad reached round the world I think I should keep ahead of you. And as for seeing the country and getting experience, why I think I should have to cut your acquaintance altogether.

76 [26v*] Before I finished my house I planted about two acres and a half of light & sandy soil near it chiefly with beans, though I had a small patch of potatoes and corn, and a few turnips beside. The whole lot contains eleven acres, mostly growing up to pines and hickories, and was sold the preceeding season for 8 dollars and 8 cents an acre. The farmer said it was good for nothing but to raise chipping squirrels on. Upon this land I put no manure nor any quickener whatever, not [27r] 45. being the owner nor expecting to cultivate so much again, and I did not quite hoe it all once. I got out several cords of stumps in ploughing which supplied me with fuel for a long time, and left small rings of virgin mould, easily distinguished through the summer by the greater luxuriance of the beans there. I had to hire a team and a man for the ploughing though I held the plough for the most part myself. My farm outgoes were

Bean-Field		
12	Ploughing—harrowing—furrowing	$ 7.50
	Beans for Seed	3.12½
	Potatoes "	1.33
	Peas	.40
	Turnip seed	6
	hoe	54
	White line for crow fence	2
	Horse cultivator and boy 3 hours	1.00
	Horse and cart to get crop	.75
	In all	$14.72½

The First Version of Walden

I got 12 bushels of beans & 18 bushels of potatoes, beside some *Economy* peas and green corn—The yellow corn and turnips were too late *76* to come to any thing. My whole income from the farm was as follows

From 9 bushels & *12 qts* of beans sold	$16.94	*Bean-Field*
[27v] 5 bushels of potatoes	2.50	*13*
9 " small " and few in the hills	2.25	
grass	1.00	
stalks	.75	
	————	
In all	23.44	
	14.72½	
	————	
net profit, not counting my labor	8.71½	

Beside produce consumed and on hand at the time this estimate *Economy* was made to the amount of 4.50 which added to the last—makes *76* the whole profit 13.21½.

By Surveying—Carpentry & day labor in the village in the *79* meanwhile I had earned
. . . .   13.34

The expense of food, excepting potatoes and a few peas which I had raised,—for 8 months, from July 4th to March 1st—the time when this was written, though I have now lived there nearly 2 years—not counting the value of what was on hand at the last date, was

Rice	1.73½
Molasses	1.73
Rye meal	1.04¾
Indian "	.99¾
Flour	.88
Sugar	.80
Lard	.65
[28r] 47. Apples	.25
Pork	.22
Dried apple	.22

129

Sweet potatoes	.10
1 Pumpkin	6
Salt	3
1 watermelon	2
	8.74 all told

Economy
80 Clothing & some incidental expenses within the same dates amounted to 8.40¾

Oil & some household utensils 2.00

So that the whole pecuniary outgoes excepting for washing & mending, which, for the most part, as we say, were done out of the house, and their bills have not *yet* been received—was

House	28.12½
Farm	14.72½
Food	8.74
Clothing &c	8.40¾
Oil &c	2.00
in all	60.99¾

And to meet this I have for farm produce sold 23.44

on hand 4.50

Earned by day labor 13.34

41.28

[28v] which subtracted from the sum of the outgoes 60.99¾ leaves

41.28

a balance of 19.71¾ on the one side, and on the other, beside the leisure & independence & health thus secured, a comfortable house for me as long as I choose to occupy it.—the 19.71¾ cents being the exact capital with which[23] I started and measure of expenses to be incurred.

23. MS: "which which."

It appears from the above estimate that my food alone cost me
about 27 cents a week. It consists at present of Rye & Indian meal
without yeast—potatoes—rice—a very little salt pork, molasses &
salt, and my drink water.

Bread I at first made of pure Indian meal & salt, genuine hoe
cakes which I baked before my fire out of doors upon a shingle or
the end of a stick of timber sawed off in building my house, but it
was apt to get smoked and to have a piney flavor. I tried flour
also but have at last found a mixture of Rye & Indian [29r] 49.
meal most convenient & agreeable. In cold weather it was no
small amusement to bake several small loaves of this in succession,
tending and turning them as carefully as an Egyptian his hatching
eggs. They had to my senses a fragrance like manna—a real
cereal fruit which I ripened—which I kept in as long as possible
by wrapping them in cloths.

I made a study of the various processes of this indispensable &
ancient art of bread-making—consulting such authorities as offered, going back to the primitive days and first invention of the
unleavened kind—when from the wildness of nuts and meats men
first reached the innocence and refinement of this diet,—and
coming gradually down through that accidental souring of the
dough which taught the leavening process, and the various fer-
mentations thereafter till you come to "good, sweet, wholesome,
bread" the staff of life.

Leaven which some deem the soul of bread, the *spiritus*[24] which
fills its [29v] cellular tissue, which is religiously preserved like the
vestal fire—some precious bottle-full, I presume, first brought
over on the May Flower did the business for America,—and its
influence is still rising, swelling, spreading in cerealian billows over
the land—this seed I regularly and faithfully procured from the
village till at length one morning I forgot the rules, and scalded
my yeast.—By which accident I discovered that even this was not
indispensable—for my discoveries were not by the synthetic but
analytic process—and I have gladly omitted it since, though most
housewives earnestly assured me that safe and wholesome bread
without yeast might not be—and elderly people prophesied a

24. Thoreau's italics.

Economy
84
speedy period to the vital functions. Yet I find it not to be an essential ingredient, and after going without it for a year am still in the land of the living.—And I am glad to escape the trivialness of carrying a bottle-full in my pocket, which would sometimes pop and discharge its contents to my discomfiture. It is simpler & more respectable to omit it. [30r] 51. Man is an animal who more than any other can adapt himself to all climates and circumstances.

85 Every New Englander might easily raise all his bread stuffs in this land of Rye & Indian corn, and not depend upon distant and fluctuating markets for them. Yet so far are we from simplicity and independence that in this village fresh and sweet meal is rarely sold in the shops—and hominy & corn in a still coarser form are hardly used by any. The farmer gives to his cattle and hogs the grain of his own producing, and buys flour which is at least no more wholesome at a greater cost at the store.

96 At present I maintain myself solely by the labor of my hands, and I find that by working about six weeks in a year I can meet all the expenses of living.

I have thoroughly tried school keeping and have found that my expenses were increased in a greater proportion than my salary, and I lost my time into the bargain. As I did not teach for the good of my fellow men, [30v] but simply for a livelihood, this was a failure—I have tried trade, but I found that it would take 10 years to get under way in that, and that then you would probably be on the way to the devil.

97 As I preferred somethings to others, and especially valued my freedom, and could fare hard and yet succeed well—I did not wish to spend my time in earning rich carpets or fine furniture—or delicate cookery, or a house in the Grecian or the Gothic style just yet.—If there are any to whom it is no interruption to acquire these things—and who know how to use them when acquired, I relinquish to them the pursuit—Some are industrious and love labor for its own sake—to such I have at present nothing to say. Those who would not know what to do with more leisure than they now enjoy—I would advise to work twice as hard as they do.

For myself I find that at present the occupation of a day laborer is the most independent of any, especially when we consider that *Economy* it requires only 30 or 40 days in a year to support one. The la- *97* borer's day ends with the going down of the sun, and he is free [31r*] to devote himself to his chosen pursuit, independent of his labor. But his employer who speculates from month to month has no respit from one year's end to another's.

One young man of my acquaintance who has inherited some *99* acres remarked to me that he thought he should live as I do if he had the means. I would not have any one adopt my mode of living on any account—for, beside that before he has fairly learned it, I may have found out another for myself—I desire that there may be as many different persons in the world as possible—and they say very truly that it takes all kinds to make a world—but I would have each one be very careful to find out and pursue his *own*[25] way—and not his father's or his mother's or his neighbor's instead—The youth may build or plant or sail—only let him not be hindered from doing that which he tells me he would like to do.

If he is reproved for being what he is he will find his only resource in being still more entirely what he is. Carry but yourself [31v*] erect and your garments will trail as they should. Disturb not the sailor with too many details, but let him be sure that he keep his guiding star in his eye. It is by a mathematical point only that we are wise, but that is sufficient guidance for all our life.

I have hitherto indulged very little in philanthropic enterprises *101* —I have made some sacrifices to a sense of duty, and among others have sacrificed this pleasure also—I may say without boasting that I have never been inside of a theatre but once, and never that I remember—subscribed a cent to any charitable object.

Professional men—Merchants—farmers—mechanics—laboring men & women—speculators and jobbers of all kinds have at various times tempted me just to take one turn at doing good to mankind—but I have been wonderfully sustained and my virtue is still unsullied in this respect.—Some have used all their arts to persuade me to undertake the support of some poor family in the town—

If I had nothing to do, for they say [32r*] the devil finds em-

25. Thoreau's italics.

Economy ployment for the idle, I certainly should try my hand at some such
101 pastime as that. When I have thought to indulge myself in this
respect, and lay heaven under an obligation by maintaining certain poor persons, in all respects as comfortably as I maintain myself, and have even advanced so far as to make them the offer—
they have one and all unhesitatingly preferred to remain poor.—
While[26] my townsmen are devoted in so many ways to the good of
their fellow men I trust that one at least may be spared to other
and less humane pursuits.—As for Doing Good—that is one of the
professions that are full. Moreover I did once try it fairly—and
strange as it may seem, am satisfied that it does not agree with my
constitution—I have a natural repugnance to it.—Probably I
should not consciously and deliberately forsake my particular
calling to do the good which society demands of me to save the
universe from annihilation—and indeed a like steadfastness
[32v *] elsewhere is all that now preserves it.

102   Men say practically begin where you are and such as you are,
not aiming mainly to become better, and with kindness aforethought go about doing good. If I were to preach at all in this
strain, I should say rather set about being good.—As if the sun
should stop when he had kindled his fires up to the splendor of a
moon or a star of the 6th magnitude, and go about like a Robin
Goodfellow peeping in at every cottage window inspiring lunatics,
and tainting meats and making darkness visible, instead of steadily increasing his genial heat and beneficence till he is of such
brightness that no mortal can look him in the face, and then, and
in the meanwhile too, going about the world in his own orbit
doing it good, or rather, as a truer philosophy has discovered, the
world going about him getting good.

When Phaeton, wishing to prove his heavenly birth by his
beneficence, had the sun's chariot but one day [33r *] and drove
out of the beaten track he burned several blocks of houses in the
lower streets of heaven, and scorched the surface of the earth, and
dried up every spring, and made the great desert of Sahara—till
Jupiter at length hurled him headlong to the earth with a thunder
bolt—and the sun through grief at his death did not shine for a year.

26. Originally "Why."

The First Version of Walden

Why, if I knew for a certainty that a man was coming to my *Economy* house with the conscious design of doing me good—I should run *103* for my life—as from that dry and parching wind of the African deserts called the Simoon, which fills the mouth and nose and ears and eyes with dust till you are suffocated.

I would not preach to men so strenuously and exclusively to practise kindness and humanity toward one another—to feed the hungry & clothe the naked, and the like, for the greater would include the less. A man is not a good man to me because he will feed me if I should be starving, or warm me if I should [33v*] be freezing, or pull me out of a ditch if I should ever fall into one— I can find you a Newfoundland dog that will do as much.

[34r*] Every class and order in the universe is the bearer of cer- *Compare* tain gifts to man. There is a whole class of musk-bearing animals *107* —and each flower has its peculiar odor—and all these together go to make the general wholesome and invigorating atmosphere. So each man should take care to emit his fragrance, and perform some such office as hemlock boughs, and dried and healing herbs —I want the flower and fruit of a man—and that some fragrance *as* of fresh spring life be wafted over from him to me—This is consolation and that charity that hides a multitude of sins.

He must serve another and a better use than any he can consciously render. We demand to discover at least some signs of life, some vegetation and putting forth of natural life in him. Some greenness, some flowering—some ripeness.

He must be a sort of appreciable wealth to us, or at least make us sensible of our own riches—In his degree an Apollo—a Mercury—a Ceres—a Minerva—or the bearer of divine gifts to me. He must [34v*] bring me the morning light untarnished, & the evening red undimmed—The hilarity of Spring in his mirth—the summer's serenity in his joy—the autumnal ripeness in his wisdom—and the repose and abundance of winter in his silence.

A man should impart his courage and not his despair—his health and ease and not his disease, and take care that this does not spread by contagion. It has been well said that our purest and loftiest joys have no memory of, or faith in, one another, and hence we need that he of our fellows who last travelled to the

Economy
Compare
107

sources of the sun—drank at the well of life—or tasted the fountain of God—should[27] communicate to us some of their inspiration.

109   If we would indeed reform mankind by truly Indian—Botanic
—magnetic—or natural means—let us strive first to be as simple
and well as Nature ourselves. It is rare that we are able to impart
wealth to our fellows, and do not [35r*] surround them with our
own castoff griefs as an atmosphere, and name it sympathy.

Compare
108

If we will think of it—there is no reformer on the globe—no
such philanthropic, benevolent, & charitable man, now engaged
in any good work any where, sorely afflicted by the sight of misery
around[28] him, and animated by the desire to relieve it, who would
not instantly and unconsciously sign off from these pure labors,
and betake himself to purer, if he had but righted some obscure
and perhaps unrecognised private grievance. Let but the spring
come to him, let the morning rise over his couch, and he will forsake his generous companions, without apology or explanation—
or the need of any.

Compare
107

I would say to the anxious philanthropist—Take up a little life
into your pores—strike root and grow—endeavor to encourage
the flow of sap in your veins—and help to clothe the human field
with green.—If [35v*] your branches wither strike your roots
wider and deeper—send your fibres into every kingdom of nature
for its contribution, and make the most of that greenness and life
which the gods allot you. Send forth your boughs into the ethereal
and starry influences—and make firm your trunk against the elements.

Who can foretel what blossoms, what fruits, what private and
public advantage may push up through this rind which we call a
man.—The traveller may stand by him as a perennial fountain in
the desert, and slake his thirst forever.

110   [36r*][29] For my own part I would fain be azad or free like the

27. MS: "should should."   28. Thoreau's italics.

29. This leaf is on version I paper, but the handwriting and ink raise some question as to whether Thoreau wrote this material before he had finished version I.
36v* has only three phrases on it: "Mercury's Reply to Poverty in Carew," "End of
Economy," "S about Hollowell Farm." 36r is numbered "137"; this number is not
part of any sequence in the manuscript.

green cypress tree—I read in the Gulistan or Flower Garden of *Economy*
Shaikh Sadi of Shiraz—that *110*

"They asked a wise man, saying; of the many celebrated trees
which the Most High God has created lofty and umbrageous,
they call none azad or free excepting the cypress, which bears no
fruit; what mystery is there in this? He replied; each has its appropriate produce, and appointed season, during the continuance
of which it is fresh and blooming, and during their absence dry
and withered; to neither of which states is the cypress exposed,
being always flourishing; and of this nature are the azads or religious independants;—Fix not thy heart on what is transitory;
for the Dijlah or Tygris will continue to flow through Baghdad
after the race of Khalifs is extinct: if thy hand has plenty, be liberal as the date tree; but if it affords nothing to give away, be an
azad, or free man, like the cypress."

[37r] 1.[30] When I first went to the pond to live my house being *Where I Lived*
unfinished for winter, and merely a defence against the rain, *8*
without plastering or chimney, uncluttered with furniture, and
with walls of rough weather stained boards, and wide chinks
which made it cool at night, was itself an inspiring object, and
reacted on me the builder. From our village houses to this lodge *Compare*
on the shore of a beautiful lake in the midst of a green forest, *9*
where hardly any traces of man were visible, was a transition as
from a dungeon to an open cage at least in a pleasant grove,
where I could glimpse the light & the flowers through the bars,
and odoriferous gales coursed through and through. It was so
open and pervious to nature that it did not seem within doors
where I sat, in unwholesome penetralia, but at most only behind
a door in the rainiest weather. The fresh & pure air penetrated
through a myriad chinks, and bathed myself and all things within
as freely as it wandered amid the [37v] boughs and needles of the
pines around, and I imbibed the influences of nature with as little
alloy as a bird in its nest amid foliage. It was invigorating only to
sit there and drink and be bathed in this unco[nta]minated cur-

---

30. The second series of page numbers begins with this leaf and runs for the rest
of this version; the numbers sometimes occur on the recto of a single leaf, sometimes
on only the first page of a four-page folio.

rent. The atmosphere of our houses has usually lost some of its life giving principle and it is necessary to our health and spirits frequently to go out, as we say, to take the air.

8   The upright white hewn studs and freshly planed door & window frames gave the house a clean and airy look, especially in the morning, when its timbers seemed saturated with the morning air, and as if by noon some sweet gum would exude from them, and incense go up from the roof. With its frame so slightly clad it seemed like a picture in outlines, a rudimental, airy and primitive hall, a crystallization around me, and reminded [me] of some mountain houses I had seen, which had this fresh auroral atmosphere about them. I had lodged in the house of a sawmiller on the Kanterskill mountains the previous summer, high up as the Pine Orchard, [38r] in the blue-berry & raspberry region, which had this ambrosial character. He was the miller of the Kanterskill Falls, & his family were clean & wholesome people like the house. The latter was not plastered but only lathed, and the inner doors were not hung. It was high-placed, airy, & perfumed; so high that only the winds that swept over the ridge of the Kanterskills passed through it.—The very light & atmosphere in which the most enduring works of art were composed.—On the tops of mountains, as everywhere to hopeful souls, it is always morning.—A clean and pure house which one would enter as naturally and gratefully as he would go under a shade, which might fitly adorn a mountain's brow—and entertain a travelling god, and where a goddess might trail her garment.—Such it seemed to me all our houses should be.

10   When I looked out on the face of the pond it reminded me of a tarn high up on the side of a mountain, and the whole region where I lived seemed more elevated than it actually [38v] was. The pond was like a mountain lake I had seen in the grey of the morning draped with mist, suspended in low weather from the dead willows and bare firs that stood here and there in the water. As the sun arose I saw it throwing off its nightly clothing of mist— and here and there by degrees its soft ripples or its smooth reflecting surface [was revealed]. The mists, like ghosts, were stealthily withdrawing in every direction into the woods, as if from the

breaking up of some nocturnal conventicle.—Both place and *Where I Lived*
time had undergone a revolution and I dwelt nearer to those eras *13*
in history which had attracted me, and as I had no clock nor
watch, but the sun & moon, I also lived in primitive time. Over
the south shore of the pond, which was a low hill covered with *12*
shrub oaks & scattered pines which seemed to rise to an illimitable
table-land—I seemed to look toward the country of the Tartars,
where tribes of men dwelt in tents.

Where I lived was as far off as many a region viewed nightly by *13*
astronomers. We are apt to imagine rare and delectable places
afar off [39r] 5. whither astronomers look, in some remote and
more celestial corner of the system, behind the constellation of
Cassiopeia's Chair, far from noise & disturbance. I imagined that
my house had its site actually in such a withdrawn, but forever
new and unprophaned part of the universe. If it were worth the
while to settle in those parts of the system near to the Pleiades or
the Hyades, or Orion or Aldeboran, then I was really there, or at
an equal remoteness from the life I had left behind—as near to the
immortal city—dwindled & twinkling with as fine a ray to my
nearest neighbor and only to be seen on moonless nights by him.
Such was that part of creation where I had squatted.

Every morning was a cheerful invitation to make my life of *14*
equal simplicity and purity with itself. The morning is to everyone
the season of his ideal life. Then, if ever, we can realize the life of
the Greeks—and we are all at some time good heathens enough to
acknowledge and worship their Aurora. The morning brings[31]
back the [39v] heroic ages—I got up early and bathed in the
pond—That was a religious exercise, and one of the best things I
did. So far the day was well spent—In some unrecorded hours of
solitude, sitting with door and windows open at very early dawn
when the stillness was audible, and the atmosphere contained the
auroral perfume I have mentioned, the faint hum of a mosquito,
making its invisible and unimaginable tour through the loaded
and drowsy air toward elysian realms, was a trumpet that recalled
what I had read of most ancient history and heroic ages. There
was somewhat of that I fancy the Greeks meant by ambrosial

31. MS: "brinks."

Where I Lived about it—more than Sybilline or Delphic. It expressed the infinite
14 and everlasting fertility of the κοσμος or world. It was θεῖον or
divine. Only Homer could have named it.

The morning, which is the most memorable season of the day,
is the awakening hour; then there is least somnolence in us, and
for [40r] an hour at least some part of us seems to awake, which
slumbers all the rest of the day & night. After a partial cessation[32]
of his sensual life, the soul of man or its organs are reinvigorated
each day, and the genius tries again what noble life it can make.
All memorable events transpire in morning time, and in a morning atmosphere. Greek poetry and art, and the fairest and most
memorable of the actions of men, date from that hour—for all
poets and heroes like Memnon are the children of Aurora, and
emit their music in the morning. If we are wakeful enough the
evening and the morning are but one. The birds sing at morning
& at evening, and their notes do not suggest on which side the sun
is rising. There is no vaunt & no weariness in them. And to him
who has kept pace with the sun it is a perpetual morning.

It matters not what the clocks say, or the attitudes and labors of
men—morning is when I am awake and there is a dawn in me.
[40v] Moral reform & improvement are the effort to throw off
sleep & somnolency. How is it that men give so poor an account
of their day[33] if they have not been slumbering? They are not such
poor calculators. If they had not been overcome with drowsiness
they would have performed something. The millions are awake
enough for physical labor—but only one in a million is awake
enough for effective intellectual exertion—only one in a hundred
million to a spiritual or divine life—To be awake is to be alive.

My thoughts, which are either the memory or the expectation
15 of my actions are the causes which determine life and death. I
know of [no] more encouraging fact than the unquestionable ability of man to elevate his life by a conscious endeavor. It is something to be able to paint a particular picture, or to carve a statue,
and so to make a few objects beautiful, but it is far more sublime
to carve and paint the very atmosphere & medium through [41r]

32. MS first read: "sensation."
33. The words "their day" were written over an erasure, possibly of "themselves."

9. which we look, which morally we can do. To affect the quality *Where I Lived* of the day—that is the highest of arts. Every man is tasked to *15* make his life, even in its details, worthy of the contemplation of his most elevated and critical hour. If we refused such paltry information as we get, the oracles would distinctly inform us how this might be done.

I went down to the pond because I wished to live deliberately, *16* and front only the essential facts of life, and see if I could not learn what it had to teach, and not when I came to die discover that I that I had not lived. I did not want to live what was not life;— living is so dear.—Nor did I wish to practice resignation unless it was quite necessary. I wanted to live deep and suck out all the marrow of life—to live so sturdily and Spartan like as to put to rout all that was not life—to cut a broad swathe and shave close— to drive life into a corner, and if it proved [41v] to be mean, why then to get the whole and genuine meanness of it, and publish its meanness to the world, and throw it in the teeth of the gods, or if it were sublime to know it by experience and be able to give a true account of it in my next excursion. For all men it seems to me, are in a strange uncertainty about it, whether it is of the Devil or of God, and have somewhat hastily concluded that it is the chief end of man here to glorify God and Him only.[34]

[42r] 11. Still we live meanly like ants, though the fable tells us *17* that we[35] were long ago changed into men, like pigmies we fight with cranes—it is error upon error and clout upon clout, and our best virtue has for its occasion, a superfluous and evitable wretchedness.—Our life is frittered away by detail. Its dish consists almost entirely of fixings & very little of the chicken's meat. An honest man has hardly need to count more than his ten fingers, or in extreme cases he may add his ten toes, and lump the rest. Simplicity—Simplicity—Simplicity. I say instead of a million count half a dozen; and keep your accounts on your thumb nail. Let our affairs be as 2 or 3, and not a hundred or a thousand. In

34. At first the text ran from what is now 41v to what is now 44r, but before Thoreau numbered the pages, he canceled the last 15 lines of 41v; they contained the beginning of "Where I Lived," 23. He then wrote the material on the next four pages, copying the canceled lines of 41v on the bottom half of 43v.

35. MS: "we we."

The Making of Walden

the midst of this civilization, such are the clouds & storms, and quicksands, and thousand and one items to be allowed for, a man has to live, if he would not founder and go to the bottom & not make his port at all, by dead reckoning, and he must [42v] be a great calculator indeed who succeeds. Simplify—Simplify. Instead of 3 meals a day, if it be necessary eat but one, instead of a hundred dishes—5—and reduce other things in proportion. Our life is like a German confederacy made up of petty states—forever fluctuating and even a German cannot tell you how it is bounded at any moment.

The nation itself with all its so-called internal improvements, which by the way are all external and superficial—is just such an unwieldly and overgrown establishment cluttered with furniture and tripped up by its own traps, ruined by luxury and heedless expense & want of calculation as the million households in the land, and the only cure for it as for them is in a rigid economy—a stern & more than Spartan simplicity of life and grandeur of purpose. It lives too fast.—Men think that it is essential that the nation make lard oil—and export ice—and talk thro' a telegraph and ride 30 miles an hour—[43r] without a doubt, but whether we should live like chimpanzees & baboons or like men is a little uncertain. If we don't get out sleepers, and forge rails, and devote days and nights to the work, but go to tinkering upon our own lives to improve them who will build railroads? And if rail-roads are not built, how shall we get to heaven in season? When I first got a cinder in my eye I suspected that I was not going to heaven. But if we stay at home and mind our business who will want rail-roads? Did you ever think what these sleepers are that underlie the rail-road? Each one is a man—an Irish-man, or a Yankee-man—The rails are laid on them, and they are covered with sand, and the cars run smoothly over them!—They are sound sleepers I assure you—And every few years a new lot are laid down and run over. So that if a few have the pleasure of riding on a rail—the rest have the misfortune [43v] to be ridden upon. And when they run over a man that is walking in his sleep—a supernumerary sleeper in the wrong position *& wake him up*, they suddenly stop the cars, and make a hue and cry about it, as if this were an excep-

tion. I am glad to know that it takes a gang of men for every five *Where I Lived*
miles to keep the sleepers down and level in their beds, as it is, for *17*
this is a sign that they may sometime get up again.

Time is but the stream I go a fishing in. I drink at it, but while *23*
I drink I see the sandy bottom, and detect how shallow it is. Its
thin current glides away, but eternity remains. I would drink
deeper—fish in the sky—whose bottom is pebbly with stars. The
Intellect is a cleaver; it discerns & splits, and rifts its way into the
secret of things. I do not wish to be any more busy with my hands
than is necessary—My head is hands & feet. I feel all my faculties
concentrated in it. My instinct tells [44r] 15. me obscurely that
my head is an organ for burrowing, as some creatures use their
snout & fore paws—and with it I would mine & burrow my way
through these hills. I cannot count one—I know not the first letter
of the alphabet. I have always been regretting that I was not as
wise as the day I was born.

I think the richest vein is somewhere herabouts—so by the
divining rod and thin rising vapors, I judge—and here I will begin to mine.

When I was fairly established in my house I sang this song,   *Not in text*

> I seek the Present Time,
> No other clime,
> Life in to-day,
> Not to sail another way,
> To Paris or to Rome,
> Or farther still from home.
> That man, whoe'er he is,
> Lives but a moral death,
> Whose life is not coeval
> With his breath.
> My feet forever stand
> On Concord fields,
> And I must live the life
> [44v]   Which their soil yields.
> What are deeds done
> Away from home?
> What the best essay

Where I Lived
Not in text

On the Ruins of Rome?
The love of the new,
The unfathomed blue,
The wind in the wood,
All fortune good,
The sun-lit tree,
The small chicadee,
The dusty highways,
What Scripture says,
This pleasant weather
And all signs together—
The river's meander,
All things, in short,
Forbid me to wander
In deed or in thought,
In cold or in drouth,
Not seek the sunny South,
But make the whole tour
Of the sunny Present Hour.
For here if thou fail,
Where canst thou prevail?
If you love not
Your own land most,
You'll find nothing lovely
Upon a distant coast.

[45r] 17. If you love not
The latest sun-set,
What is there in pictures
Or old gems set?

If no man should travel
Till he had the means,
There'd be little travelling
For Kings or for Queens.
The means! What are they?
They are the wherewithal
Great expenses to pay;—

Life got, and some to spare, *Where I Lived*
Great works on hand, *Not in text*
And freedom from care.
Plenty of time well spent,
To use,—
Clothes paid for, and no rent
In your shoes;—
Something to eat,
And something to burn,
And, above all, no need to return;—
For they who come back,
Say have they not failed,
Wherever they've ridden
Or steamed it, or sailed?
   All your grass hayed,—
   All your debts paid,—
   All your wills made?
[45v]   Then you might as well have stayed,
For are you not dead,
Only not buried?

The way unto "Today,"
The railroad to "Here,"
They never'll grade that way,
Nor shorten it, I fear,
There are plenty of depots
All the world o'er,
But not a single station
At a man's door;
If we would get near
To the secret of things,
We shall not have to hear
When the engine bell rings.

It seems as if with a little more reflection all men would be es- *Reading*
sentially students & observers—For certainly his nature & des- *1*
tiny are equally interesting to every man. It is hard to tell if that

145

Reading time which we really improve is past present or future. I might
    1 say that the student always studies antiques. In our studies we do
not look forward but backward into antiquity with [46r] redoubled pauses. Where is that lost first page of history? We have
never found the literature that dated from an antiquity sufficiently remote. The most adventurous student seeks the remotest
antiquity—the history of a time, as it were, prior to time.—Or, if
we prefer, such is the Protean character of things, we may say that
he always interprets prophecies and oracles, and is interested
solely in the future.—In accumulating property for ourselves, or
our posterity, in founding a family, or a state, or acquiring fame,
we are mortal, but in dealing with truth we are immortal, and
need fear no change nor accident.—The oldest Egyptian or
Hindoo philosopher raised a corner of the veil from the statue of
divinity, and still the trembling robe remains raised, and I gaze
upon as fresh a glory as he did, since it was I in him that was then
so bold, and he in me that now reviews the vision. [46v] No dust
has settled upon that robe—no time has elapsed since that divinity was revealed.

2   I kept a Homer on my table through the summer, though I
only glanced at his page now and then. Incessant labor with my
hands made more study impossible. Yet I sustained myself by the
prospect of such reading in future. Here of course I could read the
Iliad, if I would have books, as well as in Ionia, and not wish myself in Boston or New York—or London or Rome; in such a place
as this rather Homer lived and sung.—I read one or two shallow
books of travel in the intervals of my work, till that employment
made me ashamed of myself, and I asked myself where it was
then that I lived?

3   The student may read Homer or Aeschylus in the original
Greek without danger of dissipation or luxuriousness, for to do so
implies that he should in some measure emulate their heroes, and
consecrate morning hours to their pages. The [47r] 21. heroic
books, though printed in the character of our mother tongue, will
always be in a language dead to degenerate times, and we must
laboriously seek the meaning of each word and line, conjecturing
a larger sense than common use permits out of what wisdom and

146

valor & generosity we have. The modern cheap & fertile press has
done little to bring us nearer to the heroic writers of antiquity.
They seem as solitary, and the letter in which they are printed as
rare and curious as ever.—It is even worth the expense of youthful days & costly hours if you learn only some words of an ancient
language, which are raised out of the trivialness of the street, to be
perpetual suggestions & provocations.

We sometimes speak as if the study of the classics would at
length make way for more modern and practical studies, but the
brave and adventurous student will always study classics in whatever language they may be [47v] written, and however ancient
they may be.—For they have to be studied in the same spirit that
we study nature. They are only valuable commentaries on her
works,—never ancient, and never modern. What are the classics
but the noblest recorded thought of man? They are the only
oracles which have not decayed. There are such answers to the
most modern inquiry in them as Delphi & Dodona never gave.—
To read well, that is; to read true books in a true spirit is a noble
exercise, and one that will task the reader more than any exercise
the customs of the day esteem. It requires a training such as the
athletes underwent, and the steady *intention*[36] of the whole life to
their object. It is not enough even to be able to speak the language
in which they are written. There is a memorable interval between
the written and the spoken language—the language read and the
lan- [48r] guage heard. The one is commonly transient—a sound
—a tongue a dialect merely—almost brutish, and we learn it
unconsciously, like the brutes, of our mothers. The other is the
maturity and experience of this—If that is our mother tongue, this
is our Father tongue—A reserved and select expression which is
too significant to be heard by the ear. It does not wait to be heard,
but is content with its own truth. The one is natural and convenient, the other is divine and instinctive. The noblest written *4*
words are as far behind or beyond the fleeting spoken language,
as the firmament with its stars is behind the clouds. There are the
stars and they who can may read them. The astronomers forever
comment on and observe them. They are not exhalations like our

36. Thoreau's italics.

Reading daily colloquies & vaporous breath. When I ask myself whether
4 any unpremeditated speech or conversation of equal length, even
by the wisest of mankind and the writers [48v] of books, would
abide the myriad and impartial tests of time, which some rare &
wonderful books have so triumphantly withstood, I cannot doubt
the justice of this distinction.

3 Books must be read as deliberately and reservedly as they were
written. The herd of men who merely spoke the Greek & Latin
tongues in the middle ages were not entitled by the accident of
birth, to read the works of genius, written in those languages—for
these were not written in Greek or Latin peculiarly. The men
who glibly spoke the language of the Roman and of the Greek, for
their mother-tongue, did not learn their nobler dialects, but the
very materials on which they were written, were waste paper to
them, while they prized a cheap contemporary learning. The
classics were virtually forgotten and lost. So distinct are the
spoken & the written language. But when the several nations of
Europe had acquired rude original [49r] 25. languages sufficient
for conversation and the daily intercourse of life, then first learning revived, and scholars who were seers in their kind arose, who
could discern from this remote standpoint the treasures of antiquity; and works of genius first began to be read, and perhaps
found their truest & *fittest* audience when their language could no
longer be spoken anywhere. What the multitude could not *hear*,[37]
after the lapse of ages a few scholars *read*.[38] And a few scholars only
are still reading them.

5 A word fitly written is the most choice and select of things. No
wonder that Alexander carried the Iliad with him on his expeditions in a precious casket. It has something at once more intimate
and more universal than any other work of art. It may be trans-
lated into every language, and breathed from every human
mouth, and become anew the product as it were of our physical
organs, as its sense is recognized by our intellectual ones. It is the
work of art nearest to life itself. [49v] Such are the traces of
Zoroaster & Confucius & Moses, indelible on the sands of the

37. Thoreau's italics.
38. Thoreau's italics.

remotest times. There are no monuments of antiquity comparable *Reading* to the Classics for interest and importance. It is not necessary that *5* the scholar should be an antiquarian to study them, for these works of art have such an immortality as the works of nature, and are modern at the same time that they are ancient, like the sun and stars, and occupy by right no small share of the present hour.

As we are told, for instance, that "the serene sky and the brilliant sun of Greece merely communicate to the marble of Paros and Pentelicus a golden tint, resembling that of ripe corn, or the autumnal foliage," while in other climates "stone of the purest white soon turns black, or of a greenish hue," so time lends to the pure monuments of Grecian literature only a golden and mature tint. The poetry of the Greeks wears even now after [50r] 27. the lapse of more than 2000 summers only a cereal and autumnal hue. Enveloped still, as it were, in the inspiration which first breathed it, it carries its own serene & celestial atmosphere into all lands to protect them against the corrosions of time.

Books are the treasured wealth of the world, and the fit inheritance of generations & of nations. Books the oldest & the best stand naturally and rightfully on the shelves of every cottage. They do not have to plead their cause—but while they enlighten the reader the common sense of men will not refuse them.—The authors of great books dead or alive, are an invisible upper class and aristocracy in every civilized society, who exert the last and greatest influence.

Those who have not learned to read the ancient classics in the *6* language in which they were written must have a very imperfect knowledge of the history of the human race—for of these after all it is remarkable that [50v] no transcript has ever been made into any tongue—unless our civilization itself be a transcript and expression of them—Homer was never to my knowledge printed in English, nor Sophocles—nor Horace even. These great Geniuses and wits who have rendered memorable a remote period of the world's history—now almost its early age—works as refined as solidly done, and as beautiful as the morning itself—for I think that later writers, say what we will of their genius, have never equalled the elaborate beauty—and wonderful skill in the steady

Reading & equable exercise of their art, the life-long, heroic labors &
6 literary architecture of the ancients. Not one in many thousands
even of those who are said to have learned their language, have
ever read them.

I know that it is advised by some to overlook at last and forget
what ancient and heroic men have done, what wise and studious
men have taught, what inspired poets have sung—

[Three leaves missing; they probably contained material in paragraphs 6, 8, and 9.]

9 [51r]³⁹ only as far as easy reading—the primers and classbooks,
and when we leave school the Little Reading and story books,
which are for boys and beginners, and our reading & our conversation and thinking are all on a very low and inferior level—
low statured & feeble and worthy only of pigmies & mannikins.
10 I aspire to be acquainted with wiser men than this our Concord
soil has produced—whose names are hardly known here. Or shall
I hear the name of Plato and never read his book? As if Plato were
my townsman and I never saw him—my next neighbor, and I
never heard him speak, or attended to the wisdom of his words.
But how actually is it? His Dialogues which contain what was immortal in him, lie on the next shelf, and yet I never read them. *I
describe my own case here.* We are under-bred and low-lived, and il-
literate—and in this respect, I confess, I do not make any very
broad distinction between the illiterateness of my townsman who
cannot read at all, and the illiterateness of my townsman who
[51v] has learned to read only what is for children & feeble intel-
lects. We should be as good as the worthies of antiquity—but
partly by first knowing how good they were. We are a race of tit-
men & soar but little higher in our intellectual flights than the
columns of the daily paper.
11 There are words addressed to our condition which, if we could
hear and understand would be as salutary as the morning or the
spring to our lives, and possibly put a new aspect on the face of
things. How many a man has dated a new era in his life, a second
birth as it were from the reading of a book? The book exists for us

39. This leaf is in the Berg Collection, New York Public Library.

which will explain our miracles and reveal new ones. The at *Reading*
present unutterable things we shall find somewhere uttered. *11*
Moreover with wisdom we shall learn liberality. These same
questions that disturb & puzzle & confound us—have in their
turn occurred to all the wise men—not one has been omitted, and
each has answered them, according to his ability in his [52r] 37.
words & his life. They have had the same problems to solve.—
The solitary hired man on a farm in the outskirts of Concord, who
has had his second birth and peculiar religious experience, and is
driven as he thinks into silent gravity and exclusiveness by his
faith may think it is not true, but Zoroaster thousands of years ago
travelled the same road and had the same experience, but he
being wise knew it to be universal, and treated men accordingly,
and is even said to have invented and established worship among
men. Let him humbly commune with Zoroaster—and through the
liberalizing influence of all the worthies with Jesus Christ himself—& let "our Church" go by the board.

Most men have learned to read to serve a paltry convenience, 7
as they have learned to cypher in order to keep accounts, and not
be cheated in trade; but of reading as a noble intellectual exercise
they know little or nothing. Yet this only is reading properly
speaking—not that which lulls & soothes [52v] as a luxury, and
suffers the nobler faculties to sleep the while, but what we have to
stand on tip-toe to read, and devote our most alert & wakeful
hours to—have to gird up our robes & train ourselves for—as the
wrestler is trained for the combat.

Yet after all, while we are confined to books though the most *Sounds*
classic and study only particular languages or provincialisms, we *1*
are apt to forget the language, or rather the expression, which all
things every where, morning & evening and all events speak—
which only is copious, for the tongue is only an accidental organ
of speech serving equally the palate, and speech itself is partial,
uttering but a small part of the meaning with which the silence is
fraught.—I mean the language which things speak originally and
without metaphor—such as the life of a man hears & his instincts
speak—and at length through all his actions he learns to mutter.

I read very little however during the summer, for my [53r] 2

151

Sounds thoughts would run upon my labor mainly, or rather where they
 2   pleased, and I had not leisure to drill myself. I only read one sentence of Homer to a week of hoeing—as for instance how Ajax struggled with the Trojans to ward off fire from the ships of the Greeks, while Patroclus was supplicating Achilles for his armor & his Myrmidons. I read no more than this—at once—still remembering & repeating it—but I imagined more things than are in Homer while I hoed.

Sometimes in a spring morning when the season of work had not yet arrived *or later in the summer when it was already past*[40] having performed my accustomed ablutions, I sat in my sunny door way from the earliest dawn, wrapt in a reverie, amid the pines and hickories and sumacks, while the birds sang around and flitted noiseless over my head and out at the open window—in undisturbed solitude & stillness, except when a bough fell like a fan broken by its own weight, in my sumack grove, when the atmosphere was perfume & incense, and every sound the key [53v] to unheard harmonies, until by the sun's rays falling in at my west window, or the noise of some traveller on the distant highway, I was reminded of the lapse of time. I am sensible that I waxed and grew in these intervals, as corn grows in the night, and they were far better than any work of my hands. I realized what the oriental philosophers meant by contemplation & the forsaking of works. It was quite impossible to have performed anything, and wise persons would not propose that any deed should be substituted therefor. They were little intervals during which I journeyed, and anticipated other states of existence.

For the most part indeed I knew not how the hours went. I was accustomed to say to myself—certainly I am not living that heroic life I had dreamed of, and yet all my veins are full of life, and nature whispers no reproach. The day advanced as if to light some work of mine—and I defer to other men in my thought, as if there were somewhere busier [54r] 41. men. It was morning, and lo! it is now evening, and nothing memorable is accomplished. Yet my nature is almost content with this. What are these pines & these birds about? What is this pond adoing? I must know a little

40. Originally read "season of work was past or had not yet arrived."

more and be forever ready. Instead of singing like the birds, I *Sounds*
sometimes silently smile at my incessant good fortune. As the *2*
field-sparrow has its trill sitting on the hickory before my door, so
have I my chuckle or suppressed warble, which he may hear out
of my nest. I don't know that I bear any flowers or fruits. Methinks if the birds & flowers try me by their standard I shall not
be found wanting, but men try one another not so.

Man is still like a plant, and his satisfactions are like those of a
vegetable. His rarest life is least his own. I am not the worker but
the work. The elements are working their will with me.

I seemed to have this advantage in my mode of life over those *3*
who were obliged to look abroad for amusement—to theaters and
to society, [54v] that my life itself was now my amusement, and
never ceased to be novel. It was a drama of many scenes which
would never end. If we were always getting our living and regu-
lating our lives according to the last and divinest mode we had
learned—we should never be weary of living. Follow your genius
closely enough, and it will not fail to show you a fresh prospect
every hour.

Housework was a pleasant pastime. When my floor was dirty I
rose early and setting all my furniture out of doors on the grass,
dashed water upon the floor, and sprinkled white sand from the
pond upon it, and then with a broom I scrubbed it clean & white,
and by the time the villagers had broken their fast, the morning
sun had dried my house sufficiently to allow me to move in again
—and my meditations were almost uninterrupted—I trust that
none of my hearers will be so uncharitable as to look into my
house now—after hearing this, at the end of an unusually dirty
winter, with [55r] critical housewife's eyes, for I intend to celebrate the first bright & unquestionable spring morning by scrubbing my house with sand until it is as white as a lily—or, at any
rate, as the washer-woman said of her clothes, as white as a
"wiolet."

It was pleasant to see my whole household effects out on the
grass, making a little pile like a gipsey's pack; and my 3 legged
table from which I did not remove the books & pen & ink, standing amid the pines & hickories *bed & bedstead making but one budget.*

The Making of Walden

Sounds They seemed glad to get out themselves, and as if unwilling to be
3 brought in.—I was sometimes tempted to stretch an awning over them, and take my seat there. It was worth the while to see the sun shine on these things, and the free wind blow upon them. So much more beautiful any beautiful thing looks out of doors than in the house. A bird sits on the next bough—life-everlasting grows under the table, and blackberry vines run round its legs, pine cones & chestnut burrs, and strawberry [55v] leaves are strewn about. It looked as if this was the way these forms came to be transferred to our furniture—to tables chairs & bedsteads—because these once stood in their midst.

2 A man must find his own occasions in himself. The natural day is very calm, and will hardly reprove his indolence. If there was no elevation in our spirits the pond would not seem elevated like a mountain tarn, but a low pool, a silent muddy water & place for fishermen.

Where I Lived If men would steadily observe realities only and not allow
21 themselves to be deluded, life would be like a fairy tale, and the Arabian Nights Entertainments. If we respected only what was inevitable and had a right to be, music and poetry would resound along the streets. When we are calm & wise & unhurried, we perceive that only great and worthy things have any permanent & absolute existence—that [56r] 45. petty fears and petty pleasures are but the shadow of the reality. By closing the eyes and slumbering and consenting to be deceived by shows men establish and confirm their daily life of routine and habit everywhere which still is built on purely imaginary foundations. A more intimate and truer experience, a more practical wisdom teaches men that the trivial and commonplace are not real but apparent and superficial merely. The reality is sublime & exhilarating—If men would discriminate always and never be deluded by appearances, life would never be mean nor unworthy.—Shams and delusions are esteemed for soundest truths—while reality is fabulous. We are not prepared for the truth. Children who play life discern its true law & relations more clearly than men who fail to live it worthily but think they are wiser by experience.

All the gold all the silver we want is reality—this is sublime &

inspiring. Appearance whether [56v] fair or foul is equally shallow *Where I Lived*
and dangerous—I perceive that we inhabitants of Concord live *21*
this mean life, that we do, because our vision does not penetrate
the surface of things—we think that that *is* which *appears*[41] to be.
If a man should walk through the village and see only the reality
where think you would the mill-dam go to? If he should give us an
account of the realities he beheld there we should not recognize
the place by his description. Look at a meeting-house, or a court-
house—or a jail—or a shop or a dwelling house and say what this
thing really is before a true gaze, and they would all go to pieces
in your account of them. Men esteem truth remote in the outskirts of the system, behind the furthest star, before Adam and
after the last man.—In eternity there is indeed something true
and sublime. But all these times & places & occasions are now.
God himself culminates in the

[At some time after he had numbered the pages, Thoreau apparently removed one leaf here; it contained pages 47 and 48 of his numbering; he finished the sentence at the end of 56v on the bottom of 58v,
but he did not complete the unfinished sentence on 58v. The handwriting on 58v is not that of version I.]

[58v] present moment and will never be more divine in the lapse
of all the ages—And after all we are enabled to apprehend at all
what is sublime and noble only by the perpetual instilling and
drenching of the reality that surrounds us.

I think that the universe really needs no patching from us—and
its Maker no condolence. Let us remember that God is well

[57r] 49. Why should we live with such hurry and waste of life? *18*
We are determined to starve before we are hungry. Men say[42]
that a stitch in time saves nine, and so they take a thousand
stitches today to save nine tomorrow. Let us spend one day as *22*
deliberately as nature and not be thrown off the track by every
nut-shell and mosquito's wing that falls on the rails.

Let us rise early, and fast, or break fast gently. Let company
come and let company go—let the bells ring and the children
cry—determined to make a day of it—Why should we knock

41. Thoreau's italics.   42. MS: "say say."

Where I Lived under and go with the stream? Let us not be upset and over-
22 whelmed in that terrible rapid and whirlpool called a dinner—
situated in the meridian shallows.

Weather this danger and you are safe for the rest of the way is
down hill. With unrelaxed nerves—with morning vigor sail by
it—looking another way—tied to the mast like Ulysses. If the
engine whistles let it whistle [57v] till it is hoarse for its pains—
why should we run?—We will consider what kind of music it is
like—

18   As for work we haven't any of any consequence—Men have the
St. Vitus dance and can't possibly keep their heads still. Why, if I
should only give a few pulls at the bell rope yonder—fiery like—
that is without setting the bell, there is not a man on his farm in
the outskirts of the town—notwithstanding that press of engage-
ments which was his excuse so many times this morning, nor a boy
nor a woman—I might almost say, but will forsake all and follow
that sound, and not as we must all confess, if we are honest—to do
a deed of charity or neighborliness, & save property from the
flames—but to see it burn—since burn it must—and [we] be it
known, did not set it on fire, or to see it put out and have a hand
in it—if that is done as handsomely—yes, even if it were the very
meeting house over our heads. [58r] Hardly a man takes a half
hour's nap after dinner but when he wakes, he holds up his head
and asks what's the news—Some give directions to be waked
every half hour doubtless for no other purpose.—and then to pay
for it they tell what they have dreamed.

19   I think that there are very few important communications
made through the Post Office—and I never read any memorable
news in a newspaper in my life.

There was such a rush I hear the other day, at one of the offices
to learn the foreign news by the last arrival, as broke several large
squares of plate glass belonging to the establishment. News which
I seriously think a ready wit might write[43] a 12 month or 12 years
beforehand with sufficient accuracy—If one may judge who
rarely looks into the newspapers, I should say—that nothing new
does ever happen in foreign parts—as for Spain for instance, if

43. MS: "right."

you know how to throw in Don Carlos [58v] and the Infanta— *Where I Lived*
and Don Pedro & Seville & Granada—from time to time in the *19*
right proportions—and serve up a bullfight when other entertainments fail it will be true to the letter, and give as good an idea of
the exact state or ruin of things in Spain as the most succinct and
lucid report under this head in the newspapers. [See above for
rest of 58v]

[59r] 53. If you stand right fronting & face to face to a fact— *22*
you will see the sun glimmer on both its surfaces, as if it were a
cimeter, and feel its sweet edge dividing you through the heart
and marrow—and so you will happily conclude your mortal
career.

Be it life or death we crave only reality. If we are really dying
let us hear the rattle in our throats and feel cold in the extremeties
—If we are alive, let us go about our business.

I am glad to remember as I sit by my door that I too am a re- *Sounds*
mote descendant of a heroic race of men of whom there is tradition—in one sense a fellow wanderer and survivor of Ulysses, for *Not in text*
instance. My life passes amid the pines of New England. The pitch
pine grows before my door unlike any glyph I have seen sculptured or painted. Where are the heroes whose exploits shall appear to posterity sculptured on monuments amid [59v] such natural forms as these—as heroes and demigods amid the lotuses and
palms of the east. What new marks shall we add to the Red Pipe-
stone Quarry?

In my front-yard grow the black-berry and strawberry & the *4*
life-everlasting—Johnswort & golden rod—& shruboak and
sandcherry & blue-berry and ground-nut. The sumacks grew
luxuriantly about my house—pushing up through the embank-
ment I had made, and growing 5 or 6 feet the first season. Its
broad pinnate tropical leaf was pleasant *though strange* to look
upon. The large buds suddenly pushing out *late in the spring* from
dry and brittle sticks which had seemed to be dead, developed
themselves as it were by magic into graceful green & tender
boughs an inch in diameter—and sometimes as I sat at my window—so heedlessly did they grow and tax their brittle stems—I
heard a fresh & green bough [60r] suddenly fall to the ground,

The Making of Walden

when there was not a breath of air, broken off at its foot by its own weight.

In the fall the large masses of red berries which when in flower had attracted many wild bees to my house, gradually assumed their bright scarlet & velvety hue, and by their weight again bent down and broke the tender limbs.

5   I sit at my window this summer afternoon like a priest of Isis and observe the phenomena of 3000 years ago still unimpaired. The sacred hawks are circling about this temple—the tantivy of wild pigeons an ancient race of birds gives a voice to the air— flying by twos and threes athwart my view or perching restless on the white pine boughs behind my house—a fish hawk dimples the glassy surface of the pond, and brings up a fish—a muskrat steals out of the marsh before my door and seizes a frog in the pond— the sedge [60v] is bending under the weight of the reed-birds flitting here and there—and for the last half hour I have heard the rattle of rail-road cars, now dying away and then reviving like the beat of a partridge—conveying travellers from Boston to the country—or the faint rattle and tinkle which mark the passage of a carriage or team along the distant highway—For I did not live in such an outlandish and out of the way place as that boy who, as I hear, was put out to a farmer in the east part of the town, but ere long ran away and came home again, quite down at the heel, and homesick—He had never seen such a dull, and out of the world place—the folks were all gone away—why you couldn't

7   even hear the whistle.—The whistle of the steam engine pene- trated my woods summer & winter—[61r] 57. sounding like the scream of a hawk sailing over some farmer's yard—informing me that many restless city merchants were arriving within the circle of the town or adventurous country traders from the other side. As they come under one horizon they shout their warning to get off the track to the other, heard sometimes through the circles of two towns—Here come your groceries country—your rations countrymen—Nor is there any man so independent on his farm as can say them nay—And here's your pay for them—screams the countryman's whistle—Timber like long catapults going 20 miles an hour against the city walls—and chairs enough to seat all the

weary and heavy laden that dwell within ye.—With such huge *Sounds*
and lumbering civility, the country hands a chair to the city. All *7*
the Indian huckle-berry hills are stript—all the cranberry
meadows are raked into the city. Up comes the [61v] cotton,
down goes the woven cloth—up comes the silk—down goes the
woollen—up come the books—but down goes the wit that writes
them.

When I meet the engine with its train of cars moving off with *8*
planetary motion—or rather like a comet, for the beholder knows
not if with that velocity & that direction it will ever revisit this
system—for its orbit does not look like a returning curve—with its
steam cloud like a banner streaming behind in golden & silver
wreaths—like many a fleecy cloud that I have seen in a summer
day—high in the heavens—unfolding its masses to the light—as if
this travelling demigod would ere long take the sunset sky for the
livery of his train—When I hear the iron horse make the hills echo
with his snort like thunder—shaking the earth with his feet, and
breathing fire and smoke from his nostrils—What kind of winged
horse or fiery dragon they will [62r] put into the new mythology I
don't know—It seems as if the earth had got a race now worthy to
inhabit it—If all were as it seems, and men made the elements
their servants for noble ends. If the cloud that hangs over the
engine were the perspiration of heroic deeds—or as innocent and
and beneficent to men as that which hovers over the farmer's
fields—then the elements and nature herself would cheerfully
accompany men on their errands, and be their escort.

The stabler of the iron horse was up early this winter morning *9*
by the light of the stars amid the mountains, to fodder and har-
ness his steed—Fire too was awakened thus early to put the vital
heat in him and get him off—If the enterprise were as innocent as
it is early!—If the snow lies deep they strap on his snow-shoes, and
with the giant plow, plow a furrow from the mountains to the sea-
board, in which the cars like a following drill-barrow [62v]
sprinkle all the restless men & floating merchandise in the country for seed. All the day the Firesteed flies over the country stopping only that his master may rest, and I am awakened by his
tramp and defiant snort at midnight, when in some remote glen

Sounds in the woods he fronts the elements, encased in ice and snow and
9 will only reach his stall with the morning star—to start once more
on his travels without rest or slumber.—Or perchance at evening
I hear him in his stable blowing off the superfluous energy of the
day, that he may calm his nerves, and cool his liver & brain for a
few hours of iron slumber.—If the enterprise were as heroic and
commanding as it is protracted & unwearied!

11   What recommends commerce to me is its enterprise and bravery—It does not fold its hands & pray to Jupiter. I see these men
every day go about

[Four leaves are missing. They surely contained a few more lines of 11
(most of that paragraph was probably added in version II), and they
must have had the beginning of the following passage on the cock. For
the rest, they probably included some of paragraphs 10, 12, 13, 14, and
17, but there is no evidence as to what parts.]

Not in text [63r] 69. going & coming—with brave thoughts exalting him—
and fancies rushing thick upon him—crowing long memoriter
wise of his Indian origin & wild descent—he flew like a bird up
into the branches of a tree, and went to roost there.—And I who
had witnessed this passage in his private history immediately
wrote these verses, & inscribed them to him.

> Poor bird! destined to lead thy life
>   Far in the adventurous west,
> And here to be debarred to-night
>   From thy accustomed nest;
> Must thou fall back upon old instinct now,—
> Well nigh extinct under man's fickle care?
> Did Heaven bestow its quenchless inner light
> So long ago, for thy small want to-night?
> Why stands't upon thy toes to crow so late?
> The moon is deaf to thy low feathered fate;
> Or dost thou think so to possess the night,
> And people the drear dark with thy brave sprite?
> And now with anxious eye thou look'st about,
> While the relentless shade draws on its veil,
> For some sure shelter from approaching dews,

And the insidious steps of nightly foes.
I fear imprisonment has dulled thy wit,
Or ingrained servitude extinguished it.
But no,—dim memory of the days of yore,
By Brahmapootra & the Jumna's shore,
Where thy proud race flew swiftly o'er the heath,
And sought its food the jungle's shade beneath,—
Has taught thy wings to seek yon friendly trees,
As erst by Indus' banks & far Ganges.

Sounds
Not in text

[63v] I am perhaps the only inhabitant of the town or of the state 22 who does not hear the cock crow. Even the sailor on the Atlantic and Pacific is awakened by this familiar sound. I keep neither dog, cat, cow, pig, nor hens—so that there is a deficiency of domestic sounds—neither the churn—nor the spinning wheel—nor even the singing of the kettle, nor the hissing of the urn, nor children crying—to comfort one. An old-fashioned man would have lost his senses and died of ennui—Not even rats in the wall—for they are starved out, but only squirrels on the roof and under the floor—A whippoorwill on the ridge-pole, a blue jay screaming in the yard—a hare or woodchuck under the house—a screech-owl or a cat-owl behind it—a flock of wild geese or a laughing loon in the pond—a fox to bark in the night—But not even a lark or an oriole—those wild plantation birds ever visit my [64r] 71. clearing. No cockrils to crow nor hens to cackle in the yard—no yard! but unfenced nature reaching up to your very sills. A young forest growing up under your windows & wild sumacks and blackberry vines breaking through into your cellar—Sturdy pitch-pines rubbing and creaking against the shingles for want of room—their roots reaching quite under the house—Instead of a scuttle or a blind blown off in the gale—a pine tree snapped off or torn up by the roots behind your house for fuel. Instead of no path to the front yard gate in the great snow, no gate, no front yard—and no path to the civilized world.

Sometimes I hear the bells, the Lincoln bell—the Acton bell— 15 the Bedford bell & the Concord bell, when the wind is fair—a faint and sweet almost natural melody. An invention worth importing into the wilderness.

161

The Making of Walden

Now up they go, ding,
Then down again, dong,
And awhile they swing

[64v]   To the same old song,
And the metal goes round 't a single bound,
A-lulling the fields with its measured sound—
Till the tired tongue falls with a lengthened boom,
As solemn & loud as the crack of doom.
    Then changed is their measure to tone upon tone,
And seldom it is that one sound comes alone,
For they sing out their peals in a mingled throng,
And the breezes waft the loud ding dong along.

Bean-Field   On gala days the town fires its great guns which echo like pop
7   guns to these woods—and the waifs & loose strains of martial
music occasionally penetrate thus far. To me away there in my
bean-field at the other end of the town the big guns sounded as if
a puff ball had burst, and when there was a military turnout of
which I was ignorant I have sometimes had a vague sense all the
day of some sort of itching and disease in the horizon, as if some
eruption would break out there soon, either scarletina or canker-
rash—until some more favorable puff of wind making haste over
the fields and up the Wayland road brought me information of
the trainers

[Two leaves missing; they undoubtedly contained the last part of the
above paragraph and the first part of the following one; and probably
paragraphs 8 and 9 of "The Bean-Field."]

Sounds   [65r] 77. aldermanic with his chin upon a pad, which serves for a
21   napkin to his drooling chaps, under this northern shore quaffs a
deep draught of the once scorned water, and passes round the
cup, with the ejaculation—troonk—tr-r-r-oonk—tr-r-r-oonk.
A[nd] straight way comes over the water from some distant cove
the same pass-word repeated where the next in seniority and girth
has gulped down to his mark. And when this observance has made
the circuit of the shores then ejaculates the master of ceremonies
with satisfaction tr-r-r-oonk—and each in his turn repeats the

162

same—down to the least distended, leakiest, & flabbiest paunched *Sounds*
—that there be no mistake—And then the bowl goes round again *21*
and again until the sun disperses the morning mist, and only the
patriarch is not under the pond—but vainly bellowing Troonk—
from time to time & pausing for a reply.

When other birds are still the owls take up the strain—like *18*
[65v] mourning women their ancient U-lu-lu. Their dismal
scream is truly Ben Jonsonian—wise midnight hags. It is no
honest and blunt Tu-whit to-who—of the poets, but without jest-
ing a most solemn graveyard ditty—the mutual consolations of
suicide lovers remembering the pangs and the delights of supernal
love in the infernal groves. Yet I love to hear their wailing—their
doleful responses trilled along the woodside, reminding me
sometimes of music and singing birds, as if it were the dark and
tearful side of music—the regrets and sighs that would fain be
sung.—They are the spirits—the low spirits and melancholy fore-
bodings of fallen souls that once in human shape night-walked the
earth, and did the deeds of darkness, now expiating with their
wailing hymns and threnodies their sins, in the scenery of their
transgressions.—They give me a new sense of the vastness and the
mystery of that nature which is our common dwelling—Oh-o-o-
o-o-o—that I never had been bor-

[One leaf missing; probably contained the end of "Sounds," 18, and
beginning of "Solitude," 1.]

[66r] 81. rabbit roam the fields & woods without fear. We associ- *Solitude*
ate wildness with the night—and silence—But the repose is never *1*
complete; nature has her watchmen who are links connecting the
days of animated life.

There seems always to be sufficient space about us. Our horizon *3*
is never quite at our elbows. The *thick* wood is not just at my door
—nor the pond—but somewhat is always clearing—appropriated
and fenced in some way & familiar & worn by us—reclaimed
from nature. For what reason have I this vast range and circuit in
nature—a square mile and more of unfrequented forest for my
privacy, abandoned to me by men? Surely we do not live
crowded.—My nearest neighbor is more than a mile distant, and

Solitude no house is visible from within half a mile of my own—I have my
   3 horizon bounded by woods all to myself. I have a distant view of
the railroad where it touches the pond on the one hand, and of the
fence which skirts the woodland road on the other. [66v] But for
the most part it is as solitary where I live as on the prairies. It is as
much Asia or Africa as New England. I have as it were, my own
sun & moon and stars, and a little world all to myself. At night
there was never a traveller passed my house, or knocked at my
door, more than if I were the first or last man, unless it were in the
spring when some came occasionally from the village to fish for
pouts in the pond, and they plainly fished much more in the
Walden pond of their own natures and baited their hooks with
darkness, but they soon retreated usually with light baskets

"And left the vale to solitude & me."

and the dark kernel of the night was never prophaned by any human neighborhood. I believe that men are generally still a little
afraid of the dark—though the witches are hung—& christianity
and candles are invented.

   4   Yet I experienced occasionally that the most sweet and tender,
[67r] the most innocent and encouraging society may be found in
every natural object—even for the poor misanthrope and the most
melancholy man. There can be no very black melancholy to him
who lives in the midst of nature, and has his senses still. There was
never yet such a storm but it was Aeolian music to a healthy and
innocent ear. Nothing can rightly compel a simple and brave man
to a vulgar sadness. While I enjoy the friendship of the seasons—I
trust that nothing can make life a burthen to me. The gentle rain
which waters my beans and keeps me in the house to-day, is not
drear and melancholy but good for me too. Though it prevents
my hoeing them it is of far more worth than my hoeing.

   Sometimes when I compare myself with other men it seems as
if I were more favored by the gods than they and beyond any
deserts I am conscious of. As if I had a warrant & surety at their
hands which my fellows have not—[67v] and were especially
guided & guarded.

   I have never felt lonely or in the least oppressed by a sense of

164

solitude but once, and that was a few weeks after I went to the *Solitude*
pond to live—when for an hour I doubted if the near neighbor- *4*
hood of man was not essential to a serene and healthy life. To be
alone was something unpleasant. But I was at the same time conscious of a slight insanity in my mood, and seemed to foresee my
recovery. In the midst of a gentle rain while these thoughts pre-
vailed there suddenly seemed such sweet & beneficent society in
nature—in the very pattering of the drops, and in every sound
and sight around my house, an infinite and unaccountable friendliness all at once like an atmosphere sustaining me, as made the
fancied advantages of human neighborhood insignificant—and
I have never [68r] 85. thought of them since. Every little pine
needle expanded and swelled with sympathy—and befriended
me. I was so distinctly made aware of the presence of something
kindred to me, even in scenes which we are accustomed to call
wild and dreary, and also that the nearest of blood to me and
humanest was not a person nor a villager, that I thought no place
could ever be strange to me.

Yet I think that I love society as much as most, and am apt *Visitors*
enough to fasten myself like a blood-sucker for the time to any *1*
full-blooded man that comes in my way. I am naturally no hermit—but should probably sit out the sturdiest frequenter of the
bar-room, if my business called me that way.

What do we ask?   *Not in text*
Some worthy task;
Never to run
Till that be done,
That never done
[68v] Under the sun.
By might & main
Health and strength gain,
So to give nerve
To our slenderness,
Yet some mighty pain
We would sustain,
So to preserve

165

Our tenderness.
Strength like the rock
To withstand every shock,
Yet not be deceived,
Of suffering bereaved—
Occasion to gain
To shed human tears,
And to entertain
Still demonic fears.
Not once for all
Forever blest,
Still to be cheered
Out of the west,
Not from our heart
To banish all sighs,
Still be encouraged
By the sun-rise—
For earthly pleasures,
Celestial pains—
Heavenly losses,
For earthly gains.
[69r] Must we still eat
The bread we have spurned?
Must we rekindle
The faggots we've burned?

Solitude   I find it healthy to be alone the greatest part of the time. To be
12   in company ever with the best is soon wearisome and dissipating.
I love to be alone. I never found the companion that was so com-
panionable as solitude. We are for the most part more lonely
when we go abroad amongst folks, than when we stay in our
chambers. A man thinking or working is always alone let him be
where he will. The farmer can work alone in the field or the
woods all day hoeing or chopping wood, and not feel lonesome,
because he is employed, but when he comes home at night he cannot sit down in a room alone, at the mercy of his thoughts, but
must be where he can "see the folks," and recreate and remuner-

ate himself for his day's solitude. And hence he wonders how the *Solitude*
student can sit alone in the house all night and most of the day *12*
without [69v] ennui and the blues, but he does not realize that the
student, though in the house, is still at work in *his*[44] field, and
chopping in *his*[45] woods, as the farmer in his, and in his turn seeks
the same recreation & society that he does.

Society is commonly too cheap—We meet at very short inter- *13*
vals, not having had time to acquire any new value for each other.
We meet at meals 3 times a day, and give each other a new taste
of that old musty cheese that we are. We have had to agree on a
certain set of rules—called etiquette and politeness to make this
frequent meeting tolerable—and that we need not come to open
war. We meet at the post office and at the sociable, and about the
fireside every night—We meet incessantly and live thick, and are
in each other's way, and stumble over one another—And I think
that we thus lose some respect for one another. Certainly less fre-
quency would suffice for [70r] 89. all important and hearty communications. Consider the girls in a factory never alone—hardly
in their dreams. It would be better if there were but one inhabitant to a square mile—as where I live. The value of a man is not in
his skin that we should touch him. Solitude is not measured by the *12*
miles of space that intervene between a man and his fellows—The
diligent student in one of the crowded hives of Cambridge College
is as solitary as a dervish in the desert.[46]

I have a great deal of company in my house—especially in the *15*
morning when nobody calls. I will suggest a few comparisons—so
that some one may convey an idea of my situation. I am no more
alone than the loon in the pond that laughs aloud—or than
Walden pond itself. What company has that lonely lake, I pray?

44. Thoreau's italics.

45. Thoreau's italics.

46. The following preliminary draft of several sentences of "Solitude," 14, is on a
scrap of paper pasted to 70r at this point; Thoreau did it at later date: "I have heard
of a man lost in the woods and dying from famine and exhaustion at the foot of a tree
whose loneliness was relieved by the grotesque visions, by which owing to bodily
weakness and a diseased imagination he was surrounded and which he believed to be
relieved [real]. There are those who owing to bodily & mental health & strength are
continually cheered by the like society and never realize that they are alone."

Solitude And yet it has not the blue devils, but the blue angels in it—in the
15 azure tint of its waters. I am no more lonely than the north star.
The sun is alone, except in thick weather when there sometimes
seem to be two, but one is a mock sun. God [70v] is alone, but the
Devil, he is by no means alone, he sees a great deal of company.
The earth is alone—& Heaven is alone—but Hell is not at all, but
when Heaven receives company or goes a visiting. *Cor ne edito*[47]
"eat not the heart," said Pythagoras. You must eat something
else to be sure. I am no more lonesome than a mullein in a pasture—or a bean-leaf, or sorrel, or a single dandelion—or a horse-
fly—or a bumble bee. I am no more lonesome than the mill-brook
—or a weather cock—or the South wind—or an April shower or
a January thaw, or the only spider in a new house.

16   I have occasional visits in the long winter evenings when the
snow falls fast and the wind howls in the wood from an old settler
and original proprietor who is reported to have dug Walden
pond, and stoned it, and fringed it with pine woods, who tells me
stories of old time and of new eternity—and[48] between us we pass
a cheerful evening—with social mirth & pleasant views of things,
even without apples [71r] or cider.—A most wise and humorous
friend whom I love much. Who keeps himself more secret than
ever did Goffe or Whalley, and though he is thought to be dead
none can show where he is buried.

An elderly dame too dwells in my neighborhood, invisible to
most persons, in whose odorous herb garden I love to stroll sometimes, gathering simples, and listening to her fables. For she has a
genius of unequalled fertility and invention, and her memory
runs back further than the mythology, and she can tell me the
original of every fable, and on what fact every one is founded—for
the incidents occurred when she was a little girl.—A ruddy and
lusty old dame who delights in all weathers and seasons—and is
likely to outlive all her children yet.

17   The indescribable innocence & beneficence of nature—of sun
and wind & rain—of summer & winter—such health—such
cheer, they afford forever, and such sympathy have they ever with
our race—that all nature would be affected—and the [71v] sun's

47. Thoreau's italics.   48. MS: "and and."

168

brightness fade—and the winds would sigh humanely—and the *Solitude*
clouds weep rain—and the woods shed their leaves and put on ^17
mourning in mid summer if any man should ever for a just cause
grieve.—Shall I not have intelligence with the earth? Am I not
partly leaves and vegetable mould myself? God is my father &
my friend—men are my brothers—but nature is my mother &
my sister.

What is the pill that will keep us well—serene—contented? *18*
Not my or thy great-grandfather's—but our great grandmother
Nature's universal vegetable botanic medicines—by which she
has kept herself young always and outlived so many old Parrs in
her day—and fed her health with their decaying fatness—For my
panacea—instead of one of those quack phials of a mixture dipped
out of Acheron & the dead sea which come out of those long low
black schooner looking wagons which we sometimes see made
[72r] 93. to carry bottles—let me have a draught of undiluted
morning air.

Morning Air! If men will not drink of this at the fountain head
of the day—why then we must even bottle up some and sell it in
the shops for the benefit of those who have lost their subscription
ticket to morning time in this world. But remember that it will not
keep quite till noonday even in the coolest cellar—but drive out
the stopples long ere that & follow westward the steps of Aurora.

I am no worshipper of Hygeia, who was the daughter of that
old herb doctor Æsculapius, and who is represented on monuments "holding a serpent in one hand and in the other a cup, out
of which the serpent sometimes drank"—but rather of Hebe—
cup-bearer to Jupiter—who was the daughter of Juno & wild
lettuce, & "had the power of restoring gods & men to the vigor of
youth." She was probably the only thoroughly sound-conditioned
healthy & robust young lady that ever walked this globe, and
wherever she came it was spring.

[72v] As for men, they will hardly fail one anywhere. I have *Visitors*
had more of their society since I lived in the woods than at any ^7
other period of my life. I met many men there under more
favorable circumstances than I could anywhere else.

Who should come to my lodge this morning but a true Homeric *8*

Visitors or Paphlagonian man—Alek Therien—he calls himself—a Cana-
  8 dian—a wood-chopper and post maker—who can hole 50 posts in
a day—who made his last supper on a wood-chuck which his dog
caught. He too has heard of Homer and "If it were not for books"
would "not know what to do rainy days"—though perhaps he
has not read one wholly through for many rainy seasons. Some
priest who could pronounce the Greek itself, taught him to read
his verse in the testament at Nicolèt, away by the Trois Riviers
once, and now I must translate to him while he holds the book,
Achilles' reproof of Patroclus for his sad countenance.

[73r] "Why are you in tears Patroclus? like a young girl & &"

> Or have you alone heard some news from Phthia?
> They say that Menoetius lives yet, son of Actor,
> And Peleus lives, son of Æacus, among the Myrmidons,
> Either of whom dead, we should greatly grieve."

He says "that's good." He has a great bundle of white oak bark
under his arm for a sick man, gathered this Sunday morning. "I
suppose there is no harm in going after such a thing today?"

He had heard of Homer. Homer was a great writer, though
what his writing was about under the sun he did not know.

I have since seen Therien many times. A more simple and natural man I never saw. Vice and disease which cast such a sombre
moral hue over the world, had hardly any existence for him. He
left Canada and his father's house a dozen years ago to work in
the states, and earn money to buy a farm with at last, perhaps in
 10 his native country. He interested me because he was so happy—
so solitary—so quiet. [73v] He was a well of good humor & happiness which overflowed at his eyes. His mirth was without alloy. I
 12 heard that a wise man asked him if he didn't want the world to be
changed, and he answered with a chuckle of surprise, in his
Canadian accent—not knowing that the question had ever been
entertained before—"no—he liked it well enough."—It would
suggest many things to a philosopher to have dealings with him.
 11 He had been instructed only in that innocent & ineffectual way
in which the Catholic priests teach the aborigines—In which the
pupil is never educated to the degree of consciousness, but only to

the degree of trust & reverence—and a child is not made a man, *Visitors*
but kept a child. When nature made him she gave him content- *11*
ment for his portion, a strong body and health and propped him,
as it were, on every side with reverence & reliance—that he might
live out his 3 score years and ten a child—He was about 28 *8*
[74r] 97. years old—stout & sluggish, with a strong thick fleshy &
sunburnt neck & dark bushy hair & dull sleepy & quiet blue eye
—breathed hard and smelled of his work. He wore a flat grey
cloth cap—a dingy wool-colored great coat which draped and
concealed his body—& cow-hide boots. He was strong-limbed
and a great consumer of meat, usually carrying his dinner to his
work—a couple of miles past my house—in a tin pail—cold meats
—often cold woodchucks which his dog had caught, and coffee in
a stone bottle which dangled by a string, & sometimes he offered
me a drink. He came along early, crossing my beanfield, though
without any anxiety or haste to get to his work, such as Yankees
exhibit. Frequently he would leave his dinner in the bushes, when
his dog had caught a woodchuck *by the way*, and go back a mile
and a half to dress it, and leave it in the cellar of the [74v] house
where he boarded—often deliberating for half an hour whether
he could not sink it in the pond safely till nightfall—loving to
dwell long upon these themes. He would say as he went by in the
morning, "How thick the pigeons are! If working every day were
not my trade, I could get all the meat I should want by hunt[ing].
—Pigeons—woodchucks—rabbits—partridges, by George, I
could get all I should want for a week in one day."

If others had cultivated their intellectual faculties till they *11*
astonished him—his physical contentment and endurance—like
the cousin to the pine & the rock was equally astonishing to them.
I asked him once if he was not sometimes tired at night after working all day, and he answered with a sincere and serious look—
quite truthful—"Gorrappit I never was tired in my life." It
sounded like the triumph of the physical [75r] man. It suggested
what a rigorous and true training might accomplish for all.

Sometimes I saw him at his own work in the woods felling trees, *10*
and he would greet me with a laugh of irrepressible satisfaction
and a salutation in Canadian French—though he spoke English

Visitors as well—and when I asked him in which he thought now, or if he
  10 spoke aloud to himself which language he used—You know we
sometimes talk to ourselves—"Yer—sometimes" answered he—
He said it was in English. When I approached him he would
suspend his work and with half suppressed mirth lie along the
trunk of a tree he had felled and peeling off the inner pine bark,
roll it up in a ball, and chew it—while he laughed & talked.—
Such an exuberance of animal spirits had he that he would sometimes tumble down and roll on the ground with laughter—at any
thing which [75v] made him think and tickled him. Sometimes
when at leisure he would amuse himself all day in the woods with
a little pocket pistol, firing salutes of powder to himself, at regular
intervals as he travelled—and would occasionally steal up behind
my house and fire a stout charge—& laugh loudly at my surprise.
He loved also to frighten his dog when alone with him in the
woods—by pointing his pistol at him & firing powder only.

  13   His only books were an almanack and an arithmetic—in which
last especially he was quite expert. The former was a sort of universal lexicon to him—which he supposed contained an abstract
of human knowledge—I loved to sound him on all the reforms of
the day—and he rarely failed to look at them in the most simple
& practical light—and as they concerned him. He had never
heard of such things before. He allowed that he might dispense
with many articles of commerce to [76r] 101. advantage. He had
worn the homemade Vermont gray—and that was good—If I
didn't like factories—was it necessary to send abroad for our
drink? Did he ever drink anything beside water which the country afforded? He had soaked hemlock leaves in water and drank it
in Canada, and that was better than water in warm weather.
Could he do without money? And he showed the convenience of
money in such a way as to suggest and coincide with the most
philosophical accounts of the origin of this institution & the very
derivation of the word *pecunia*.[49] If an ox were his property & he
wished to get needles or thread at the store he thought it would be
inconvenient and impossible soon to go on mortgaging some
fraction of the creature each time to that amount.

49. Thoreau's italics.

The First Version of Walden

Speaking of Plato's definition of a man one day, he said that the *Visitors* knee of the cock turned the other way from man's, and that was *13* an important difference. [76v] He was so simply & naturally *11* humble that humility was no distinct quality in him—nor could he conceive of it. Wiser men were demigods to him. He particularly reverenced the writer and the preacher. Their performances were miracles. When I told him that I wrote a good deal he thought for a long time that it was merely the hand writing I meant. I asked him if he ever wished to write his thoughts—He said that he had read and written letters for those who could not —but he never tried to write thoughts—no—he could not—he could not tell what to put first—it would kill him & then there was spelling to be attended to at the same time.

He would exclaim sometimes—"How I love to talk! By George, *13* I could talk all day. You make me think of things I never thought of before."

Sometimes there would come half a dozen men to my house at *Not in text* once—healthy and sturdy working [77r] men, descended from sound bodies of men, and still transmitting arms & legs & bowels from remote generations to posterity. They had a rude wisdom and courtesy which I love. I met them so often in the woods— that they began to look upon me at last as one of their kin. One a handsome younger man a sailor-like—Greek-like man—says to me to-day—"Sir, I like your notions—I think I shall live so myself. Only I should like a wilder country, where there is more game. I have been among the Indians near Apallachicola. I have lived with them. I like your kind of life. Good-day, I wish you success and happiness."

They came in troops on Sundays in clean shirts, with washed hands & faces, and fresh twigs in their hands.

There appeared in some of these men even at a distance, a genuine magnanimity equal to Greek or Roman, of unexplored and uncontaminated descent—The expression of their grimmed & sunburnt features made me think of Epaminondas of Socrates & Cato. [77v] The most famous philosophers & poets seem in some respects infantile beside the easy and successful life of natural men. These faces—homely—hard and scarred like the rocks,

The Making of Walden

Visitors but human & wise—embracing Copt, and Mussulman and all
Not in text tribes & nations. One is a pacha or Sultan—Selim—or Mustapha
or Mahmoud in disguise.

Circumstances and employment may conceal for a season but
they do not essentially alter the finer qualities of our nature. I
observe among these men when I meet them[50] on the road an
ineradicable refinement & delicacy—as old as the sun & moon.—
A fineness which is commonly thought to adorn the drawing
rooms only. There is no more real rudeness in laborers & washer
women—than in gentlemen and ladies. Under some ancient
wrinkled, almost forlorn visage of an Indian chieftain slumbers
all that was ever writ or spoken of man. You can tell a nobleman's
head though he may be shovelling gravel beneath it six rods off
in the midst of a gang [78r] 105. with a bandanna handkerchief
tied about it. Such as are to succeed the worthies of history. Their
humble occupation which allows them to take no airs upon themselves seems their least disadvantage.—Civilization seems to
make bright only the superficial film of the eye. Most men are
wrecked upon their consciousness.

2   I had 3 chairs in my house—1 for solitude—2 for friendship 3—
for society. When visitors came in larger and unexpected numbers
there was but the 3d chair for them all—but they generally econo-
mized the room by standing up. It is astonishing how many great
men and women a small house will contain. I have had 25 or 30
souls and bodies at once under my roof—and yet we often parted
without being aware that we had come very near to one other.
Our houses generally with their huge halls & garretts & cellars,
seem to me extravagantly large for their inhabitants. One would
certainly be somewhat astonished, if when [78v] the herald blew
his summons before the Middle-sex House he should see come
creeping out over the piazza for all inhabitants a ridiculous
mouse.

3   One inconvenience I sometimes experienced in so small a house
—the difficulty of getting to a sufficient distance from my guest
when we began to utter the big thoughts in big words. You want
room for your thoughts to get into sailing trim and run a course or

50. MS: "them them."

174

two before they make their port. The bullet of your thought must
have overcome its lateral and ricochet motion and have fallen
into its last and steady course, before it falls into the ear of the
hearer, else it may plough out through the side of his head. Our
sentences wanted room to unfold and form their columns in the
interval. We need a considerable neutral ground—though it be
disputed territory, for individuals like nations must have suitable
broad and natural boundaries between them.—The [79r] reason
why the Kilkenny cats quarrelled and ate each other all up but
the tails in that hollow sphere, certainly is that there was not room
in that small space for their several spheres to revolve.

We were so near that we couldn't hear and we couldn't speak
low enough to be heard—As when you throw two stones into calm
water, but so near that they break each other's undulations. If we
are very loquacious & loud talkers then we can afford to stand
very near together—cheek by jowl—& shoulder to shoulder. But
if we speak reservedly and thoughtfully we want to be further
apart. But if we would be silent we must commonly be so far apart
that we cannot possibly hear each other's voices in any case.

As the conversation began to assume a loftier and grander tone
we gradually shoved our chairs further apart till they touched the
wall in opposite corners—and then sometimes there was not room
[79v] enough. If you don't want the fire to smoke you mustn't
stand too near it—so as to divert the current of the chimney's
inspiration.

My best room, always ready for company—on whose carpet the *4*
sun rarely fell—for its green blinds were kept always closed, was
the pine wood behind my house. There when distinguished guests
came in summer days I took them—and nature was my domestic
that swept the floor and dusted the furniture, and kept the things
in order.

If one guest came he sometimes partook of my frugal meal, and *5*
it was no interruption to conversation to be stirring a hasty pud-
ding in the meanwhile or watching the rising and maturing of a
loaf of bread in the ashes in the meanwhile. But if 20 came and sat
in my house there was nothing said about dinner—though there
might be bread enough for two—more than if eating [80r] 109.

Visitors were a forsaken habit—but we naturally practiced abstinence.
5 To copy an old joke—we were hungry enough for one but not enough for 20—and this was never felt to be an offence against hospitality, but the most proper and considerate course. The waste and decay of physical life which so often needs repair seemed miraculously retarded—and the vital vigor stood its ground. I could entertain thus a thousand as well as 20, and I am not aware that any ever went away disappointed or hungry from my house—when they found me at home. So easy is it—though many house-keepers doubt it—to establish new and better customs in the place of the old—to quote the lines which one of my visitors inscribed upon a yellow walnut leaf—and which make part of the motto of my house—

> "Arrived there, the little house they fill,
> Ne looke for entertainment, where none was:
> Rest is their feast, and all things at their will:
> The noblest mind the best contentment has."

6 [80v] When Winslow—afterward Governor of the Plymouth colony went with a companion on a visit of ceremony to Massassoit on foot through the woods, and arrived tired and hungry they were well received by the king—but nothing was said about eating that day. When the night arrived to quote their own words "He laid us on the bed with himself & his wife, they at the one end, and we at the other, it being only planks laid a foot from the ground, and a thin mat upon them. Two more of his chief men, for want of room, pressed by and upon us; so that we were worse weary of our lodging than of our journey." At one o'clock the next day Massassoit "brought two fishes that he had shot" about "thrice as big as a bream." "These being boiled there were at least forty looked for a share in them. The most ate of them. This meal only we had in two nights and a day; and had not one of us bought a partridge, we had taken our journey fasting." For fear they should be lightheaded for want of sleep on account of "the [81r] savages' barbarous singing (for they used to sing themselves asleep)" and for want of food, and that they might get home while they had strength to travel—they departed. The fact was—the

Indians had nothing to eat themselves—and they were wiser than   *Visitors*
to think that apologies & ceremony could supply the place of food   *6*
and so said nothing about it—This was a time of fasting with
them. At another time when Winslow visited them—he[51] got as
much to eat as he got little before.

Meanwhile my beans, whose continuous length of row was 7   *Bean-Field*
miles already planted were impatient to be hoed. What was the   *1*
meaning of this so steady and self respecting labor I knew not. I
came to love my rows—my beans—so many more than I want.
Why should I raise them? This had been my curious labor all
summer—why—only heaven knows. To make this portion of the
earth's surface which yielded only blackberries and Johnswort
and cinqfoil—sweet wild fruits and pleasant flowers, produce
[81v] instead this pulse. What shall I learn of beans or beans of
me? I cherish them I hoe them early & late I have an eye to them,
and this is my day's work. It is a fine broad leaf to look upon. My
auxiliaries are the dews and rains to water this dry soil—and
what fertility is in the soil itself, which for the most part is lean and
effete. My enemies are worms, cool days, and most of all woodchucks. They have nibbled for me a quarter of an acre clean. But
what right had I to oust Johnswort and the rest, and break up
their ancient herb garden? But soon the remaining beans will be
too tough for them, and will go on to meet new foes.

24 years ago I was brought from the city to this very pond—   *2*
through this very field—so much further into the world I had but
recently entered. It is one of the most ancient scenes stamped on
the tablets of my memory. That woodland vision for a long time
occupied my dreams. [82r] 113. The country then was the world
—the city only a gate to it. And now tonight my flute has waked
the echoes over this very water. One generation of pines has fallen
and I have cooked my supper with their stumps—and a new
growth of oaks and pines is rising all around the pond to greet
other infants' eyes. Almost the same Johnswort springs from the
same perennial root in this pasture. Even I have at length helped
to clothe that fabulous landscape of my dreams, and the result of

51. The word "he" was written over "they."

Bean-Field my presence and influence is seen in these bean leaves and corn-
2 blades, and potatoe vines.

3   I planted about 2 acres and a half of upland and as it was only
about 15 years since the land was cleared and I myself had got out
2 or 3 cords of stumps, I did not give it any manure, but in the
course of the summer it appeared by the arrowheads which I
turned up in hoeing that an extinct nation had anciently dwelt
here and planted beans ere white men came to cut & clear the
land, and so to some extent had [82v] exhausted the soil for this
very crop. However, as it had lain fallow so long I got a good
crop.

4   Before yet any woodchuck or squirrel had run across the road,
or the sun had got above the shrub oaks, while all the dew was
on—though the farmers said that would never do—I began to
level the ranks of haughty weeds in my beanfield, and throw dust
upon their heads.—Early in the morning I worked barefooted—
dabbling like a plastic artist in the dewy & crumbling sand, but
later in the day the sand blistered my feet.—There the sun lighted
me to hoe beans—pacing slowly backward & forward over that
yellow gravelly upland, between the long green rows 15 rods—the
one end terminating in a shrub-oak copse where I could rest in the
shade, the other in a blackberry field where the green berries
deepened their tints by the time I had made another bout—Removing the weeds—putting fresh soil about the bean stems & encouraging this weed I had sown—making the yellow soil [83r]
express its summer thoughts in bean leaves & blossoms, rather
than in wormwood and piper and millet grass—making the earth
say beans instead of grass—This was my work. As I had little aid
from horses or cattle—or hired men or boys—or improved implements in husbandry, I was much slower and became much more
intimate with my beans than is usual. But labor of the hands—
even when pursued to the verge of drudgery, is never the worst
form of idleness. It has a constant and imperishable moral—to the
scholar it yields a classic result—to the literary it is literary. It is
oftenest honest & honorable.

A very *agricola laboriosus*[52] was I to travellers bound westward

52. Thoreau's italics.

through Lincoln & Wayland to nobody knows where.—They *Bean-Field* sitting at their ease in gigs—with elbows on knees & reins loosely *4* hanging in festoons.—I the homestaying laborious native of the soil—and soon my homestead was out of their sight & thought. It was the only open & cultivated field for some dis- [83v] tance on either side, so they made the most of it—And sometimes the man in the field heard more than was meant for his ear, of travellers' gossip and comment—"Beans so late!—peas so late!"—for I continued to plant when others had begun to hoe—The ministerial husbandman had not suspected it—"Corn—my boy—for fodder —corn for fodder!"—"Does he *live*⁵³ there?" asks the black bonnet of the grey coat. And the hard featured farmer reins up his grateful dobbin—to know what he is doing where he sees no manure in the furrow, and recommends a little chip-dirt or any little waste stuff—or ashes or plaster. But here were two acres & a half of furrows, and only a hoe for cart and two hands to draw it—and chip dirt far away. Fellow travellers as they rattled by compared it aloud to the fields they had passed—so that I came to know how I stood in the agricultural world—This was one field [84r] 117. not in Mr. Coleman's report. And by the way—who estimates the value of the crop which nature yields in the fields unimproved by man. The crop of English hay is carefully weighed, the moisture calculated—the silicates and the potash; but in all dells and pond holes, in the woods & pastures & swamps grows a rich and various crop only ungathered and unimproved by man. Mine was, as it were, the connecting link between wild and cultivated fields—as some states are civilized—and others— half-civilized—and others savage or barbarous—so mine was, though not in a bad sense,—a half-cultivated field—They were beans cheerfully returning to their wild & primitive state, that I cultivated—while my hoe played the *Ranz des Vaches*⁵⁴ for them.

Near at hand upon the topmost spray of a birch, sings the *5* brown-thrasher—or red mavis as some love to call it—all the morning—glad of your society—[84v] that would find out another farmer's field if you were not there. While you are planting

53. Thoreau's italics.
54. Thoreau's italics.

Bean-Field the seed he cries "Drop it—drop it—cover it up—cover it up—
⁵ pull it up—pull-it-up—pull-it-up." But this was not corn, and so
it was safe from such enemies as he. You may wonder what his
rigmarole—his amateur Paganini performances on one string or
on 20 have to do with your planting and yet prefer it to leached
ashes or plaster.

6   As I drew a still fresher soil about my rows with my hoe—I disturbed the ashes of unrecorded nations who in primeval days lived
under these heavens—and their small implements of war and
hunting were brought to the light of this modern day—They lay
mingled with other natural stones some of which bore the marks
of having been burned by the Indian fires, and some had only
been burned by the sun—and also with bits of pottery and glass
brought by the recent cultivators of the soil.

[85r] When my hoe tinkled against the stones in my bean-field
—that music *echoed to the woods & the sky &* was an accompani-
ment to my labor which yielded an instant and immeasurable
crop—*It was no longer beans that I hoed, nor I that hoed beans,* and I
confess that I sometimes remembered with pity my acquaintances
who had gone to the city to attend the oratorios—The night-hawk
circled over head in the sunny afternoons—like a mote in the eye,
or in heaven's eye—falling from time to time with a swoop & a
sound as if the heavens were rent—torn at last to very rags &
tatters—and yet a seamless cope remains. Small imps that fill the
air & lay their eggs on the ground—on bare rocks on the tops of
bare hills, where few have found them. In their flight they were
graceful and slender—like waves & ripples caught up from the
pond—as leaves are raised by the wind—to float in the heavens—
such kindredship is in nature. The hawk is aerial brother of the
wave which he sails over and surveys [85v] those his perfect air
inflated wings answering to the elemental unfledged pinions of the
sea.—When I pause to lean upon my hoe these sights & sounds I
saw and heard anywhere in the row—the inexhaustible entertainment which the country offers.—Sometimes I was attracted by
the passage of wild pigeons from this wood to that, with their
slight tantivy & carrier haste—or from under some rotten stump
my hoe turned up a sluggish portent[ous] outlandish spotted

salamander—a trace of Egypt and the Nile—yet our contem- *Bean-Field* porary—Or when I rested in the shrub-oaks I watched a pair of *6* henhawks circling high in the sky—alternately soaring & descending, approaching & leaving one another—as if they were the imbodiment of some of my own thoughts which soar as high & circle as majestically there.

It was a singular experience—that long acquaintance I culti- *10* vated with [86r] 121. beans *what with planting & hoeing & harvesting and threshing and picking over and selling them.* I was determined to know beans. When they were growing I used to hoe from 5 o'clock till 12—and spent the rest of the day about other affairs. Consider the intimate and curious acquaintance one makes with various kinds of weeds—disturbing their delicate organizations so ruthlessly—and making such invidious distinctions with his hoe— levelling whole ranks of one species, and sedulously cultivating another.—That's Roman wormwood—that's pig-weed—that's sorrel—that's piper-grass—have at him chop him up—turn his roots up-ward to the sun—don't let him have a fibre in the shade —if you do he'll turn himself tother side up and be as green as a leek in 2 days.—A long war, not with cranes, but with weeds— those Trojans who had sun and rain and dews on their side. Daily the beans saw me come to their rescue armed with a hoe, and thin the ranks of their enemies, filling up the trenches with weedy dead. [86v] Many a lusty crest-waving Hector that towered a whole foot above his crowding comrades, fell before my weapon and rolled in the dust.

Those summer days which some of my contemporaries devoted *11* to the fine arts in Boston or in Rome—and others to contemplation in India, and others to trade in London or in New York—I with the other farmers of New England devoted to husbandry.— Not that I wanted beans to eat—for I am by nature a Pythagorean—but perchance—as some must work in fields if only for the sake of tropes & expressions—to serve a parable-maker—one day.

However, it was on the whole a noble amusement—though my labor there had not much to do with the crop that was to be harvested in the fall.

This is the result of my experience in raising beans. Plant the *14*

181

Bean-Field common white bush bean about the first of June in rows 3 feet
14 [87r] by 18 inches apart, being careful to select fresh round &
unmixed seed. First look out for worms & supply vacancies by
planting afresh. Then look out for woodchucks, if it is an exposed
place for they will nibble off the earliest tender leaves almost clean
as they go, and again when the young tendrils make their appearance they have notice of it and will shear them off with both buds
and young pods, sitting erect like a squirrel. But above all harvest
as early as possible, if you would escape frosts and have a fair and
saleable crop. You may save much loss by this means.

15   This further experience also I gained. I said to myself I will not
plant beans and corn with so much industry another summer, but
such seeds, perhaps, if the seed is not lost, as sincerity—truth—
simplicity—faith—innocence—and see if they will not grow in
this soil even with less toil & manurance and sustain me. [87v]
Commonly men will only be brave as their fathers were brave,
but why should not the New Englander try new adventures—&
not lay so much stress on his grain his potatoe and grass crop, and
his orchards! raise other crops than these?—We should in some
degree be cheered and fed if when we met a man we were sure to
see that some of these qualities we so much prize, but which are
for the most part broadcast and floating in the air had taken root
and grown in him. Here comes such a subtle and ineffable quality, for instance, as truth or justice, though the slightest amount of
it, along the road. We should never stand upon ceremony with
sincerity. We should never cheat and insult—and banish one another by our manners—if there were present the kernel of worth
& friendliness—We should not meet thus in haste. Most men I do
not meet at all for they seem not to have time—they are busy
about their beans.

16   [88r] 125. Husbandry was anciently a sacred art but it is pursued with heedlessness and haste by us. Our object is to have large
farms and large crops. Our thoughts on this subject should be as
slow as the pace of oxen. The difference between the ancients and
us may be seen in their different treatment of their fellow laborer
the ox. We are accustomed to say that the ox is more profitable
than the horse, because it not only costs less to keep it, but when it

is past labor we can slaughter it, and it will furnish food for our *Bean-Field*
families—we treat it as a slave rather than as a servant. If other *16*
nations, as the Egyptians, have been idolators in this respect, and
made animals objects of adoration, we have gone to the other and
an equally fatal extreme—for every animal should be approached
with a feeling of reverence.—"According to the early laws of
Greece, the ploughing ox was held sacred, and was entitled when
past service, to range the pastures in freedom [88v] and repose. It
was forbidden, by the decrees of Triptolemus, to put to death this
faithful ally of the labors of the husbandman, who shared the toils
of ploughing & threshing. Whenever therefore an ox was slaugh-
tered, he must first be consecrated or devoted as a sacrifice
(ἱερεῖον), by the sprinkling of the sacrificial barley; this was a
precaution against the barbarous practice of eating raw flesh
(Βουφαγία). A peculiar sacrifice (Διπόλια) at Athens, at which
the slayer of the ox fled, and the guilty axe was thrown into the
sea, on the sentence of the Prytanes, yearly placed before the
people a visible type of the first beginnings of their social institutions."

Ancient writers on agriculture speak of such things as the "dignity of the herd." Varro suggests that the object of the Argonautic
expedition was a ram's fleece—The golden apples of the Hesperides were by the ambiguity of language goats and sheep which
Hercules imported. The stars and constellations [89r] 127. bear
their names. The Ægean sea has its name from the goat—and
famous mountains & straits—as the Bosphorus or ox-passage.
Ovid makes Italy to be from *vitulas*.[55] The fine or tax (mulcta a
mulgendo) anciently paid in kind refers to this. The oldest coins
bore the figures of cattle—Our word pecuniary is from the Latin
pecunia which is from *pecus*[56] or herd—which was the oldest currency or medium of exchange. Celebrated Roman families have
derived their names from the same source. As Porcius Ovinius—
Capritius—Equitius—Taurus—Capra—Vitulus &c.

By avarice and selfishness and a grovelling habit of regarding
the soil as property or the means of acquiring property solely,

55. Thoreau's italics; he first wrote "*vitulis*."
56. Thoreau's italics.

Bean-Field
17 husbandry is degraded with us and the farmer leads the meanest of lives. He knows not nature but as a robber. We are apt to forget that the sun looks on our cultivated fields, & on the prairies and forests without distinction. They reflect and absorb his rays alike. In the light of the [89v] sun the earth is all equally cultivated like a garden and yields every where to an irresistible civilization.— What though I value the seed of these beans & harvest that in the fall of the year,—this broad field which I have looked at so long— looks not to me as the farmer but away from me to influences more genial to it. It matters little after all whether the fields fill the barns of the husbandmen. The true husbandman will cease from anxiety—as the chestnut woods are not concerned whether they bear chestnuts this year or not—and finish his labor with every day relinquishing all claim to the produce of his fields—The landscape is deformed when there is an attempt to appropriate what cannot be appropriated.

Village
1 After sitting still in my house or working in my field in the forenoon, I usually bathed again in the pond swimming across one of its coves for a stint, and shook the dust of labor from my feet & clothes, and [90r] 129. for the afternoon was as free as the bird that has built its nest and reared its brood.

Every day or two—I strolled to the village to hear some of the gossip which is incessantly going on here—either circulating from mouth to mouth, or from newspaper to newspaper—and which taken in homeopathic doses was really as refreshing in its way as the rustle of leaves and the peeping of frogs. As I walked in the woods to see the birds & squirrels—so I walked in the village to see the men and boys—instead of the wind among the pines I heard the carts rattle.

The village seemed to me a great news room, and one side to support it—as at Redding and Company's in State Street—they kept nuts & raisins—salt & meal and other groceries.—Some have such a vast appetite for the former commodity—and such sound digestive organs that they can sit forever in public avenues without stirring and let it simmer and whisper through them like the Etesian winds—or as if inhaling ether—it only producing numbness [90v] and insensibility to pain, without affecting the

consciousness. I hardly ever failed when I rambled thro' the vil- *Village*
lage to see a row of such worthies either sitting on a ladder sun- *1*
ning themselves—with their bodies inclined forward, and their
eyes glancing along the line this way and that from time to time
with a voluptuous expression of satisfaction—or else leaning
against a barn with their hands in their pockets,—like caryatides
as if to prop it up.

They being commonly out of doors, heard whatever was in the
wind. These are the coarsest mills in which all gossip is first rudely
digested or cracked up, before it is emptied into finer and more
delicate hoppers—I could not help observing that the vitals of the
village were the grocery—the bar-room—the post-office—and the
Bank—and as a necessary part of the machinery—they kept a
bell—a big gun—and a fire engine at convenient places.—And
the houses were so arranged as to make [91r] the most of the
world and of mankind in lanes and fronting one another so that
every traveller had to run the gauntlet, and every man woman
and child might get a lick at him. Of course those who were sta-
tioned nearest to the head of the line, where they could most see
and be seen, and have the first slap at him, paid the highest prices
for their places, and the few straggling inhabitants in the outskirts
where long gaps in the line began to occur, where the traveller
could get over walls and turn aside into cow paths, and so escape
—paid a very slight ground or window tax.

I would here observe, in a parenthesis, that it costs me nothing *Economy*
for curtains—for I have no gazers to shut out but the sun & moon *89*
—and I am willing they should look in. The moon will not sour
milk or taint meat of mine—nor will the sun injure my furniture
or fade my carpet—and if he is sometimes too warm a friend—I
find it still better economy to retreat [91v] behind some curtain
which nature has provided than to add a single item to the details
of house keeping.—It is best to avoid the beginnings of evil.—But
to return to the village—Signs were hung out on all sides to allure *Village*
the traveller—some to catch him by the appetite as the tavern & *1*
victualling cellar—some by the fancy as the dry-goods store & the
jewellers—and others by the hair—or the feet—or the skirts as the
barber—the shoemaker—or the tailor. Besides, there was a still

Village
1   more terrible standing invitation to call at every one of these houses—and company expected about these times—For the most part I escaped wonderfully from these dangers either by proceeding at once boldly and without deliberation to the goal as is recommended to those who run the gauntlet—or by keeping my thoughts on high things like Orpheus—who "loudly singing the praises of the gods, to his lyre, drowned the voices [92r] 133. of the Sirens, and kept out of danger."—Sometimes I bolted suddenly & nobody could tell my whereabouts, for I did not stand much about gracefulness, and never hesitated at a fence or a hole in a wall. I was even accustomed to make an irruption into some houses where I was well entertained, and after learning the *kernels* & very last seine-full of news—what had subsided—and the prospects of war and peace & whether the world was likely to hold together much longer—I was let out through the rear avenues, and so escaped to the woods again.

Ponds
1   Sometimes having had a surfeit of human society & gossip—and worn out all my village friends—I rambled still further westward than I habitually dwell—"to fresh woods and pastures new"—into unfrequented parts of the town—to solitary swamps and meadows, and pine woods & oak-thickets and rocky pastures—or while the sun was setting made my supper of huckleberries & blueberries on Fair-Haven hill—and laid up a store for several days.

2   Sometimes, after my hoeing [92v] was done for the day I joined some impatient companion who had been fishing since morning on the pond—as silent and motionless as a duck or a floating leaf—who after practicing various kinds of philosophy—had concluded commonly by the time I arrived that he belonged to the ancient sect of Coenobites.

4   Occasionally after staying in a villager's parlor till the family had all retired—I have returned to the woods, and spent the hours of midnight fishing in a boat on the pond by moonlight—serenaded by owls and the barking of foxes, and hearing from time to time the note of the woodcock or the booming of snipes a mile off circling over the river meadows, or the croak of a bittern close at hand. These private hours were very memorable & valu-

able to me—anchored in 40 feet of water and 20 or 30 rods from *Ponds* the shore—surrounded sometimes by thousands of small perch *4* and shiners—[93r] 135. dimpling the surface with their tails in the moonlight—communicating by a long flaxen line with mysterious vespertinal fishes which had their dwelling 40 feet below, or sometimes dragging 60 feet of line about the pond, as I drifted in the gentle night air—now and then feeling a slight vibration along it —indicative of some life prowling about its extremity—of dull uncertain blundering purpose there, and slow to make up its mind—at length you slowly raise, pulling hand over hand, some horned pout squeaking & squirming to the upper air.—It was very queer—in dark nights, when your thoughts had wandered to vast and cosmogonal themes in other spheres—to feel the *faint* jerk which came to interrupt your dreams and link you to nature again.

It seemed as if I might next cast my line upward into the air— as well as downward into this element which was hardly more dense.—

The main reason and inducement to fish was that it introduced *Higher Laws* me to the night and detained me there. [93v] Fishermen and *1* hunters see nature at an advantage which the philosopher can never enjoy. They go through the fields with freedom and abandonment—not formally, and see nature without looking at her, as members of her family—without etiquette—& in a deshabille.

Flint's or Sandy pond our greatest lake and inland sea, con- *Ponds* taining 190 acres lies about a mile east of me, and a walk through *28* the woods thither by such paths as the Indians used was sometimes my recreation in the summer. It was worth the while if only to feel the wind blow and see the waves run and remember the life of mariners. I went a nutting there in the fall one windy day when the nuts were dropping into the water and were washed ashore; and as I crept along its sedgey shore—the fresh spray blowing in my face I came upon the mouldering wreck of a boat, the sides gone and hardly more than the impression of its flat

[One leaf missing; it undoubtedly contained more of "The Ponds," 28, and a little of 5, and probably some material on the ground nut of "House-Warming," 1. See note 2, p. 101.]

Ponds [94r] midst of pine woods—without any visible inlet or outlet but
5
8 by the clouds and by evaporations. Successive nations have drank
at it and passed away. Perhaps on that spring morning when
Adam & Eve were driven out of Eden Walden pond was already
in existence, and even then breaking up in a gentle spring rain—
accompanied with mist and a southerly wind—and covered with
myriads of ducks and geese that had not heard of the fall.—Even
then it had commenced its periodical rise and fall, and had clari-
fied its waters, and had colored them of the hue they now wear—
and obtained a patent of heaven to be the only Walden pond in
the world,—and distiller of celestial dews—Who knows in how
many unremembered nations' literatures this has been the Casta-
lian fountain—or what nymphs presided over it in the golden age!

7   It is surrounded by a belt of paving stones extending a rod or
two into the water, and then the bottom is pure sand, except in
the deepest parts—or where [94v] it is more than 40 feet deep
where there is usually a little sediment and a bright green weed is
brought up on anchors.

6   It is so pure and clear that the bottom can easily be seen in 25
or 30 feet of water. Once in the winter, many years ago, when I
had been cutting holes through the ice in order to catch pickerel,
as I stepped ashore I heaved my axe back on to the ice—but as if
some evil genius had directed it, it slid 4 or 5 rods directly into one
of the holes—where the water was 20 feet deep. Out of curiosity I
lay down on the ice and looked through the hole, when I saw the
axe a little on one side, standing on its head—with its helve erect
and gently swaying to and fro with the pulse of the pond—and
there it might have stood erect & swaying till in the course of time
the handle rotted off if I had not disturbed it. Is a thing lost when
you know where it is—and how to get it? Making another hole
directly over the axe with an ice chisel which I had—and cutting
down the

[Probably three leaves missing; they undoubtedly contained the rest
of "The Ponds," 6, and probably "Baker Farm," 3 and 4.]

Baker Farm [95r] 147. hoping to get a sight of the well bottom—to complete
5 my survey of the premises—but there, alas, are shallow quick-

sands, and rope broken & bucket irrecoverable—Meanwhile the *Baker Farm* right culinary vessel was selected—water was seemingly distilled *5* and at length, after consultation and long delay, passed out to the thirsty one—not yet suffered to cool—nor yet to settle—such gruel sustains life here I thought—so shutting my eyes and excluding the motes by a skillful undercurrent—I drank to genuine hospitality the heartiest draught I could.—I am not squeamish in such cases where manners are concerned.

My haste to catch pickerel wading in retired meadows in sloughs and 6 bog holes, in forlorn & savage places seemed for an instant trivial to me who had been sent to school & college but as I ran down the hill to the pond—with the rain-bow over my shoulder—and some slight tinkling sounds borne to my ear through the cleansed air—from I know not what quarter *my Genius said—grow wild according to thy nature like these ferns & brakes which endeavor not to become English hay. Let the thunder rumble in thy own tongue—what if it brings ruin to farmers' crops in season that is not its errand to thee. Take shelter under the cloud while they flee to carts & sheds* & I said to myself—Why not live always a rude and frontier life—full of adventures and hard work—learn much—travel much—though [95v] it be only through these woods & fields! There is no other country than this—here is the field and the man.—The daily boundaries of life are expanded & dispersed and I see in what field I stand. Roam far and wide—grasp at life and conquer it. Learn much and live. You are really free—stay till late in the night—be unwise and daring. See many men far & near in their fields & cottages before the sun sets—though as if many more were to be seen—Rest not every night in villages nor in the same place. The noblest life is continuous and unintermitting without pauses or waste. Men come meanly home at night only from the next field or street *8* where their household echoes haunt—and their life pines because it breathes its own breath over again. But we should go beyond our shadow at sunrise, and come home from far—from adventures and perils—from enterprises and discoveries every day.

[One leaf missing here; probably contained "Baker Farm," 9, and perhaps some of "Higher Laws," 1, as well as the beginning of 5.]

Higher Laws [96r] 151. revives from time to time, but always when I have done
5 I feel that it would have been better if I had not fished. I think I
am not mistaken. It is a faint intimation—yet so are the first
streaks of morning. It tempts me continually because it is a means
of becoming acquainted with nature—not only with fishes—but
with night and water—and the scenery—which I should not
otherwise see under the same aspects.—and occasionally, though
3 not so often, because I wish to add fish to my fare for variety—I
actually fish sometimes as naturally—and from the same kind of
1 necessity—as the first fishermen did. I love sometimes to take rank
hold on life, and spend my day more as the animals do. The
novelty and adventure that are in this pursuit recommend it to
3 me. Whatever humanity I may conjure up against it is all factitious, & concerns my philosophy more than my actual feelings—
not that I am less humane than [96v] others—but I do not perceive that these are affected very much. I do not pity the fishes nor
1 the worms. This is habit. But the ramble by the river and meadow
seems to be incomplete, and to want a sufficient aim for itself—
without this purpose. The traveller of the prairie is a hunter—of
the head-waters of the Missouri & Columbia—a trapper. Those
who go to the Falls of St. Mary are fishermen. The traveller who
is only a traveller learns things by the halves, and at 2d hand—
3 and is poor authority.—When *some of* my friends have asked me
anxiously about their boys—whether they should let them hunt
or not—I have answered yes—remembering that it was the best
5 part of my education. There is unquestionably this instinct in me
which belongs to the lower order of creation. Yet with every year
I am less a fisherman, though without more humanity. When I
have caught my fish & cooked them, I have gained nothing by it,
but perhaps lost

[One leaf missing; probably contained material of "Higher Laws,"
but there is no evidence as to what.]

7 [97r] 155. If I listen to the faintest but constant suggestions of my
genius I see not to what extremes or insanity it would lead me.—
And yet that way as I grow more resolute and faithful my road
lies. The faintest assured objection which one healthy man feels

will at length prevail over the arguments & customs of mankind. *Higher Laws*
—No man ever followed his genius till it misled him. Though the *7*
result were bodily weakness, yet no man perhaps can say that the
consequences were to be regretted—for these were a life in conformity to higher principles.—If the day and the night are such
that you greet them with joy—and life emits a fragrance like
flowers and sweet scented herbs—more elastic—more immortal—
more starry—that is your success. All nature is your congratula-
tion—and you have cause momentarily to bless yourself. The
greatest gains and values are furthest from being appreciated.
We can easily come to doubt if they [97v] exist. We soon forget
them. They are the highest reality. The facts most astounding &
most real are never communicated by man to man. The true
harvest of my daily life is somewhat as intangible and indescribable as the tints of morning or evening. It is a little star-dust
caught. It is a segment of the rainbow I have clutched.

Generally I was the friend and defender of such of the brute *Brute*
creation as were my neighbors. Walden was formerly a place of *Neighbors*
eagles—and the woods are still extensive & various. I amused my- *Not in text*
self with watching what life still remains—my only companions.

While I was building my house a pair of robins were forward to *Compare*
take advantage of this protection against birds of prey and built *10*
their nest in one day in a pitch pine which I had left growing
against the rear within 3 feet of my ham- [98r] 157. mer and
though the scraps of shingles were falling all over the tree—and
there they dwelt, till at length some boys destroyed the eggs.

Sometimes a phoebe came and looked in at my door or window *Spring*
to see if my house was enough like a cave for her—sustaining her- *25*
self on humming wings with her talons clenched as if she held by
the air, while she surveyed the premises—and frequently she
flitted through and out at the opposite window.

A long-eared-red-bellied field mouse had her nest underneath *Brute*
my house, and before I had laid the second floor, and swept out *Neighbors*
the shavings, would come out to pick up the crumbs at my feet *9*
when I took my lunch. It had probably never seen a man before,
and soon became quite familiar. It would come out regularly at
lunch time, and run over my shoes and up my clothing, and my

191

Brute legs inside clinging to the flesh. It would run readily up the sides
Neighbors of the room by short impulses like a squirrel—which it resembled
9 considerably in its motions. At length as I leaned [98v] my elbow
on the bench one day, it ran up my clothes, and along my sleeve,
and round and round the paper which held my dinner while I
kept it close dodging and playing at bo-peep with it, and when at
last I held still a piece of cheese between my thumb and finger, it
came and nibbled it, sitting in my hand, and then cleaned its face
and paws like a fly, and walked away.

Winter There were scores of pitch pines in my field from 1 to three
Animals inches in diameter, which had been gnawed by the mice the pre-
13 vious winter. A Norwegian winter it was for them—for the snow
lay long & deep, and they had to mix a large proportion of pine
[bark] meal with their other diet. These trees were alive and apparently flourishing at mid-summer, and had many of them
grown a foot—though completely girdled—and sometimes laid
bare for the space of a foot—but now after the lapse of another
winter I perceive that such are already without exception dead.
For this

[One leaf missing; certainly contained some of "Brute Neighbors,"
11, and possibly some of 10, on the partridge.]

Brute [99r] 161. cled round and round me—nearer and nearer, till with-
Neighbors in 4 or 5 feet, pretending broken wings & legs, to attract my atten-
11 tion—and get off her young—who had already taken up their
march with faint peep single file through the swamp as she directed. I frequently heard the young afterward, when I could not
see the parent.

So much lives free, though secret and skulking in the woods.

Here too the pigeons sat over the spring—or fluttered from
bough to bough of the white pine over my head in the heat of the
day.

There is always a wild and yet a wilder life somewhere sustaining itself at any moment than we allow for—which corresponds to
the rareness of some of our thoughts.

I have formerly seen the racoon in the woods behind my house
and probably still hear their whinnering at night.

The First Version of Walden

In the fall the loon came as usual to moult and bathe himself in *Brute*
the pond, making the woods ring with his wild laughter [99v] *Neighbors*
before I had risen—at rumor of whose arrival all Concord sports- *16*
men are on the alert, in gigs & on foot—two by two—and three by
three—with patent rifles & patches and conical balls—and spy-
glass or pin-hole on barrell. They come rustling through the
woods—like October leaves—at least 10 to one seeming already to
hear the loon laugh. Some station themselves on this side of the
pond—some on that—for the poor loon cannot be omnipresent, if
he dive here—he must come up there. But now the kind October
wind rises, rustling the leaves and ruffling the surface [of the
water] so that no loon can be seen or heard though our sportsmen
sweep the pond with spy glasses, and make the woods ring with
their discharges. The waves generously rise and dash angrily taking sides with all water-fowl.—But no thanks to the rising wind
this time—for the dweller by the pond heard when the loon went
off in that morning rain without loud long hearty

[Five leaves missing; these leaves and the one leaf missing between
leaves 102 and 103 probably contained material for "House-Warming,"
18, and "Winter Animals," 7, 9, and 10. See p. 98.]

[100r] 173. with the most harsh and tremendous noise I ever *Winter*
heard from any inhabitant of the wood, responded at regular in- *Animals*
tervals to the goose, as if determined to disgrace and expose this *2*
intruder from Hudson's bay, by exhibiting a greater compass and
volume of voice in a native, & boo-hoo him out of Concord horizon. It was the most thrilling concert I ever heard—What do you
mean by alarming the citadel at this time of night—consecrated
to me—Do you think I am ever caught napping at such an hour
as this, and that I have not got lungs and a larynx as well as yourself? boo hoo! boo hoo! boo-hoo!

   I hardly ever opened my door in a winter or even in a summer
evening without hearing the note of this owl—though never so
near at hand and loud before.

   The booming of the ice in the pond—my great bed-fellow in *3*
that part of Concord—as if it were restless in its bed, and would
[100v] fain turn over—It was hypsy, and nervous and did not

Winter sleep well—and the cracking of the ground by the frost—these
Animals were other memorable sounds in a winter night.

3
4
    Sometimes in clear nights I heard the foxes, as they ranged over
the snow crust in search of a partridge or other game—barking
raggedly and demonically—like forest dogs—as [if] laboring with
some anxiety—struggling to be dogs outright and run freely in the
streets. They seemed to me like imperfect & rudimental men—
burrowing men—still standing on their defence—awaiting their
transformation. Sometimes one came near to my window at night
—attracted by the light, and barked a vulpine curse at me—and
then retreated.

5   Usually the red squirrel waked me in the dawn coursing over
the roof and up and down the sides of my house, by fits & starts,
as if sent out of the woods on purpose to arouse me. During [101r]
the winter, I threw out some sweet corn which had never got ripe
upon the snow crust by my door, and was amused by watching
the motions of the various animals that were baited by it. In the
twilight and the night the rabbits came regularly and made a
hearty meal. By day-light & in fact all day long the red squirrels
came and went, and afforded me much entertainment by their
manoeuvres. One would approach at first warily through the
shrub oaks running over the snow by fits and starts like a leaf
blown by the wind—now a few paces this way with wonderful
speed and waste of energy, making inconceiva[ble] haste with his
trotters, as if it were for a wager—never getting on more than half
a rod at a time and then suddenly pausing with a ludicrous expression—and a gratuitous sommerset—as if all the eyes in the
universe were fixed upon him—wasting more time in delay &
circumspection—than would have sufficed [101v] to walk the
whole distance.—I never saw one walk.—And then suddenly, before you could say Jack Robinson it would be in the tip top of a
young pitch pine—screwing up its clock—and chiding all imaginary spectators—and soliloquizing & talking to the universe
and itself—for no reason that I could ever detect, or itself was
aware of—I suspect. At length it reached the corn—and selecting
a suitable ear, would frisk about in the same uncertain trigono-
metrical way to the topmost stick in my wood-pile, before my

window, looking me in the face—and there sit for hours nibbling *Winter*
at first voraciously ear after ear and throwing the half naked cobs *Animals*
about wastefully—till at length it grew dainty and played with its *5*
food—tasting only the inside of the kernel—and the ear which
was held balanced over the stick by one paw slipped from its careless grasp, and fell to the ground—when it would [102r] 177. look
over at it uncertain—as if suspecting that it had life—with a mind
not made up, whether to get it again, or a new one or be off. And
so the little impudent fellow would waste many an ear in a forenoon—till at last seizing some longer & plumper one—considerably bigger than itself—and skilfully balancing it—it would set
out with it to the woods—like a tiger with a buffaloe—by the
same zigzag course and with frequent pauses.—He scratched
along with it as if it were too heavy for him & falling all the while
—making its fall a diagonal between a perpendicular and hori-
zontal—being determined to put it through at any rate. A singularly frivolous and whimsical fellow. And so he would get off with
it to where he lived and carry it to the top of a pine tree 40 or 50
rods distant—and I afterwards noticed the cobs strewn about the
woods in various directions.

All the emotions and the life of the [102v] squirrel imply spectators—They grew at last to be quite familiar and sometimes
stepped upon my shoe when that was the nearest way. Sometimes
they got under my house two at a time—directly under my feet as *Spring*
I sat writing—and kept up the queerest chuckling & chirruping— *12*
and vocal pirouetting and gurgling sounds that ever were heard—
and when I stamped they only chirruped the louder—as if past
all fear and respect in their mad prank—and defying all humanity
to stop them.—No you don't—Chickaree! They were wholly deaf
to my arguments—or failed to perceive their force—and fell into a
strain of invective that was irresistible.

At length also the jays arrive—whose discordant scream had *Winter*
been [heard] long before, as they were warily making their ap- *Animals*
proaches—a quarter of a mile off—and in a stealthy sneaking and *6*
cowardly manner—they drew near flitting from tree to tree—and
picked up the kernels which

[One leaf missing; see note between 99v and 100r.]

Winter [103r] I opened my door in the evening off they would go with a
Animals squeak and a bounce.—They only excited my pity near at hand.
14 One evening one sat by [my] door three paces from me, at first
trembling with fear, yet unwilling to move.—A poor wee thing—
lean and bony—with ragged ears and sharp nose—scant tail &
slender paws. It looked as if nature no longer contained the breed
of nobler bloods, but the earth stood on its last legs. Its large eyes
looked young & unhealthy—almost dropsical.—I took two steps
—and lo! he scud away with an elastic spring over the snow
crust—straightening its body and its limbs into graceful length,
and soon put the forest between me and itself—The wild free
venison—asserting his vigor and the dignity of nature—not without reason was his slenderness. Such then was his nature.

15   What is a country without rabbits and partridges? They are the
most natural and simple [103v] animal products.—Ancient &
venerable families known to antiquity as to modern times—of the
very hue and substance of nature—nearest allied to leaves and to
the ground—and especially to one another—it is either winged or
it is legged. It is hardly as if you had seen a wild creature when a
rabbit or a partridge burst away—but only a natural one—as
much to be expected as rustling leaves.

[Thoreau canceled the first six or seven lines of "The Pond in Winter," 16, which at first followed here, when he decided to have material
of "Former Inhabitants" come next; he probably canceled some more
of "The Pond in Winter," 16, in the first of the three leaves that are
missing at this point. Most of the material on these leaves probably consisted of material for the early paragraphs of "Former Inhabitants."]

Former [104r] 189. men with earthen ware—and left descendents to suc-
Inhabitants ceed him. I was pleased when in mid-summer—a man who was
10 carrying a load of pottery to market—stopped his horse against
my field and inquired concerning Wyman—he said that he long
ago bought a potter's wheel of him—and he wished to know what
had become of him.

I had heard read[57] of the potter's clay and wheel in scripture,
but I thought that latterly such as we used had either come down

57. The word "read" was canceled later.

unbroken from those days—or that they grew on trees like gourds
somewhere.

Now only a dent in the earth marks the site of most of these dwellings—with buried wall stones—and strawberries raspberries & thimbleberries growing in the sunny sward there—some pitchy pine or gnarled oak in the chimney nook—and the sweet scented black birch waves where the door stone was—Sometimes the well dent is visible, where once a spring oozed—now dry and tearless grass—or *it is* covered deep not to be discovered till some late [104v] day, with a flat stone under the sod, when the last of the race departed.

These dents—like deserted fox-burrows—old holes—are all that is left where once was the stir and bustle of human life—and man's destiny was being consummated—& fate, free-will, foreknowledge absolute—in some dialect or other were all in turns discussed.—"Cato and Brister—as tradition says—pulled wool."

Still grows the vivacious lilack a generation after the door and 13 lintel and the sill are gone—unfolding still its early sweet-scented blossom in the spring—to be plucked by the musing traveller—planted and tended once by children's hands—in front-yard plot —now standing by wall-sides in retired pastures—and giving place to new-rising forests.—The last of that stirp—sole survivor of that family. Little did the dusky children think that the little slip with its two eyes only which they stuck in the ground in the shadow of the house—and daily watered—would root itself [105r] so, and outlive them, and house itself in the rear that shaded it—and grown man's garden and orchard, and tell their story to the lone wanderer a half century after they were dead—blossoming as fair, smelling as sweet, as in that first spring. I mark its still tender—civil—cheerful lilack colors.

But this small village—germ of something more why did it fail 14 —while Concord grows apace? Were there no natural advantages —no water privileges—forsooth? Aye—only the deep Walden pond and cool Brister's spring—privilege to drink long & healthy draughts at these—all unimproved by these men, but to dilute their glass. They were universally a thirsty race. Might not the basket—stable-broom mat-making—corn parching—linen-spin-

Former ning—& pottery business have thrived here—making the wilder-
Inhabitants ness to bloom—and a numerous posterity have inherited the land
14 of their ancestors? The sterile soil would at least have been proof
against a lowland degeneracy. Again, [105v] perhaps, Nature will
try, with me for a first settler—and my house raised 2 springs ago
15 to be the oldest in the hamlet.—And with such thoughts as these I
lulled myself asleep.

Pond in Early in the morning while all things are crisp with frost, come
Winter men with fishing reels, and slender lunch—men of unquestionable
3 faith,—and let down their fine lines through the snowy field to
take pickerel and perch—Who pursue their trade with as much
self-respect as any mechanic or farmer does his—wisely taught by
their instinct to follow other fashions and trust other authorities
than their townsmen. Wild men who frequent the river meadows
and solitary ponds in the horizon—connecting links between
towns—who in their goings & comings stitch towns together in
parts where they would be ripped and with the hunter race pre-
vent wild animals from multiplying.—Who sit and eat their
luncheon in stout fear-noughts on the dry oak-leaves on the shore
of the pond—as wise in natural lore—as the citizen is in artificial.

[Four leaves apparently missing; a good deal of the material may
have been devoted to the freezing, melting, and qualities of Walden and
other waters. See p. 99.]

Spring [106r] 201. it was 36° or 3 degrees higher than Walden. In the
1 middle $32\frac{1}{2}$ degrees. This difference of $3\frac{1}{2}$ degrees between the
temperature of the deep water and the shallow in Flint's pond—
and the fact that a great proportion of it is comparatively shallow
—show why it should break up so much sooner than Walden.

The temperature of the river the same day was $32\frac{1}{2}$ the same
with the middle of Flint's pond—and nearly the same with that of
snow just melted and running in a sluice which[58] is 32 or freezing
point. The temperature of Martwell Bigelow's well—which was
neither the warmest nor the coldest that was tried—was 43—that
Ponds of the boiling spring 45 or the warmest of any, but it is perhaps
13 the coldest in summer when *shallow &* stagnant snow and surface
water is not mixed with it.

58. MS: "which which."

The First Version of Walden

As I was desirous of recovering the long lost bottom of Walden *Pond in* pond, before the ice broke up last winter,[59] I surveyed it carefully *Winter* with compass and chain, and sounding line, and found it to con- *6* tain a little over $61\frac{1}{2}$ acres, and [106v] to be 102 feet deep in the middle. As I sounded through the ice I could determine the shape *8* of the bottom with greater accuracy than is possible in harbors which do not freeze over—and was astonished at its general regularity—In the *deepest part*[60] it was more level than any field which is exposed to the sun and wind and the plow. In one instance on a line arbitrarily chosen it did not vary more than one foot in 30 rods—and generally near the middle I could calculate the variation for each 100 feet before hand within a few inches. Some are accustomed to speak of deep and dangerous holes in running streams and ponds—but these are contrary to the law of nature, the tendency of water being to level all inequalities unless there are rocks in the way.

Indeed the regularity of the bottom and its conformity to the shores and the range of the neighboring hills, was so perfect that a distant promontory betrayed itself by the soundings even in the middle, and its direction was determined by observing the opposite shore. Cape

[Three leaves missing; they probably contained some of the material of paragraphs 9 through 15, and certainly the beginning of 16.]

[107r] 209. house of fishes, and carts off their very element and air, *16* held fast with chains and stakes like corded wood all through the favoring winter air, to wintry cellars to underlie the summer there. It looks blue as amethyst or solidified azure afar off as it is drawn through the streets. They are a merry race, these ice cutters full of jest & sport—and when I went among them they were wont to invite me to saw pit-fashion with them—I standing underneath.

This winter,[61] as you all know, there came a hundred men of *17* Hyperborean extraction swoop down on to our pond one morning with a shriek from the engine—with many carloads of ungainly

59. Later changed to "early in 1846."
60. The word "middle" was canceled.
61. Later changed to "In the winter of 46 & 7."

Pond in looking farming tools—sleds plows—drill-barrows—turf-knives—
Winter spades—saws—rakes—and each [man] was armed with a double-
17 pointed pike staff—such as are not described in the N. E. Farmer
or the Cultivator.

At first I did not know [107v] whether they had come to sow a
crop of winter rye, or some other kind of grain recently introduced
from Iceland. As I saw no manure I judged that they meant to
skim the land—thinking the soil was deep and had lain fallow
long enough—as I had done with my field the year before. They
said that a gentleman farmer, who was behind the scenes, wanted
to double his money—which as I understood amounted to half a
million already—but in order to cover each one of his dollars
with another, he took off the only coat and the skin itself of Walden pond in the midst of a hard winter.—They went to work at
once plowing, harrowing, rolling, furrowing, in admirable order,
as if they were bent on making this a model farm but when I was
looking sharp to see what kind of seed they dropt into the furrow
—a gang of fellows by my side suddenly began to hook up the
virgin mould itself—with a peculiar jerk—clean down to the
sand—or rather

[One leaf missing; undoubtedly contained material for 17 and 18.]

18 [108r] 213. in the almanack—his shanty. In a good day they told
me they could get out a thousand tons which was the yield of
about one acre.

The ice was put to many novel uses. The horses ate their oats
out of cakes of ice hollowed out like a bucket.

19 Ice is a curious subject for our contemplation. They have some
in the houses at Fresh Pond 5 years old. Why is that a bucket of
water soon becomes putrified, but frozen it remains sweet forever?
One suggests that this is the difference between the affections and
the intellect.

Spring They have not been able to break up our pond any earlier than
1 usual this year as they expected to—for she has got a thick new
garment to replace the old.
Pond in
Winter From my window for 16 days I saw a hundred men at work,
20 like busy husbandmen, with teams and horses, and apparently all

the implements of farming—such a picture as we see on the first *Pond in*
page of the almanack—and when I looked out I thought of the *Winter*
fable of [108v] the lark and the reapers & the parable of the ²⁰
sower and such like things—And now they are all gone, and in 16
days more perchance I shall look from the same window on the
pure sky-blue Walden water there, reflecting the clouds and the
trees, and sending up its evaporations in solitude—and no traces
will appear that a man has ever stood there.—Or I shall see perchance a solitary fisher in his boat—like a floating leaf—pursuing
the contemplative man's recreation, and beholding his form reflected in the waves where lately a hundred men securely labored
—or I shall hear a solitary loon laugh as he dives and plumes
himself there.

Thus it appears that the sweltering inhabitants of Charleston 21
and New Orleans & Havanna of Madras and Bombay and Cal-
cutta—drink at my well.

In the morning I bathe my intellect in the stupendous & cosmogonal philosophy of the Bhagvat-Geeta—since whose composition years of the gods have elapsed—and in comparison with
which this [109r] modern world and its literature seem puny and
trivial—and I doubt if these things are not to be referred to another state of existence than this of ours—so remote are that re-
ligion & sublimity from our conceptions.—I lay down the book
and go to my well for water, and lo! there I meet the servant of
the Brahmen priest of Brahma & Veeshnoo & Indra, who still sit
in his temple on the Ganges reading the Vedas—the descendant
of the religious devotee who once dwelt at the roots of trees with
his crust and his water jug.

I meet his servant come to draw water for his master, and our
buckets grate together in the same well.

The pure Walden water is mingled with the sacred water of the
Ganges. With favoring winds it is wafted past the site of the
fabulous [109v]⁶² [110r] 217. islands of Atlantis and the islands of

62. It appears that 109v was originally blank. Later, Thoreau copied the last
lines of "The Pond in Winter," 21, that are on 110r on the bottom of 109r and top of
109v. This change clearly marked the separation between this chapter and "Spring."
Thoreau probably made the change when he was adding to the beginning of
"Spring" and dividing his book into chapters.

Pond in the Hesperides. It makes the periplus of Hanno—and floating by
Winter Ternate and Tidore and the mouth of the Persian Gulf, it melts in
21 the tropic gales of the Indian seas, and is landed in ports of which
Alexander heard only the names.

Spring The ice in the pond at length begins to be honey-combed, and
3 I can set my heel in it as I walk.[63] Fogs and rains & warmer suns
are gradually melting the snows. The days have grown sensibly
longer and we see how we shall get through the winter without
adding to our woodpile—for large fires are now no longer necessary—and I am on the alert for the first signs of spring—if I can
hear the striped squirrels bark—or the chance note of some
migratory bird.

On the 13th of March after I had heard the song sparrow and
the black-bird the ice was still a foot thick on the pond. As the
weather grew warmer, it [110v] was not sensibly worn away by
the water, nor broken up & floated off as in rivers, but became
porous & honey-combed and *saturated with*[64] water—so that you
could put your foot through it when 7 or 8 inches thick—though it
was melted for half a rood, around the shore but by tomorrow [?]
evening—after a warm rain followed by fog it would have wholly
disappeared—all gone off with the fog—Last year I went across
the middle 5 days before it had disappeared entirely. In 1845
House- Walden broke up on the 1st of April in 1846 on the 25th [of][65]
Warming March—it froze entirely over the former year on the 22nd of
12 Dec.—last year on the 16 of December—in both years a week or
two later than Flint's pond and the river probably on account of
Spring its greater depth. The sun warms shallow water through ice a
1 foot thick—as you may make a burning glass with a piece of ice
and kindle a fire with it from the sun. The ice in the shallowest

[One leaf missing; it probably contained more of "Spring," 1, and the
first part of 4.]

4 [111r] river—and he dropped down without obstruction, from
Sudbury, where he lived, to Fair Haven pond, which he found,
unexpectedly, was covered with a firm field of ice. It was a very

63. Thoreau first wrote "began," "could set," and "walked"; exactly when he
changed them to the present tense is uncertain.
64. The words "imbibed more" were canceled.   65. MS had ditto mark.

warm spring day, and he was astonished to see such a body of ice *Spring* remaining. Not seeing any ducks he hid his boat on the backside *4* of an island in the pond, and then concealed himself in the bushes on the south side to await them. The ice was melted out 3 or 4 rods from the shore, and there was a smooth and warm sheet of water, with a muddy bottom such as the ducks love within, and he thought it likely that some would be along pretty soon. After he had lain still there about an hour he suddenly heard a low[66] and seemingly very distant sound, but singularly grand and impressive, and unlike anything he had ever heard before, gradually swelling and increasing as if it would have a universal and memorable ending—a sullen rush and roar, which seemed to him, all at once, like the sound [111v] of a vast body of fowl coming in to settle there—and seizing his gun he started up with excitement and found that the whole body of the ice had started while he lay there, and drifted in to the shore, and the sound he had heard was made by its edge grating on the shore and at first gently nibbling and crumbling off—and at length heaving up and scattering its wrecks along the island to a considerable height before it became still and silent again.

But we must not let the winter go so easily. When the ground is *11* completely bare of snow and a few warm days have dried its surface, it is pleasant to compare the faint tender signs of the infant year just peeping forth, with the stately beauty of the withered vegetation which has withstood the winter—the various thistles and other strong stemmed plants which have not even yet sown their seeds—and graceful reeds and rushes whose winter is more gay and stately than their [112r] 223. summer—as if not till then was their beauty ripe.—Wild oats perchance and life-everlasting whose autumn has now arrived—those unexhausted granaries of winter, whose seeds entertain the earliest birds.

I never tire of admiring their arching drooping and sheaflike tops. They bring back the summer to our winter memories—and are among the forms which art loves to perpetuate. They are an antique style—older than Greek or Egyptian—a lighter and more graceful Ionic—a richer Corinthian—a simpler Doric—a more

66. MS originally read "slow."

Spring various Composite. The beauty of the drooping and sheaf-like
11 head of the rush all men have admired in all ages—and it must
have some such near and unaccountable relation to human life,
as astronomy has to those laws and figures which first existed in
the mind of man.

All the phenomena of winter are suggestive of an inexpressible
tenderness, and fragile delicacy—We are accustomed to hear this
king almost tyrant described as rude and boisterous—but with the
gentleness of a lover he adorns the tresses of summer.

5 [112v] At length the sun's rays have attained the right angle,
and warm winds blow up mist and rain and melt the snow banks
—and the sun dispersing the mist smiles on a chequered landscape
of russet and white—smoking with incense—through which the
traveller picks his way from islet to islet cheered by the music of a
myriad rills and rivulets whose veins are filled with the blood of
Compare winter which they are bearing off.—As I go back and forth over
6 the rail-road through the deep cut I have seen where the clayey
sand *like lava* had flowed down when it thawed and as it streamed
it assumed the forms of vegetation, of vines and stout pulpy leaves
—unaccountably interesting and beautiful—which methinks I
have seen imitated somewhere in bronze—as if its course were so
to speak a diagonal between fluids & solids—and it were hesitat-
ing whether to stream in to a river, or into vegetation—for vegetation too is such a stream as a river, only of slower current.

Spring [113r] The first sparrow of spring—the year beginning with
13 younger hope than ever—the faint silvery warblings heard over
the bare and moist fields from the song-sparrow—the blue-bird—
and the red-wing as if the last flakes of winter tinkled as they fell—
What at such a time are histories—chronologies—traditions, and
all written revelations?

The brooks sing carols and glees to the spring—the marsh-hawk
—sailing low over the meadow—is already seeking the first slimy
life that awakes. The sough of melting snow is heard in all dells
and on all hillsides—and by the sunny river banks—and the ice
dissolves apace in all ponds. The earth sends forth an inward heat
to greet the returning sun—not yellow like the sun—but green is
the color of its flame.

The First Version of Walden

The grass flames up on all hillsides like a spring fire. Grass is the *Spring* symbol of perpetual youth its blade like a long green ribbon— *13* longer than was ever woven in the factories of men—streaming from the sod into the summer—checked [113v] indeed by the frost, but anon pushing on again—lifting its last year's spear of withered hay with the fresh life below.—It is as steady a growth as the rill which oozes out of the ground, and indeed is almost identical with that—for in the fertile and growing days of June, when the rills are dry—the grass blades are their channels—and from year to year the herds drink at this green stream—and the mower cuts from this outwelling supply—what their several needs require.—So our human life but dies down to the surface of nature —but puts forth its green blade still to eternity.

The change from storm & winter to fair and serene weather, *15* from dark and sluggish hours to bright and elastic ones, is a memorable crisis which all things proclaim. It is instantaneous—at last. Suddenly an influx of light fills the house—though the clouds of winter still over hang it *and the eaves are dripping with sleety rain.* I look out on the pond which was [114r] 227. cold grey ice but yesterday—and already the signs of fair weather were there and it was become a calm & smooth lake, full of promise as a summer evening—seeming to have some intelligence with distant horizons, as if a summer evening sky was already reflected in its bosom, though none was visible over head—I heard a robin in the distance the first I had heard for many a thousand years, methinks, whose sound has the same meaning it was wont to have. But where does the minstrel really perch, who could ever find the twig he sits on? This at least is not the *turdus migratorius.*[67] The pitch pines about my house, which had so long drooped—suddenly looked brighter, more green & more alive and erect, as if entirely cleansed by the rain—and fitted once more to express immortal beauty, and make a part of this world which is called κοσμος. I knew that it would not rain any more.

As it grew darker, I was startled by the clank of geese fly[ing] low over the woods—like weary travellers late getting in from southern lakes, and indulging at last in unre- [114v] strained com-

67. Thoreau's italics.

The Making of Walden

Spring plaint and mutual consolations. As I stood at the door I could
₁₅ hear the rush of their wings as driving toward my house, they sud-
denly spied my light, and with hushed clamor wheeled and
₁₆ settled in the pond. In the morning I watched them from my
door through the mist sailing in the middle of the pond, 50 rods
off—so large and tumultuous that the pond seemed like an artificial pond for their amusement. But when I stood on the shore—
they at once rose up with a flapping of wings, at the signal of their
commander, and when they had got into rank circled about over
my head—29 of them, and then steered straight to Canada with a
regular clank clank from the commodore at intervals,—trusting
to break their fast in muddier pools.

A compact flock of ducks also rose up at the same time and
took the route to the north in the wake of their noisier cousins.

[One leaf missing; it probably contained paragraph 17 and part of
19; 18, part of 19, 20, and 21 were added in later versions.]

₂₂ [115r] 231. On the 29th of April, as I was fishing from the
banks of the river near the Nine-Acre-Corner bridge, standing on
the quaking grass and willow roots, where the muskrats burrow, I
heard a singular rattling or perhaps shuttle-like sound, not musi-
cal but almost like the rattling sticks which boys play with their
fingers, when, looking up I observed a very slight & graceful
hawk, like a night-hawk, alternately soaring like a ripple and
tumbling a rod or two over and over, and showing the under side
of its wings which gleamed like a satin ribbon in the sun, and was
of the pearly color of the inside of a shell. This sight reminded me
of falconry and what nobleness and poetry is associated with that
sport. The Merlin it seemed to me it might be named. It was the
most etherial flight I had ever witnessed. It did not simply flutter
like a butterfly, nor soar like the noblest hawks, but it sported
with [115v] proud reliance in the fields of air; mounting again and
again with its strange chuckle it repeated its free and beautiful
fall, turning over and over like a kite. It was most high and lofty
tumbling, as if it had never set its foot on terra-firma. It seemed to
have no companion in the universe,—sporting there alone,—and
to need none, but the morning and the ether with which it

played. It seemed not lonely, but made all the earth lonely be- *Spring*
neath it, though it had no mate in the world. Where was the 22
parent that hatched it, its kindred, and its father in the heavens?
The tenant of the air, it seemed related to the earth but by an egg
hatched some time in the crevice of a crag,—or was its native nest
made in the angle of a cloud, woven of the rain-bow's trimmings
and the sunset sky, and lined with some soft haze caught up from
earth? Its eyrie was perchance some cliffy cloud.

Beside this I got a rare [116r] mess of golden and silver, and 23
bright cupreous fishes—which looked like a string of jewels—This
spring ramble was very invigorating and purgative of wintry
fumes and dumps.

Our village life would stagnate, I think, if it were not for the 24
unexplored forests and meadows which surround it. We need the
tonic of wildness,—to wade sometimes in meadows where only the
bittern and the meadow-hen lurk, and hear the booming of the
snipe; to smell the whispering sedge where only some wilder &
more solitary fowl builds her nest, and the mink crawls with its
belly close to the ground.

At the same time that we are earnest to learn and explore all
things, we require that all things should be mysterious and unex-
plorable by us that land and sea be infinitely wild, unsurveyed
and unfathomed by us. We can never have enough of nature. We
must be refreshed by the sight of inexhaustible vigor, vast features
and titanic—the sea coast with its wrecks, the wilderness with its
living and [116v] its decaying trees,—the thunder cloud—and the
rain that lasts 3 weeks and produces freshets. We need to witness
our own limits transgressed, and some life pasturing freely where
we never wander. We are cheered when we observe the vulture
feeding on the carrion that disgusts and disheartens us, and deriv-
ing health & strength from the repast. There was a dead horse in
the hollow by the path to my house, which compelled me sometimes to go round & out of my way, especially in the night when
the air was heavy; but the assurance it gave me of the strong appetite and inviolable health of nature was my consolation for this.
—I love to see nature so rife with life that myriads can be afforded
to be sacrificed, and suffered to prey on one another—the tender

Spring organizations that can be so serenely squashed out of existence
24 like soft pulp,—tadpoles which herons gobble up, and tortoises
and toads run over by a wheel in the road; and that sometimes it
has rained flesh & blood! [117r] 235. With the liability to accident we must see the trivialness of it, and the little account that is
to be made of it. The impression made upon a wise man is of universal innocence—Poison is not poisonous after all, nor are any
wounds fatal. Compassion is a very untenable ground to occupy
long at a time. It must be very expeditious. Its works will not bear
to be stereotyped.

25　　Early in May or by the last of April, the oaks hickories—maples
and other trees just putting out amidst the pine woods around the
pond gave them the appearance, especially in cloudy days, of the
sun just breaking through mists and shining on them. Their green
bursting buds and expanding leaves scattered a slight brightness
like sun shine over the hill sides.

> When the oaks are in the gray
> Then Farmers plant away.

The 3rd or 4th of May I saw a loon in the pond—and during the
first week of this month I heard the whippoorwill—the brown-
thrasher—the veery—the wood pewee, the chewink, and other
birds—the wood thrush I had heard [117v] long before—The
pollen of the pitch pine already covered the pond, and the stones
and rotten wood along the shore with its yellow dust—

　　And so the seasons went rolling on into summer as one rambles
into higher & higher grass—

26　　Thus was my first year's life in the woods completed.[68]

68. This is clearly the end of version I. Two additional leaves of light-blue paper
contain material that Thoreau developed further in "Conclusion," 16 and 17; but
the material is in no respect an integral part of version I, and the handwriting and
ink are certainly not those of version I. There is no clear evidence as to when
Thoreau wrote this material.

PRINTED IN U.S.A.